The RUODLIEB

edited with translation and notes by

C.W. GROCOCK

BOLCHAZY-CARDUCCI PUBLISHERS / ARIS & PHILLIPS LTD

U.K.   ISBN 0 85668 292 6 *cloth*
            ISBN 0 85668 293 4 *limp*

U.S.A.   ISBN 0 86516 098 8 *cloth*
            ISBN 0 86516 073 2 *limp*

Published in England by ARIS & PHILLIPS LTD, Warminster, Wiltshire, England.
Published in the U.S.A. by BOLCHAZY-CARDUCCI PUBLISHERS, Chicago, Il.

CONTENTS

Editor's Preface

It is several years since a cursory attempt at reading through
some of the principal works in the medieval latin corpus brought me
into contact with the *Ruodlieb*. The poet's obscure latinity gave
him the victory on our first encounter, but could not prevent at
least a little of the attractiveness of his story, with its noble
themes blended with wit and humour, from reaching me.   In the course
of preparing this edition I have read through the poem many times
more, and found a way round most (though not all) of the obscurities
which baffled me on a first reading, but the sense of romance which
I saw in the work at first has not been dispelled, and I hope never
will be.

As far as my own efforts at editing this notoriously difficult
poem are concerned, *alea iacta est*, no doubt to the releif of my
publishers, my wife, and to the many friends who have cheerfully put
up with hours of enthusiatic explanations of details of plot and
character.   If I have been able to pass on to one of them, or
to any student who may in the future have cause to read this book,
something of my own love for the remarkable story contained in its
pages, then I shall consider all my labours to have been well spent.

My thanks are due to the staff of the library of the University
of London, for their courtesy, patience and help; to my publisher,
for his longsuffering, frequent encouragement, and good advice, and
not least for the provision of a typewriter on which I have been
able to originate the work; and most of all, to Dr J.B. Hall, my
friend, mentor and adviser, whose careful attention to detail and
copious criticisms have saved me from blundering into error on more
than one occasion, and without whose valuable help in proofing the
work I should have been considerably disadvantaged; *non est
discipulus super magistrum*.   Such mistakes and errors as remain in
the work are entirely my own.

Thanks are also due to James Catford, for interest and encouragement; and, most of all, to my wife, whose patience has been inexhaust-
ible and whose interest in the progress of *Ruodlieb* has been genuine
and precious during the two years that it has taken up both our time;
multae filiae congregauerunt diuitias: tu supergressa es uniuersas.

Godalming, June 1985.

1

I.   Previous Editions And Translations

If the story of Ruodlieb, the young knight who goes abroad in search
of better fortune than he can find at home, is one which merits the
description 'romantic', then the story of the poem's survival from
the medieval monastic library at Tegernsee to its present status and
renown is no less wondrous.   The poem itself rivals the hero whom
its verses celebrate in the miraculous way in which both escape near-
disaster and attain to a position far above that which they held at
first.   Fortune appears to have played just as commanding a role
in the preservation of the work as she does in the ultimate
exaltation of the hero from whom the poet takes its name.   Like him,
the poem has gained an undreamed-of status in medieval literature.

The hero, we are told, left his homeland 'despairing that he would
ever live anywhere in peace' (I.15), and with only his squire and
his dog for companions.   But even this is a healthy state of affairs
compared to that of the principal manuscript of *Ruodlieb*, Munich
clm 19486, which suffered the fate of many an unwanted text in the
late Middle Ages; no longer prized as one presumes it once was, it
was cut up in its home, the ancient monastery of Tegernsee (a major
centre of learning and culture in medieval Germany) and was used as
binding for other volumes.   At this point the poem passed into an
oblivion from which it was to emerge only after the passing of
several hundred years; the manuscript still bears the legend *attinet
monasterio Tegernsee* in two places in a fifteenth-century hand.
These words were perhaps written when the destruction of the manuscript was taking place or had already happened, and they provide a
rough clue to the date of this event.

It was not, in fact, until 1803 that *Ruodlieb* re-emerged into
the light of day.   Many of the libraries of German monasteries
were secularized, and their contents sequestrated by the state.   Books
from Tegernsee were taken to Munich, some 30 miles north-west, and in
the Royal Bavarian Library they were examined by B.G. Docen, who
discovered some of the poem among bindings and inside the wooden
covers of various volumes.   Carefully cutting the fragments free and
piecing them together, he found that they made up what had once been
a number of quarto leaves of parchment folded over into octavo pages.
They were in appalling condition: in some instances half the page had
been cut away vertically, leaving a row of half-lines.   There were
also breaks, incisions, and stitches, and the writing itself was worn
and blurred in places.   Examination of these pages shows that although
some of them may have been bound together, this was never true of them
as a whole.   All the fragments are written in the same hand, but with
different pens and inks. Frequent erasures, corrections and glosses
suggest that this is the author's own copy (cf. Strecker in *Neue
Jahrbücher f. klass. Altertum* XXIV, 1924).

Docen set to work transcribing the text, and made the briefest of reports of it in his *Miscellaneen zur Geschichte der deutschen Literatur* in 1807. He was promoted to keeper of the Royal Library in 1811, but made no attempt to publish his transcription of the text.

Docen was succeeded in 1829 by Andreas Schmeller, the associate of Jacob Grimm, and he found the fragments of the poem among Docen's papers, as well as discovering more himself, bringing the total number of leaves then known to 34. This was augmented by the discovery in 1830 of another double parchment leaf, containing all of fragment XI in the present edition, in the Austrian monastery of St. Florian. This was published by Maurice Haupt in 1834. It clearly belongs to a different manuscript, being written in a different hand and having its text divided into sections or 'strophes' with roman numerals in red. It is dated a little later than the Munich fragments on palaeographical grounds, and is thought to be a fair copy.

The first edition which might have any claim to be 'complete' was produced by Schmeller (with a good deal of assistance from Jacob Grimm) in 1838 in *Lateinische Gedichte des X. und XI. Jahrhunderts*. While no longer satisfactory for scholarly purposes, Schmeller's edition has a vast number of conjectures, most of which are obvious ones. These are of such a quantity that in the present edition I omit mention of him; all uncredited conjectures (denoted in the text by square brackets) are from Schmeller. His edition is deficient primarily because of its necessary omission of the text contained in another double parchment leaf which was not brought to light until 1840. This is a further fragment of the Tegernsee manuscript and was found among the papers of Baron von Moll at Dachau, not far from Munich. All editions since Schmeller include it as foll. 4a and 4b, and it is kept in the library at Munich with the other fragments. These new discoveries were not included in the text as a whole until 1882, the year in which Freidrich Seiler's *Ruodlieb: der älteste Roman des Mittelalters* made its appearance. This edition includes a lengthy analysis of the poem and a detailed introduction, dealing with linguistic features, metre, and the background to the work; much of this has stood the test of time, though many of Seiler's conclusions have been overtaken by more recent research. As Zeydel notes (p.3) 'he was the last German editor of a critical edition'. His text represented a substantial improvement over that of Schmeller, though in some of his readings he shows 'an uncanny ability...to decipher what is practically obliterated' (Zeydel, pref. p.2).

Seiler's work was defective in some respects, as was pointed out in a lengthy and scholarly review of the work by Ludwig Laistner in the *Anzeiger* IX, pp.70 - 106 of the *Zeitschrift f. d. Altertum*. Apart from numerous corrections to Seiler's introduction and commentary, Laistner made an important breakthrough in revising the order of the fragments in a second article in *Zeitschrift f.d. Altertum* XXIX, pp.1 - 25. The revised sequence he sets out here has been accepted by all critics ever since. In order to facilitate reference to the Schmeller and Seiler editions, I include here a list of their comparative orders.

Laistner	I	II	III	IV	V	VI	VII	VIII	IX	X	XI	XII
Seiler	I	II	III	IV	V	VI	VII	VIII	XII	XIII	IX	X
Schmeller	I	-	-	II	III	IV	V	VI	XI	XII, XIII	VIII	IX

Laistner	XIII	XIV	XV	XVI	XVII	XVIII
Seiler	XI	XV	XIV	XVI	XVII	XVIII
Schmeller	X	XIV	VII	XV	XVI	XVII

Thus, Seiler XV is XIV in the present edition, and Schmeller X is XIII. Schmeller's fragments XVIII and XIX are the epigrams included by Seiler and myself at the end of the work, after the poem proper.

Apart from Moriz Heyne's German rendering of 1897, the next edition to appear was by Karl Langosch, *Waltharius, Ruodlieb, Märchenepen: lateinische Epik des Mittelalters mit deutschen Versen* (Berlin, 1956). Langosch's text is substantially that of Seiler, arranged in Laistner's order, with a facing translation in rather doggerel German. As Ford notes (Tr. p.7) 'he did not make any original textual contributions'. In fact, some of the misreadings introduced by Schmeller in 1838 persist via Laistner as far as Langosch, as at VII.48, where all three print *rediens* against the manuscript's *ridens*. Langosch also included a brief résumé of research carried out up to that time and a short introduction.

Only three years elapsed before the next edition of *Ruodlieb*, this time the work of a scholar based in the USA, Edwin Zeydel. His *Ruodlieb: The Earliest Courtly Novel (After 1050)* appeared as no. 23 of *University of North Carolina Studies In The Germanic Languages And Literatures* (Chapel Hill, 1959). His text was based on a fresh examination of the manuscript evidence, and included a fairly full introduction and a rather sparse commentary and textual notes. The major fault in his work lies in his translation, which is slavish in its retention of awkward constructions and varying tenses, and is thus awkward and disjointed. On the credit side, he contributed over 30 more conjectures, reducing the number of incomplete lines to fewer than 90. His edition was the first to be produced outside Germany, and incorporates the first English translation of the work.

Gordon B. Ford Jr.'s translation appeared 6 years later (Leiden, 1965) but took the retrograde step of being based on Langosch's text with a few variants introduced by Ford himself, instead of using Zeydel's edition. Ford also produced a facsimile edition (Louisville, Ky., 1965) and a printed edition, again incorporating his own emendations and using a fresh examination of the manuscripts, the following year (Leiden, 1966). This last includes a linguistic glossary which is purely descriptive, and contains needless lists of *exempla*. His translation includes a rather superficial introduction of 8 pages. In my own treatment of linguistic phenomena in *Ruodlieb* I have abandoned the order adopted by Seiler and Ford (who followed him) and tried to include references to the text to illustrate various features of medieval latin, rather than aiming at completeness. I give more detailed discussion of the various linguistic phenomena in the commentary.

Finally, note should be taken of the facsimile edition produced in 1974 as part 1 of a projected 3-part series, with an introduction by Walter Haug (*Ruodlieb. Faksimile-Ausgabe der Codex Latinus Monacensis 19486 der Bayerische Staatsbibliothek und der Fragmente von St. Florian*, bd.1, Wiesbaden 1974). It is this very clear facsimile edition which I have chosen to use as a basis for my text; the work of previous editors was then compared with it.

It should also be noted that not all editors include the epigrams which occur on fol.1^v and 34^v of the Munich manuscript. Schmeller included them as fragments XVIII and XIX of his work; I follow Seiler and include them after the main body of the text. Zeydel provides a full discussion of them in 'Die elf Epigramme der Münchener Ruodliebshandschrift', *Deutsche Vjs. f. Literatur. und Geistes.* XXXVIII, 1959, pp.257ff.

II.   Authorship, Provenance And Date

The poet who wrote *Ruodlieb* does not give us his name, but neverthe-
less he does supply us indirectly with a good deal of information
about himself by the way he worked his material - points he noted,
details he lingered over, and so on - and by the physical means he
employed in putting the work down on paper.   It is generally agreed
that the fragments which make up Munich clm 19486 constitute the
author's own fair copy;   the numerous corrections and substitutions
(some of which have been erroneously interpreted as glosses by past
editors) go beyond what one might expect from a mere scribe engaged
in transcribing the text.

The poem was probably never completed.   Dronke (p.36) notes various
'loose ends' in the narrative, inconsistencies (though these are
occasionally to be found in other medieval poems, such as Beroul's
Tristan, where one of King Mark's barons is killed early on, only to
reappear later) and instructions not properly carried out.   When
Ruodlieb is given the loaves by Rex Maior, he is specifically told
not to open them all on his homecoming.   Nonetheless this is what he
does, and as Dronke notes (p.31 n.2) 'there is no suggestion of dis-
obedience in the episode'.   Again, a parallel can be seen in Beroul's
Tristan, in which Ewert notes no less than five instances of incon-
sistent prophecy, at vv. 270, 292-4, 320, 581-648, and 2752-64.   One
might conclude that for these two medieval poets (and perhaps for
their audience also) the main focus of interest lay elsewhere than in
seeing all the loose ends of the story tied up.

The relationship of the two surviving manuscripts is clear.   The
Munich text is cramped and crowded, some pages even containing verses
crammed vertically in the right-hand margin.   It has been supposed that
it formed the basis for a now-lost clean copy at Tegernsee;   at all
events, it bears the marks of the author's own revision, as has been
noted above.   The St. Florian fragment, on the other hand, looks more
like a part of a 'clean' copy, and is dated on palaeographical grounds
to about 20 years after the Munich text (Zeydel, p.2).

The original length of the poem has been the subject of much debate.
From the clear evidence that the text breaks off unfinished before
the bottom of the last leaf, 34^r, it seems that the poet never finished
his work, or at least did not complete transcribing it.   Laistner
conjectured that the poem originally contained 3881 verses (that is
to say, almost half is now missing), and his analysis is discussed at
length by Braun (p.6).   Hauck, in the *Paul-Brüne Beiträge* 70 (1948)
thought the number of missing verses to be a good deal smaller.   Yet
earlier, Singer supposed the loss to be even greater than Laistner
thought.   The most recent analysis of the Munich fragments, by Walter
Haug in the introduction to the Wiesbaden edition of 1974, concludes
that the text encompassed 'ursprünglich drei Binionen, vier Ternionen,
einen Quaternio und einen Quinio, insgesamt also 54 folia umfasste'

(p.39). Unfortunately the nature of the poet's transcription makes it impossible to judge precisely how much text is missing; an average estimate of, say, 33 verses per side (assuming that as in some of the extant sides, extra verses are written in the margin) gives a figure of 3465 verses for 105 sides (the other sides are occupied by the Epigrams). Possible reasons why the poet never completed his work will be discussed below, in 'Literary Features Of Ruodlieb'.

We may not know who the author was, but the poem does give important clues about what he was. It is clear that his native tongue was German. There are the names he gives to some of his characters, the glosses in German that he added to the text, some German idioms found in Latin guise, and the delightful *Liebesgruss* at XVII.12-13 to back up this argument. Furthermore some of the fish names in X are left in German. Seiler (pp.136ff.) made great play with the German idioms in particular, though he has been shown to have gone too far in this, as Ottinger demonstrated in *Historische Vjs*. XXVI, pp.449ff. Most of what Seiler held to be 'Germanisms' are in fact part and parcel of medieval Latin, though expressions such as *mantel* (X.130) and *mordrita* (VIII.20) are clear exceptions.

It is probable, too, that the poet had a clerical background; his latinity demonstrates this above all else. Dronke sees him as a 'cultured, sensitive man, who has received the normal Latin education, sacred and secular, of his day'. At V.210 he lists monks ahead of abbots, which might suggest that he was a monk himself. The later references to Tegernsee in the manuscript point to this Bavarian found-ation as the almost certain place of composition. On the other hand, the poet is no cloistered figure, sheltered from the ways of the world; his descriptions of courts, diplomatic proceedings, and the like are a strong indication that he was familiar not only with the ideals of Christian kingship (the major thrust of Braun's thesis; see also below, 'Literary Type And Synopsis Of Plot') but also with its reality. He also has some knowledge, perhaps at second-hand, of the contemporary Byzantine and Saracen world of southern Italy and Sicily; Zeydel suggests that 'he was in all probability a nobleman and courtier'. The poem itself shows how well he put this background to good use in his literary enterprise. Zeydel (p.9) suggests that 'with the writer of *Ecbasis Captiui*, with Wipo and the poet of the Cambridge Songs...our author probably belonged to the circle of writers at the court of Henry III'. Certainly the identification of the poet with Froumond, the monk of Tegernsee, which was originally proposed by Schmeller, has long been discounted; the manuscript itself cannot be dated so early (Frou-mond died before 1025) and the style and prosody of the work show that *Ruodlieb* is the product of a quite different poet.

Mention of Froumond brings us to consider the date of *Ruodlieb*. on palaeographical grounds the Munich fragments have been dated to about 1060 - 1070. Chroust suggests (*Monumenta Palaeographica* II.1, 1.2, plate 7) that they are from the time of either Abbot Sigfrid (1048 - 1069) or Abbot Eberhard (1069 - 1091). Ford prefers the date 1060 - 1070 (tr. p.2), and Zeydel the period 'after the decade 1040-1050'. A much earlier date was presumed by Grimm and Schmeller, mainly on the basis of the identification with Froumond.

Other evidence from the poem has also been adduced to give a more precise indication of its date of composition. Giesebrecht suggested (*Geschichte der deutschen Kaiserzeit* II, p.625) that the meeting of the two kings described in fragment V bore a remarkable similarity to the actual meeting of Henry II of Germany with Robert II of France on the banks of the Meuse in 1023. So long as this identification was accepted, a date c. 1030 could be assumed, and the poem treated as an elaboration of an eye-witness report. However, this early date does not fit with the palaeographical evidence if the Munich manuscript is to be regarded as the author's own copy. A more likely historical inspiration has been suggested by Hauck; this is the Act of Indulgence promulgated by Henry III in 1043. As Braun points out (p.19) the tenor of this Act ties in very closely with the Christian idealism to be found in fragments IV and V (treatment of prisoners, terms laid upon the defeated enemy), and furthermore Henry's Act met with the explicit approval of successive abbots of Tegernsee, Herrand and Bern, in 1043 and 1044. Zeydel concludes that 'the peace-loving "major" king in *Ruodlieb* reminds one strongly of an idealised Henry, whose efforts between 1043 and 1047...were bent on pacifying the realm by urging forgiveness to all feuders' (p.9). In conclusion, then, historical and palaeographical evidence both point to a date of 1050 - 1070 for the composition of the *Ruodlieb*.

8

It is acknowledged by all studies of *Ruodlieb* that the poem is in
many respects enigmatic, *ein Rätsel*.   'It has been variously called
an heroic epic, an epic romance, a courtly novel and a didactic poem'
(Ford, Tr. p.5).   'Little agreement has so far been achieved on the
question to what literary type *Ruodlieb* belongs' (Zeydel, p.13).
'To define its genre and intent, and to explain its literary and cultural
context, the poem *Ruodlieb* has been showered with more suggestions
than the Sleeping Beauty with presents at her birth' (Dronke, p.33; cf.
Braun, pp.2ff.).   The truth of the matter is that *Ruodlieb* bears a
close affinity to several genres while fitting none exactly, and in this
respect is a poem likely to irritate those with tidy minds.
Ford, following Kögel and Strecker (refs. in Braun, p.52) calls his
translation 'The First Medieval Epic Of Chivalry' but drops this sub-
title from his Latin text.   Strecker and especially Kögel claimed
that there were affinities between *Ruodlieb* and *Waltharius*, though most
of the supposed parallels that they adduce are single words used in the
same place of a line of verse.   Braun analyses two more promising
supposed parallels (III.40-43 with W.215-220, and V.269-277 with W.
125-140) but concludes that the similarities are too vague to presume
any but the slightest of links.   Such similarities as there are are
best explained as the result of a common background in latin learning.
Furthermore, Ruodlieb bears little resemblance himself to the 'epic hero'
exemplified in the characters of Aeneas, Walther, Siegfried or Roland.
The poem as a whole is remarkable for the complete absence from it of
any portrayal of any fighting or killing (though one surmises that the
execution of the redhead may have been described in the missing portion
of text after the end of VIII).   Braun attributes this feature to the
Benedictine and Cluniac influence on the poet and to its roots in
Christian idealism (p.97).
The claim that the work is first and foremost a romance was made by
Maurice Wilmotte in a greatly overstated form in 1916.   His prime
motivation seems to have been one of nationalism, in that he claimed the
work as a whole for France.   In this respect his conclusions are risible
but there are some grounds for regarding the poem as 'courtly'.   In
many ways the narrative depicts standards of behaviour and taste
normally associated with such works as those of Chrétien de Troyes
which were written over a century later.   The central character is
himself a man of some rank, with a small retinue of his own.   Feudal
relationships play an important part in the background to the story,
and women are also pictured as important and influential characters.
These characteristics are assessed in the next section, 'Literary And
Cultural Features Of *Ruodlieb*'.
Is the poem primarily didactic, as Singer suggested, with particular
reference to the lessons given to Ruodlieb by Rex Maior?   Langosch,

too, regards the work as a didactic poem in medieval novel form. Braun
also sees the ultimate nature of the poem as didactic, and traces its
origins in the Christian idealism transmitted through the monastic
culture at Tegernsee and other Cluniac houses. Ultimately, this
Christian idealism finds its earliest poetic exponents in poets like
Venantius Fortunatus (cf. notes on I.1, 86, IV.86). 'Just like the
Rule of St. Benedict in the sphere of monastic and spiritual life,
so was Fortunatus one of the principal transmitters of the spirit of
later antiquity to the Middle Ages in the field of courtly life and
secular poetry in latin through his chosen poetic types such as
epigrams and letters,(Braun pp 100-101, my trans.). It is Braun's
thesis that *Ruodlieb* is to be best explained in the terms of the
monastic culture from which it sprang, and that it marks the point
where the ideal of *militia Christi* breaks into literary form. The
acceptance of soldiers by the church is illustrated by a prayer from
the Pontifical of Guillaume Durand, which shows what role the church
assigned to knights. The latin text runs as follows:

> 2. *Benedictio ensis. exaudi, quesumus, Domine, preces nostras*
> *et hunc ensem, quo hic famulus tuus circumcingi desiderat,*
> *maiestatis tue dextera dignare benedicere, quatenus esse*
> *possit defensio ecclesiarum, uiduarum, orphanorum, omniumque*
> *Deo seruientium, contra seuitiam paganorum, aliisque sibi*
> *insidiantibus sit terror et formido, prestans ei eque persec-*
> *utionis et iuste defensionis effectum. per Christum.*

(Text in M. Andrieu, *Le Pontifical au Moyen-Age* III p.448; Andrieu
says the prayer is part of the *benedictio ensis* of the Romano-German
Pontifical. Translation in Barber, *The Knight And Chivalry* p.39).

According to the 'didactic' interpretation, the framework of the
poem from V onwards is governed by the advice given to Ruodlieb by Rex
Maior (cf. Braun, p.59). However, even granting the occurrence of
inconsistencies in medieval storytelling generally (see the remarks at
the start of the previous chapter on Beroul's *Tristan*) it is clear
that not all of the precepts actually find an illustration in what surviv
of the poem. Furthermore, the narrative preceding the advice has to
be regarded either as leading up to the advice-giving or as mere scene-
setting. It is also clear from the space given over to certain
aspects and characters in the fabliau-like stories which occur to
illustrate some of the precepts that the poet was himself more interested
in the literary aspects of his writing than in a straightforward
didactic composition.

The various attempts to divide up *Ruodlieb* into various sections
all prove defective in some respect, though they do help to see the
different parts of the work in perspective. Laistner divided the
narrative into 5 'books':

1.	*Ruodlieb exul*	I.1. - V.219
2.	*Ruodlieb reuocatus*	V.220 - VIII.129
3.	*Ruodlieb redux*	IX.1 - XI.81
4.	*Ruodlieb herus*	to XVII.84
5.	*Ruodlieb heros*	to the end

Heyne divided his German translation into three sections:

1. *Ruodlieb in exile*   I.1 - V.584
2. *Ruodlieb's return*   V.585 - X.32
3. *Ruodlieb at home*   X.33 - end

Langosch, like Laistner, saw five sections in the narrative:

1. *At the king's palace*   I.1 - V.219
2. *The lessons and their illustration* V.220 - VIII.129
3. *At the lady's castle*   IX.1. - X.32
4. *Ruodlieb with his mother*   X.33 - XVII.84
5. *The 'Heldensaga'*   XVII.85 - end

Overall, it seems that in view of the continuity of the narrative in the manuscripts (there is nothing to denote breaks at V.219 or X.32, as Langosch proposes) it is best to regard the work as a unity, and thus the didactic element becomes secondary. The poet may have had a didactic aim when he began the work, but it does seem to have been overtaken by his sheer delight in writing the poem itself; that is to say, the narrative element has swamped the didactic element. The poet does seem to have made a continuous revision of his poem (this is perhaps the most satisfactory explanation of the insertion of the name *Ruodlieb* in the same hand as the rest at V.223. It is true that Chrétien's *Le Chevalier De La Charette* is similar in not naming the hero until v.3660, but here it is for the deliberate reason that the knight must remain incognito, which is hardly the case with Ruodlieb). Langosch is probably correct in assuming that the poet's aim altered as he progressed, though I would turn round the idea, and suggest that the author found certain parts of the story, and perhaps even some of the Rex Maior's precepts, more interesting than others while the process of composition was in progress; perhaps he even found the poem changing despite himself. As the end of the extant fragments is approached, more Germanic names are found, but to suggest as Zeydel does (p.16) that the author lost interest in his work 'after changing its type from a realistic mirror of knighthood to a romantic romance of heroism' makes too much of the 'different' styles in the one work: there are magical elements in the early part of the poem (the herb *buglossa* in particular has fantastic powers) as well as in the latter part. Furthermore, the fairytale elements introduced near the end might not have affected the poet's manner too much: cf. the essay by Helen Cooper, 'Magic That Does Not Work' in *Medieval Poetics* (*Medievalia et Humanistica New Series*, 7, New York 1976). Lack of interest is not the only reason why an author should break off in mid-stream, and the sudden ending is reminiscent of that in Wolfram von Eschenbach's *Parzival*.

What of possible sources for the poem? Again, a remarkable diversity of suggestions has been put forward (cf. Dronke, p.33). It should be noted that no conscious borrowings from the poetry of antiquity such as populate the *Waltharius* are to be found in *Ruodlieb*, and such reminisc- ences as do occur are vague, perhaps even unconscious. Classical allusions are also rare; there are some affinities in characterisation with the plays of Plautus(cf. the redhead knocking at the door with scenes from *Miles Gloriosus*) but this is not entirely surprising when one considers that the plays of Hrotswitha derive much of their substance from them (Braun, p.65). Such classical reminiscences as do occur are noted in the commentary, as are the claimed (and spurious) borrowings from the Elder Pliny.

Oral tradition has been suggested as a source of the poem (Zeydel p.9), and Singer insisted on the primacy of mimes and jongleurs in the derivation and stylistic nature of the poem. Braun notes links with sagas (pp.9-12) while Zeydel proposes a parallel in Icelandic literature (the *Hakonssaga Harekssonar*) for Rex Maior's 8th precept (p.11). Seiler detected a Cornish-Irish antecedent for precept 3 (p.71). The story as a whole has loose parallels in Russian folk-literature (Seiler, Laistner in *Zeitschr. f.d. Altertum*. XXIX) and in a Cornish folk-tale preserved by Wilhelm Grimm. As Zeydel points out (p.10) rags-to-riches stories like that of Dick Whittington are a commonplace in folk literature generally.

As already noted, *Waltharius* was once thought to have influenced the poet, but such similarities as there are are far too vague to support any definite conclusions (so Braun, pp.52ff.). If a latin source is to be sought for the poem, it lies (for its ethos) in the Christian idealism of Venantius and his successors, and (for its form) in the prose-novels of Apuleius and his later imitators (Braun, pp.23-27, 104).

One thing is certain: *Ruodlieb*'s affinities with the poetic world of the *Nibelungenlied*, of Chrétien de Troyes and of Gottfried von Strasbourg, put it a good many years ahead of its time in medieval literary history. 'There is nothing like it in literature before 1050 or for hundreds of years after' is Zeydel's rather exaggerated claim (p.15). Braun, rightly I think, sees the explanation of this prematurity in the poem's close links with the monastic world, found in the works of Augustine and seen in both *Ruodlieb* and in Henry III's Act of Clemency, but whose general ethos took the best part of another century to filter down to the secular world and to have a real influence on courtly behaviour as it was to be portrayed in the later romances (Braun, p.76).

Helena M. Gamer stressed the importance of *Ruodlieb* as 'the unique and precious literary testimony for important aspects of medieval life in Germany in the eleventh century' (cited in Ford, Tr.p.8). The poem's importance goes beyond its cultural witness, though; it is, according to Burdach, 'the first freely-invented courtly novel'. Its uniqueness must not be allowed to detract from the background against which the work was composed, and it is better to regard it, as Braun does, as the culmination of a monastic and Christian literary tradition in contact with secular reality. The poet's genius lies in creative adaptation, rather than pure invention. Similar values to those found in *Ruodlieb* are found elsewhere in medieval latin literature, but they are to be seen in Odo's *Vita Geraldi* and in Hrotswitha rather than in *Waltharius*. In this respect the latin antecedents of the poem are not the epics of antiquity but what Braun calls the 'spätantiker Kleindichtung', the lesser poems of rhetorical poets such as Sidonius or Venantius. On the other hand, it is important to bear in mind the poet's own creative genius, as Dronke does in regarding the work as a 'poetic experiment'. In his narrative technique and powers of description, as well as the way he explores his characters, the author of *Ruodlieb* demonstrates unique and unparalleled powers of literary creation.

In order to avoid confusion it seems best to include a synopsis of the complete narrative at this point in order to demonstrate how the story probably proceeded. Seiler included a detailed analysis in his intro-duction, but since the present edition includes a translation into English the synopsis here serves just to give an overall outline of the story.

A young man of noble birth and character is cheated and harassed by his feudal lords, and leaves his mother and home to seek his fortune abroad, with only a squire to accompany him. As he enters a neigh-bouring country he meets a huntsman, who turns out to be the servant of a great king (Rex Maior). He extols the virtues of this king, takes the young man to the capital city, and introduces him at court (Fragment I). The young man impresses the Rex Maior by his skill at fishing with the magic herb *buglossa*. Meanwhile the kingdom in which the young man has just arrived, and which has been at peace with its neighbours for some time, suddenly finds itself at war (Fragment II).

The young man assumes a position of command in the army, and the neighbouring kingdom is subdued in battle. Its army is taken prisoner. Its general tries to justify his warmongering (gap after Fragment II) but the young man dismisses these excuses, and sends word to his lord the Rex Maior, who orders the young man to come home and to bring the prisoners with him (Fragment III). In order to arrange peace, Rex Maior sends the young man as an emissary to Rex Minor, the defeated king, and the latter summons his barons to discuss the terms laid down (gap after Fragment III). The barons consider the emissary's words, and agree to a meeting with Rex Maior. The young man returns to Rex Maior, reports at length on the negotiations, and also tells him of a game of chess he played with Rex Minor. They make ready for the meeting (Fragment IV).

The two kings meet with all ceremony, and Rex Maior shows great clemency to his vanquished foe. Rex Minor offers him many gifts, but all save a few are refused; the gifts are described at great length. Rex Maior gives very lavish gifts to the former prisoners.

Meanwhile, Ruodlieb (named for the first time at V.223) receives a messenger from his mother. His former enemies have repented of their evil towards him, and he asks the king's permission to return home. The Rex Maior prepares gifts of gold and jewels and has them hidden in two large loaves for Ruodlieb to take home with him. Then he summons his barons and tells them that Ruodlieb wishes to leave. He tells the young man that he wishes to give him some gift, and offers him gold, but Ruodlieb chooses wisdom instead. Accordingly, Rex Maior gives him 12 precepts, and also presents him with the two 'loaves'. Ruodlieb sets out, and on his journey he meets a redhead (precept 1 illustrated) who joins him, and then cuts across some fields because the road is a sea of mud (breaking precept 2: Fragment V ends here). Peasants drive off the redhead (gap after Fragment V) and Ruodlieb tells him that he deserved all he got. The two men seek lodging for the night; Ruodlieb seeks a young man with an old wife, the redhead the reverse (precept 3 illust-rated). A shepherd they meet tells the story of a young man who served an old miser and then married his widow, as well as that of an old man with a young wife (Fragment VI ends here). Ruodlieb goes to the house of the first couple (gap after Fragment VI) and spends the night there. The redhead goes to the old man's house and flirts with his coquettish

13

young wife (precept 6 illustrated). (Fragment VII ends). The old man surprises the redhead with his wife, a fight ensues, and he is mortally wounded (gap after Fragment VII). A trial takes place, and the young woman and the redhead are brought before the people. The young woman defends herself and admits to the crime; she repents of her past life and breaks down. The judge hands her over to her children, and her later life of religious dutifulness is described. The redhead then protests his innocence (end of Fragment VIII).

After the redhead is executed (one presumes), Ruodlieb continues on his way and meets a nephew of his who is in the clutches of a mistress (gap after Fragment VIII). He urges the nephew to return home with him (Fragment IX) and they arrive at a noblewoman's castle (gap after Fragment IX). She receives them well, and Ruodlieb again demonstrates his skill at fishing with *buglossa*. A banquet is held, and they put on fresh clothes (Fragment X). The people there amuse themselves with pet birds, and then Ruodlieb plays the harp while his nephew dances with the noble lady's daughter; soon, the two young people are deeply in love (Fragment XI). Ruodlieb asks his hostess about his mother's circumstances, and they start to arrange the wedding of the young lovers (Fragment XII). Then the two men return home, and Ruodlieb opens the two loaves the Rex Maior gave him (Fragment XIII).

The scene switches to the wedding of the nephew, which is described in playful detail (Fragment XIV). Ruodlieb's mother advises him to marry too, and warns him of the perils of old age (Fragment XV). She stresses his need of an heir, and so he summons his barons (precept 7) who suggest a possible wife (Fragment XVI). Ruodlieb sends his nephew to the lady to woo her, but discovers that she has another lover (gap after Fragment XVI). He sends his nephew again with some garters that the lady dropped when she was with her lover, a mere clerk, and thus reveals to her that he is aware of her deceit (Fragment XVII). Meanwhile, his mother has some dreams which predict his future glory (end of Fragment XVII). The dream sees the beginning of its fulfilment in an adventure involving a cave full of treasure guarded by a dwarf and belonging to two kings. Ruodlieb captures the dwarf, who tells him of the two kings and of the beautiful princess Heriburg whom he is to marry. It is at this point that the poem breaks off (Fragment XVIII).

IV.   Literary And Cultural Features Of *Ruodlieb*

Ruodlieb is a valuable source for information about the customs of
the society depicted by the poet, although as a work of fiction it must
be remembered that the descriptions it contains may owe as much to the
author's fertile imagination as to an imitation of the real world he
knew.   We shall return to this point later, first spending a little
space on the cultural features of the work, and then passing on to the
Ruodlieb-poet's abilities in description and characterisation.   A
fuller discussion of individual cultural aspects will be found in the
commentary.

One of the features of *Ruodlieb* which does most to set it ahead of its
time is its portrayal of courtly life.   Kingship itself is held in high
esteem, and the Rex Maior character serves as a vehicle, as Braun does
not tire of pointing out, for Christian idealism (cf. III.12ff, IV.84ff).
He is firm and yet gentle, and merciful in victory, though he was no
doubt resolute in his military campaign against his aggressor (sadly, this
part of the narrative is lost).   He is loved by his people as a father
(VI.109) and is on the other hand Solomon-like in his wisdom (V.451ff.).
All in all, he behaves in an identical fashion to Rabelais' later ideal
Christian King, Pantagruel.   The court over which he holds sway is one
marked by strict rules of etiquette, and the king consults his barons
before making any decisions (V.394.   Cf. also Rex Minor in IV.1ff, and
Ruodlieb himself in XVII.20ff.   This is a commonplace in medieval literature).   Wine is employed as a symbol of greeting (V.161; cf. *Nibelungenlied* 126.4) and as a sign of peace (IV.48, 162).   Kisses are also used in
a formal, ritual way (I.119,120, V.18, 221, 284, 582, IV.167, XIV.8, XVII.
101; cf. *Nib*.297.3,4) and greetings in general are stylised (IV.93. VII.
45.   Zeydel claims that these involve raising or doffing hats).   When in
the presence of a superior, and especially the king, it is proper to stand
up (IV.49, 118, V.448;   cf. *Nib*.1780).   A shared meal is regarded both
as part of courtly behaviour (as the meal recorded in XIII.18) and as a
sign of intimacy (X.65ff.).   It is also depicted in idealistic, Christian
terms (VII.1ff.).   This last idea of the shared meal has clear links with
the Eucharist, but also has roots in German paganism (cf. note on VII.4).
Washing before the meal is also part of the ceremonial (X.59).   On the
other hand, the duels, jousts and tournaments which play such a vast
part in the later romances are utterly absent from the *Ruodlieb*.

Music plays an important part in the life of these people: the poet
uses a fairly technical vocabulary, which indicates that he was himself
familiar with the *mimi* (V.87) and the *harpatores* (XII.26).   Ruodlieb
himself, like Tristan in the later stories, is the best of all harpists.
The young lovers' dance is described (XI.25ff.) in terms which Hauck
and Winterfeld have regarded as a portrayal of a folk-dance imitating
the flights of birds.   I prefer Dronke's interpretation (p.55) of this
passage as being symbolic of their courtship;   it encapsulates a relationship which has already begun, but has yet to find its consummation.

The character of the young girl is one which the poet clearly found very interesting, and his psychological portrayal of her and of their 'falling in love' is noteworthy. According to Colin Morris the poet perhaps 'deprives Chrétien of his claim to complete originality' in this exploration of romantic love (*The Discovery Of The Individual 1050-1200*, New York 1972, p.134n.).

The two most valuable sections of the poem for the student of medieval customs are undoubtedly the wedding (XIV) and the village trial (VIII). The wedding has been the subject of much discussion (Wackernagel *Zeitschr f.d. Altertum* II, 548ff; Meyer, *Zeitschr. f. Rechtsgeschichte* LII, 276ff.). As the poet describes it the wedding and its formalities come fairly close to what is known of the practice in ancient Germanic law. The three stages, *desponsatio* or betrothal, *traditio* or giving away of the bride, and *nuptiae* are all referred to (*pace* Zeydel p.19). All take place in a secular context: marriage in church was only made necessary much later, during the papacy of Alexander III, and lay ceremonies continued even after this. The *desponsatio* here is undertaken by the lovers themselves over their meal (X.61ff.) and at the dance (XI.50ff.), and is finalised in their dice-game (XI.62ff.; note the remark at XI.58). This is clear from Ruodlieb's own words at XIV.18ff. The *traditio*, or handing-over, is not specifically mentioned (perhaps because the girl's father is dead) but Ruodlieb performs the function done in modern times by both the father of the bride and the priest/registrar. The other men look on and affirm their consent (XIV.41ff.). Zeydel notes that the *Friedelehe* or consent of the bride was sought in later periods; *Ruodlieb* provides us with early evidence of its existence. The spirited young bride withholds her consent until the bridegroom accepts the same terms as have been offered to her. The poet obviously found her character a delight to portray, as she moves from a lighthearted argument about her having 'won him at dice' (XIV.52-56) to the more serious point about equality in marriage (XIV.69ff). The groom agrees, and they then proceed to the giving of the rings, the ceremonial whetting of the sword against a pillar, and the giving of gifts (the *nuptiae* proper). There is no need to regard the earlier exchange of rings (XI.62ff.) as anything more than the giving of love-tokens. As Zeydel notes, the few occasions where marriage is mentioned in the *Nibelungenlied* add little to the above picture; they do provide some useful literary parallels, though, and these are noted in the commentary.

The village trial in VIII gives another detailed picture of contemporary life. The *rector* (= OHG *Schuldheizo* as early as Paul the Deacon's time) presides, the jurors are seated, and the people stand looking on. Once again the poet's interest and sympathies lie with the woman, whose character-portrayal is vivid. Much more space is given to her speech than to the details of the trial proper.

The poet's interest in detail is revealed by the careful descriptions he gives of various manufactured goods such as jewellery and goblets, clothing, and the tack of Ruodlieb's horse. He also gives vivid vignettes of animals, such as the dancing bears. On the other hand we are given few physical details about these, and furthermore there is no landscape in the narrative. The poet's interest in description is confined to the courts, the castles and (briefly) to the muddy village street - never to the open countryside, to forests or mountains.   On occasion the details are very precise: the thigh-bands worn by Ruodlieb and his nephew, for example, are from Lucca (XI.114).   The poet uses details like this to enhance the richness of his characters, and to reinforce the splendour of their behaviour: hence the lavish tunics, fur coats and cloaks with lining and borders, hats and chaplets.   These last hint at Byzantine influence; the other items became stock-in-trade for poets from 1200 on.   The jewellery mentioned at V.308ff. has been likened to the Gisela treasure from Mainz (see note on V.340ff.).   Zeydel includes photographs of some of the best pieces in his edition, and sees some resemblances, though he admits (p.20) that much of the detail in the poem is pure invention on the part of the poet.   Both gold and enamel manufacture were carried out at Tegernsee in the 11th century.

Many of the preconceptions about medieval latin poetry being trapped by a fixed, rhetorical tradition are destroyed by an examination of the poet's handling of his characters.   His skill is such that they come to life through their speeches, despite Ford's peculiar claim that the poet 'must have looked on them as representative types and not as specific individuals' (Tr.p.2).   Dronke's study is very valuable in this respect, and goes into far more detail than there is space for here; cf. pp.37ff. of his essay.   The poet's *pièces de résistance* are undoubtedly the young bride and the country wife; his portrayal of Rex Maior is stately, as an ideal Christian king ought to be, and perhaps as a result is less developed in some ways than the minor characters are.   The same is true to a certain degree of Ruodlieb.   Only in the chess game do we see any kind of 'sparkle' about his personality: the poet seems hampered by the idealism he wishes to portray in these two characters.   Even in his relations with his mother Ruodlieb seems stiff and stilted, because his behaviour is so 'proper'.   The redhead, on the other hand, is a colour-ful if unsympathetic character, bustling with energy; the country wife is seen to be a woman of extremes in her lustful passion and then her excessive expressions of remorse.   Even the old shepherd is portrayed in some detail.

Little of our knowledge of these characters is physical (save for the young girl, depicted through fairly common imagery at X.55).   We are given details mainly about their clothes and personal possessions in order to throw more light on the characters themselves.   Our main knowledge of the figures in *Ruodlieb* is rather psychological, derived from the poet's ability to create 'personality through dialogue, individualizing his characters through their tone and manner of speech' (Dronke p.36).

Such creativity, bordering on a precise representation of real events, led earlier critics to believe that such passages as the diplomatic neg-otiations conducted by Ruodlieb are faithful transcriptions of events the poet had witnessed.   The likening of the jewellery in the poem to the Gisela treasure, noted above, is another example of this.   It seems nearer the mark, however, to regard such descriptions as products of the poet's own invention, perhaps derivative in part from reality, but always going beyond it.   Thus Rex Maior is such an ideal that he is almost in-human, unfeeling, in his perfection at times like a saint without a spot on his character.   Similarly the jewellery described at V.308ff. is 'a far more spectacular work of art than even Gisela's brooches' (Dronke p. 47) and in fact belongs to the same world as the *buglossa* and the jewels

formed from the lynx's urine.   It is therefore excessive to regard the
latter part of the poem, with its dwarves and hidden treasure, as a complete departure from the earlier ethos of the poem (cf. Ford, Tr.pp.4-5).
    The same is true of the poet's geography. Apart from the reference to
Rex Maior's territory as *Africa* (see note on XIII.42, 47) and to leg-
bands from Lukka and coins from Byzantium, there is nothing which locates
the story in the known world.   Apart from the German names, the story
could be set anywhere in medieval Europe geographically speaking.   Such
detail is clearly not an important part of the poet's overall aim, which
lies in his characterisation (or in the ideal he sets out, according to
Braun pp.1-2, 81).   The humour latent in the story of the redhead and
elsewhere is explored by Dronke (pp.48ff.).
    There are some notable instances of imagery.   Young women are twice
likened to the moon (X.55, XV.3) and the image of gliding movement is
twice used of the young girl (X.57, XI.53).   In the dance the young
man is likened to a falcon, the girl to a swallow (XI.51);   the swallow-
image is also used earlier in a different context at I.51.   A whole
spate of images occurs in Ruodlieb's mother's account of the ageing of
women and men (XV).   The woman becomes *par uetule simie* (4; cf. VII.28,
63 for parallel imagery) and wrinkled like a plucked magpie (XV.15),
with breasts like wizened toadstools (16) and a mouth as though full
of flour (11).   She hangs her head like a vulture on the prowl (22).
The commonplace metaphor of 'floods' or 'rivers' of tears is found at
VIII.32 and 105 (the country wife).   As Seiler remarks (p.198) this
poet rarely uses epithets: *pectora pulchra* is found at XIV.94 (and cf.
XVIII.29), *equus equipedans* at IV.239, *chorea altisona* at V.93, *rubeta
fundicola* X.43, *crines auricolores* at XV.18.   Dronke points out that
many of the objects mentioned by the poet are used symbolically, like
the salt in the story of the old farmer (VII.86ff. and note) or the
clothes the nephew receives from Ruodlieb: 'the new coat is, we might
say, more than a wedding present: it is an augury of the young man's
Vita Nuova' (Dronke, p.60).
    Seiler noted the existence of many proverb-like lines in the work.
They derive in part from the rhetorical style of poets like Sidonius
Apollinaris and the genre represented by the *Dicta Catonis*;   cf. I.95,
III.14-14, 62, 538, V.425-32, 443-5, 456 474ff., 491ff., 501-503,VI.32,
XVIII.22.   Such pithy sayings as are found here stand in the medieval
rhetorical tradition, and according to Friend (*The Medieval Literature
Of Western Europe* p.30) 'it is very likely that one method for teaching
Latin was to translate proverbs into rhyming latin verse'.
    The poet's storytelling ability sets him apart as a true master of
medieval latin literature.   Braun points out that after 'where did he
get his material?' the question we must ask of this poet is 'where did he
learn to arrange it so?'(my paraphrase).   His characterization has been
discussed;   it now remains to examine his latinity.   Brunhölzl regards
the poet's use of language as poor, being full of 'weaknesses' ('Zum
Ruodlieb', *Deutsche Vjs*. XXXIX, 1965, pp.506ff.).   This is unfair to the
poet;   many of the 'weaknesses' Brunhölzl identifies are in fact 'medi-
evalisms'.   Dronke takes the opposite view, saying that 'his use of
language did not thwart (his aims) but realized them' (p.64).   This is
also a little wide of the mark;   some of the tense-changes and awkward
constructions do seem deliberate, but others needed glossing by the poet,
and obscurities remain.   For all his genius the poet seems to have
wrestled with the latin on occasion, and he did not always win.

V. Linguistic Features Of *Ruodlieb*

This section is of necessity synoptic in its references to the text, and fuller discussion of salient points will be found in the commentary. Reference is made to the following works: *Grandgent* = C.H. Grandgent, *An Introduction To Vulgar Latin*, Boston 1910; *Palmer* = L.R. Palmer, *The Latin Language*, London 1961; *Strecker* = K. Strecker (trans. and revised R.B. Palmer), *Introduction To Medieval Latin*, Dublin/Zürich 1968; *Woodcock* = E.C. Woodcock, *A New Latin Syntax*, London 1959.

Ruodlieb's text contains some interesting morphological features: *natabus* is found for *natis* at XII.11, and *dominabus* for *dominis* at XIV.10. At V.119 *aluus* is masculine, not feminine, and the same is true of *fores* at XVI.36. Distributives are used in the place of cardinals at V.333, 374, VI.65, VII.2, VIII.99, X.42, and XIII.40. *Bini* is found in the singular at III.62 and V.253, and *gemini* is used for *duo* at VII.102 and XVII.89. Some verbs also occur in unusual forms: *saliuit* for *saluit* (I.42), *resalire* for *resilire* (II.15), *duruit* for *durauit* (II.58), *consiliar* for *consiliabor* (XVIII.13), *coquitura* for *coctura* (XV.26), *stupefiri* for *stupefieri* (VI.14), *rediebamus* and *preteriebant* for *redibamus* and *preteribant* (IV.165, XI.52). *ipsus* is found at V.31 for *ipse* (see note) and *quis* for *quibus* at IV.48, V.492, and X.3. Many of these forms are found in late latin verse, and *ipsus* is pre-classical.

The text reveals that the poet had more than a passing acquaintance with Greek words. From Carolingian times it had been the fashion to add some spice to poetry by including Grecisms, and the poet Abbo of St. Germain, writing on the fall of Paris at the end of the ninth century, shows that the custom persisted. Some of the Greek words found in *Ruodlieb* are clearly derived from late and Carolingian latin: *diastema* (XI.48), *oda* (XI.39), *pincerna* (XIII.27 and XIV.16), *pixis* (XVII.21,23,29), *sistema* (XI.48), *smigma* (I.34), *sophia* (IV.86, etc.), *sperula* (V.365), and *trochus* (XV.16). Others have changed meanings: *doma* (III.25, etc.), *entheca* (I.19, etc.), *heros* (XI.31), *paranimphus* (V.543), *podismus* (V.6, glossed *gang*), *simnista* (V.194), *sinaxis* (V.11, glossed *cursus uel hora*). A third group derive either from glosses, or, as Löwenthal thinks in one or two instances, from direct contact with the Byzantine world: *cosmus* (XIV.30), *decapenta* V.81, 124, 194), *enesis* (XIV.88), *piramis* (XIV.63), *polis* (V.323); and to these must be added some grecisms which the poet may have coined himself, such as *amphiprehensus* (V.1, 163), *finipolis* and *mercipolis* (III.28, Ep.VII.7) and *parafredus* (VI. 57). Other *hapax legomena* are dealt with below.

Wilmotte detected Romanisms by the score in his study of 1916, and Seiler sought to demonstrate numerous Germanisms (pp.135ff.). The arguments put forward by Wilmotte were rightly exploded by Strecker; words such as *causa* and *gamba* (I.7, etc., V.85 etc.) form a normal part of the latin of the period. Seiler's claims have been scrutinised by Ottinger (*Historische Vjs.* XXVI, 1931, pp.449ff.), with the conclusion

19

that most of the 'Germanisms', like Wilmotte's 'Romanisms', were in fairly widespread use among German-latin writers in the eleventh century. There are, however, some words worth noting as derivations from the poet's native tongue. The word *lorifregi* is not entirely unknown, but the poet saw fit to gloss it *zugilprechoto* to assist future readers. *faida* (I.63), *mordrita* (VIII.20), *mantel* (X.130) and *marhmanni* (II.52) show clear German descent, though again their use is not without some parallels. *podismus* at V.6 also required a German gloss, *gang,* and *uuerra* (II.63) is obviously of non-latin descent. The names of fish (X.39ff.) show strong German traits, some being latinised forms of German, and some left in their original form; X.41 has been called 'the first German hexameter'! The *liebes-loubes/wunna-minna* couplets at XVII.12-13 and 68-69 also deserve inclusion in this category.

In addition to the above categories, the *Ruodlieb*-poet makes use of a number of words which find no parallel usage (and often no mention whatsoever) in the dictionaries. Future research may well unearth some other uses of these, but for the time being they appear to be unique: *adhiare* (XI.19; confused with *inhiare*?), *anuatim* (XV.21), *circumcapere* (XIV.66), *congeneralis* (XVI.11, cognate of *congener*), *corilinus* (X.110), *?dix/dicis* (V.228), *deizare* (IV.146), *equipedans* (IV.239), *facultare* (XI.61), *gulatus* (X.124, from *gula*= 'throat-fur'), *migalina* (XIV.97, ?from *migale* = *pica* = 'piebald'), *nulligenus* (XI.44), *neutrim* (V.72, XVI.16), *peccunnus* (V.423), *promptifacere* (VI.92), *recircuitura* (V.361), *suates* (IV.95, cognate of *nostrates*), *torridula* (II.2). *anuatim* is one of the many adverbs in *-im* of which the poet is very fond (*alterutrim, dextrim, diatim, discretim, minutim, neutrim, nostratim, sintrim, transuersim* are the others). Another form for which the poet displays a fondness are nouns in *-amen*, such as *iuuamen* (XVI.31), *legamen* (IV.22), *oramen* (V.190, 580), *sagi[men* (VI.73) and *tribulamen* (V.390) as well as the rare *famulamen* (IV.136) and two possible neologisms, *uariamen* (V.171, XI.40) and *demandamen* (IV.132, XVII.54, possibly coined from *demandamentum*). For such neologisms and their occurrence in medieval latin, cf. *Strecker* p.56.

The peculiar variety of tenses used by the poet is probably best explained as being due to the exigencies of the hexameter. Classical poets made free use of the historic present, but not even the poets of late antiquity come close to *Ruodlieb*'s diversity, which is illustrated in many passages in the poem. Cf. the sequence of tenses in the narrative from V.1-19: *fuit...posset cenare...stat...posuere...fixerunt... fuit...est posita...solet...vēnit...audit...demandat...qui fuerat...ut uideant...quam prandia sumant...ut uidit...recipit...dat...ait,* or from III.27ff.: *subeunt...reseruant...numerant...gaudebant...tribuebant... dirigitur...qui loquatur...ut remandet...poscit...fert...dat...insedit... coegit.* In the indicative mood, the present is found for the future (V.126, 507, 517, 518, 521; cf. *Grandgent* 126.1), for the imperfect or perfect (I.5, 62, IV.78, 79, 230, V.66, etc.) and for the pluperfect (VII.16, X.103, etc.). Present tenses are replaced by futures (I.106, XVI.48, XVII.8), by perfect (I.5, III.29, VIII.4, XI.53, XII.7, etc.) and even by the pluperfect at V.575. The pluperfect also replaces the imperfect (IV.184, V.255,546, etc.) and the perfect (V.449,543, 608, etc.). The future perfect is used for the future at I.97, V.418, 454, etc.

Strecker p.67 notes that past tenses in particular were subject to much confusion in medieval writers.

Turning to the subjunctive mood, the confusion is equally great. A certain amount of confusion is detectable even by the time of late antiquity, and is certainly present in pre-classical latin (so *Palmer* p.331: 'Plautus' usage fluctuates even in one and the same sentence...in late latin...the pluperfect subjunctive gradually supplanted the imperfect'). In *Ruodlieb* we find present for imperfect (V.98, 317, XVI.40), perfect for present (II.34, V.571, VII.41, XVIII.18), present for pluperfect (XVII.113), pluperfect for imperfect (VII.69, X.3, XI.29) and vice versa (VIII.31, XI.72). Pluperfect also replaces perfect at XVI.68. To be fair to the poet, some of this confusion is also found in other contemporary poets, and may derive from his knowledge of pre-classical latin. Since medieval poets took pre- and post-classical authors as well as classical ones for their models, it is scarcely surprising that they found few real guidelines in this respect. Some of the tense-changes are discussed by Dronke, and shown to be deliberate.

There is also a deviation from classical norms in the case of moods (cf. *Strecker* pp.66, 67): *cum* always takes the indicative when used to mean 'since' and sometimes in narrative meaning 'when' (cf. I.14, V.243, VII.107, XI.18; I.55, IV.100, etc.). Again, this phenomenon is to be found frequently in Plautus (*Palmer* p.335). Ford (Ed. p.13) lists some occasions where he claims that the subjunctive is used for the indicative, but on examination all these can be explained as careful use of the subjunctive with jussive or optative force.

The poet's imitation of the writers of antiquity is reflected in the cases which some verbs govern: *libet, requirere* and *penitere* govern the accusative (I.130, V.103, II.41, XVII.37, VIII.3, 70). The following verbs govern the genitive: *ouare* (IV.173, V.563), *dominari* (IV.98), *replere* (V.313), *saturare* (VI.39) and lastly *fraudare* (IV.183, unparalleled in any of the dictionaries). The adjectives *longus, par, promptus* and *sollicitus* also govern the genitive at I.28, XIV.60, IV.59 and I.97. *deficere, ledere* and *miserari* are found construed with the ethic dative popular in medieval writers (IV.101, VI.28, 98, VIII.7, 51). Other verbs whose usage is so far without parallel are *condono* used absolutely in the sense 'give one leave to go' (IV.166, but cf. Plautus *Amph.* 534), *consuefacio* (probably confused with *consuesco* at XI.5), *hilaro* used intransitively at IX.8, and *intersedeo* (VII.9; cf. note on this verse).

Deponent verbs are sometimes used passively (I.13, 125, IV.89, VIII.19; cf. *Strecker* p.61) or are found in an active form (IV.2, 75, VII.23, X. 97, XI.27, 34, 44, 61, XIV.77, XV.65). The latter are found in late latin writers. According to Seiler (p.142) many of these usages are forced on the poet by the metre. The infinitive is found used a a noun at I.82 (*posse:* also IV.143, XIV.60), at I.114 (*uelle,* also IV.15, 56, 143, V.494, 541); XIV.14 (*famulari*), XVII.117 (*uigilare*) and XII.8 (*uiuere,* also at VIII.8). These usages, including infinitives governed by prepositions, can be paralleled from pre-classical and classical times (*Palmer* p.318).

Ford notes two occasions when a participle does not agree with its antecedent I.72 and V.306; the first of these may be considered an ablative absolute, the second one of the loose appositional phrases of

21

which the poet is fond.   The ablative absolute is also used at V.266 and
(very abruptly) at I.78.   *Palmer* p.305 gives some pre-classical
parallels.   The gerund is very commonly used, especially in the ablative
form.   This is a regular feature of medieval latin (cf. *Strecker* p.61)
and is also pre-classical (*Palmer* p.324).   Both gerund and gerundive
are used with a future sense to stress purpose (IV.123, VI.9) or intent
(XVIII.12;   cf. *Strecker* p.61, *Palmer* p.321).

The poet exhibits common medieval practice in his use of pronouns (cf.
Strecker p.63).   The genitive is used as a possessive at II.60, IV.13,
154, etc.   The reflexives (especially *sibi*) are used often in a non-
reflexive sense (I.59, 83, 113, etc.).   *ipse* is used as a possessive or
demonstrative at V.396, VIII.12, 48, 94, etc.   *ille* and *is* are also used
possessively (XIV.4, 11, 14, I.43, V.513, etc.).   *unus* is used as the
indefinite article at VI.10, IX.14, and XVI.29.
possessively at XIV.4, 11, I.43, V.513, etc.   *unus* is found used as the
indefinite article at VI.10, IX.14, and XVI.29.

There are various deviations from classical practice in the poet's use
of adjectives.   He uses the comparative for the positive on several
occasions (though many of these are used like *sepius* at I.4, 9, with the
force 'fairly frequent').   Cf. V.13, 52, 119, 246, 515, VII.48, 64, 92,
98, VIII.56, 87. etc.   *plures* is also used frequently (I.3, IV.213, V.
147, 427, etc.).   The positive is used instead of a comparative at
XIV.56, and with *quam* instead of a superlative at I.8, III.60, IV.205,
248, V.303, and XVI.58;   the comparative is used once in this way at III.
169.

Prepositions are also used in noteworthy ways (cf. *Strecker* p.64).
de replaces *a* at I.84, IV.200, V.19, VI.76;   *per* replaces *a* at V.309.
Both phenomena are noted in *Grandgent* 14.   *post* is found frequently after
verbs of motion or emotion, as at I.52, 54, IV.164, etc.   Although some
have seen this as a Germanic trait, it is not unknown in late latin: cf.
note on VIII.25.   *in* reinforces a plain ablative at IV.120.   *dum*
replaces *cum* in all senses of the latter (cf. *Palmer* p.336;   *Woodcock* 221
n.iii).   *quo* and *quatinus* replace *ut*, as they commonly do in Carolingian
writers (cf. Aethelwulf's *De Abbatibus*, in which *quatinus* = *ut* throughout).   *quia* and *ut* replace the accusative-infinitive construction of
classical times;   again, this is common in late latin (*Grandgent* 82).

A distinct peculiarity of the *Ruodlieb*-poet is his use of *uel* or *ue*
and *siue*, which disappeared in Vulgar Latin according to *Grandgent* 11:
cf. II.20, V.108, 579, VI.51, 56, VII.105, XIV.63, 67.   Other unusual
usages are *duellum* and *bellum* in distinct senses at IV.242; *fenus* with th
sense 'stake' at XIV.53;   *murcus*, 'cut short', at V.131;   *nucerina* at
VII.12;   *recuruatus* at XV.12;   *similagineus* at VII.67.

VI.   Metrical Features Of *Ruodlieb*

As in syntax, so in prosody the *Ruodlieb*-poet deviates from the
practice of classical times, though most of the phenomena of his work
can be paralleled in later latin writers and in medieval authors.
Vowels are frequently shortened, as for example *cottidianus* at V.196,
connubium at XV.20, *zizania* at II.61, *desiderat* at V.219, and *lorifregi* at IV.226.   Final *-o* is frequently shortened, especially in
the case of the ablative of the gerund: *Strecker* p.72 notes that in
this last case, final *- o* is almost always short in twelfth-century
verse.   Similar treatment is afforded to adverbs in *-e*, as at I.69.
Siguinus, *Ars Lectoria* p.41, treats *-o* as indefinite.   On the other
hand, final syllables are sometimes lengthened, as in the case of *ausus*
(V.219), *illius* (XI.28), *stet* (II.62) etc.
There is confusion over vowel-length in *sed* (IV.138 and V.263), *bonus*
(V.198 and VI.95), *mater* (XII.39, 41), *libra* (V.338 and 360), *fiunt*
(V.368, X.105 and XI.8) and *psitacus* (V.135 and 173).   The Greek words
used by the poet (listed in the previous chapter) are also afforded a
very loose treatment.   However, lest the author of *Ruodlieb* be thought
slipshod in these matters, one should consult Siguinus' *Ars Lectoria*,
which illustrates the confusion over syllable-length which obviously
reigned in the eleventh century.   Cf. also *Strecker* pp.58, 59.
The poet avoids hiatus, save at XI.22, and elision also;   in this he
resembles the author of *Waltharius*.   This practice may in part explain
the awkward word-order so common in the poem.   The use of the leonine
rhyme-scheme throughout tends to fix the caesura in the third foot,
though this is not always the case, and one line (XVIII.5) is defective
in that it has no caesura at all.   XIII.2 has a 'caesura' at the end of
the third foot.
The leonine is almost ubiquitous in the poem, sometimes in double-
rhyme but usually in mono-rhyme and sometimes even using assonance.   Lines
without rhymes are to be seen at V.524, 551, VI.62, 73, 98, VII.18, 116,
VIII.50, XIII.3, XVII.52, 72, 113, 128, XVIII.21.   Leonine verse
reached the height of its popularity in the tenth and eleventh centuries,
but declined in the twelfth (*Strecker* p.74).   The predominance of mono-
rhyme is consonant with the date of the poem, and rhymes such as *sepes/
plebs* at I.53 or *tres/figens* at IV.163 can be paralleled in later
poets: cf. Hugh Primas' *Diues eram et dilectus,* where this master
of rhyming latin poetry rhymes *ante/dante/sancte/diligam te.*   *Ruodlieb*
also has sporadic end-rhyme (perhaps fortuitous) at II.30, 35, III.25,
32, IV.71, V.535, 544, etc.   Occasionally the caesura-rhyme links up
with a preceding or following verse, as (for example) at V.317, VI.90,
X.97 or XI.69.   Such internal rhyme was later cultivated greatly, as
in Bernard of Cluny's *Hora nouissima tempora pessima sunt, uigilemus.*

R. Barber, *The Knight And Chivalry*, London 1974

K. Bartsch, H. de Boor, *Das Nibelungenlied*, 20th ed. Wiesbaden 1972

W. Braun, *Studien zum Ruodlieb: Ritterideal, Erzählstruktur und Darstellungstil*, Berlin 1962

F. Brunhölzl,'Zum Ruodlieb', *Deutsche Vjs f. Litt. und Geist.* XXXIX, 1965, pp.506ff.

E.R. Curtius, *European Literature And The Latin Middle Ages* (trans. W.R. Trask) London 1953

P. Dronke, *Poetic Individuality In The Middle Ages*, Oxford 1978

J. Engels, C.H. Kneepkens, H.F. Reijnders, *Magister Siguinus: Ars Lectoria*, Leiden 1979

A. Ewert, *Marie De France: Lais*, Oxford 1969

A. Ewert, *The Romance Of Tristan: Introduction And Commentary*, Oxford 1970

E. Faral, *Les Arts Poétiques du XIIe et XIIIe Siècles*, Paris 1924

J.H. Fisher (ed.), *The Medieval Literature Of Western Europe: A Review Of Research, Mainly 1930 - 1960*, New York 1966

G.B. Ford, Jr., *The Ruodlieb: The First Medieval Epic Of Chivalry From Eleventh-Century Germany. Translated From The Latin With An Introduction*, Leiden 1965

G.B. Ford, Jr., *The Ruodlieb· Linguistic Introduction, Latin Text And Glossary*, Leiden 1966

Helena M. Gamer, 'Studien zum Ruodlieb', *Zeitschr. f.d. Altertum* . LXXXVIII, pp.249ff

C.H. Grandgent, *An Introduction To Vulgar Latin*, Boston 1910

J.L.C. Grimm, A. Schmeller, *Lateinische Gedichte des X und XI Jahrhunderts*, Göttingen 1838

A.T. Hatto, *The Nibelungenlied*, Harmondsworth 1965

L. Laistner, Review of Seiler, *Anzeiger f. d. Altertum und d. Lit.* IX, 1885, pp.70ff.

L. Laistner, 'Die Lücken im Ruodlieb', *Zeitschr. f.d. Altertum und d. Lit.* XXIX, 1885, pp.1ff.

K. Langosch, *Waltharius, Ruodlieb, Märchenepen. Lateinische Epik mit deutschen Versen*, Berlin, 1956

F. Löwenthal, 'Bemerkungen zum Ruodlieb', *Zeitschr. f.d. Altertum und d. Lit.*, LXIV, 1927, pp.128ff.

E. Muret, L.M. DeFourques, *Beroul: Le Roman de Tristan*, 4th ed. , Paris 1974

L.R. Palmer, *The Latin Language*, London 1961

T.B.W. Reid, *Chrestien de Troyes: Yvain*, Manchester 1942

L.D. Reynolds (ed.), *Texts And Transmission: A Survey Of The Latin Classics*, Oxford 1983

M. Roques, *Chrétien de Troyes: Erec et Énide*, Paris 1973

Ruodlieb. Faksimile-Ausgabe.......bd.1, Wiesbaden 1974

F. Seiler, *Ruodlieb, der älteste Roman des Mittelalters, nebst Epigrammen*, Halle 1882

K. Strecker (trans. and revised R.B. Palmer), *Introduction To Medieval Latin*, Dublin/Zurich 1968

F. Whitehead, *La Chanson de Roland*, Oxford 1975

P. von Winterfeld, *Deutsche Dichter des lateinischen Mittelalters*, 2nd ed. 1917

E.C. Woodcock, *A New Latin Syntax*, London 1959

E.H. Zeydel, *Ruodlieb: The Earliest Courtly Novel (After 1050)*, Chapel Hill 1959

E.H. Zeydel, 'Die elf Epigramme der Münchener Ruodliebshandschrift', *Deutsche Vjs. f. Litt. und Geist.* XXXIII, 1959, pp.257ff.

SIGLA

M = Munich clm 19486

F = St Florian Port. 22

RUODLIEB

quidam prosapia uir progenitus generosa $\qquad$ M2^r
moribus ingenitam decorabat nobilitatem,
qui dominos plures habuisse datur locupletes,
sepius ad libitum quibus is famulans et honor[um
5   nil deseruisse potuit, putat ut meruisse,
quicquid et illorum sibi quis commisit herorum
aut ulciscendum causeque sue peragendum
non prolongabat, quam strennuiter peragebat.
sepius in mortem se pro dominis dat eisdem
10   seu bello seu uenatu seu quolibet actu.
nil sibi fortuna prohibente dabant malefida:
semper promittunt promissaque dissimulabant.
ast inimicicias horum causa sibi nactas
cum superare nequit, super hoc quid agat neque dic[it,
15   nusquam secure se sperans uiuere posse
rebus dispositis cunctis matrique subactis
tandem de patria pergens petit extera reg[na;
nullus et hunc alius sequitur nisi scutifer ei[us,
qui uehat enthecam rebus uariis oneratam,
20   a puero sibi quem docuit sufferre labore[m.
balenam dextrim, parmam uehit atque sinistri[m,
dextra lanceolam, sub scuto fertque pharetra[m,
annone saccum modicum sub se satis aptu[m.
ast loricatus dominus super et tunicatus
25   pro] mitra galeam rutilam gestat chalibinam,   M2^v
accinctus gladio compto capulotenus auro.
pen]det et a niueo sibimet gripis ungula collo,
un]gula non tota, medii cubiti modo longa,

I.1-28   11 male fida *Langosch*   14 dicit *Seiler*: dicat
Schmeller   21 balenam *edd.*: balneam *cod.*   23 annone *m.alt.*:
ad fodrum *m.pr.*   26 accinctus *Seiler*: ...ictus *cod.*,
Schmeller

I

There once was a man, born of a noble family, who enhanced   1
his innate nobility with his good behaviour.   He is said to
have had many rich lords and frequently served them at their
bidding, though he could win none of the honours he thought
he deserved.   Whatever any one of those masters gave him to
do - avenging an enemy, or furthering their own interests -
he wasted no time in energetically carrying it through.   He
frequently put his life at risk for these same liege-lords,
whether in war, out hunting, or in every manner of deed.
They gave him nothing - faithless fortune held them back -
and they were always making promises, only to pretend that
they had not.

He, however, could not overcome the hatred which rose up   13
against him on account of those things, and he could not say
what he ought to do about it;   despairing that he could ever
live anywhere in peace, he settled all his affairs, left them
in his mother's charge, and at last left his home country for
a foreign land.   No-one went with him save his squire, who
was to carry the pack laden with various items.   The knight
had taught him since he was a lad to endure hardship on his
account.   He carried a basin on his right shoulder and a
shield on his left;   his right hand gripped a lance, he carried
a quiver beneath the shield, and sat upon a fair-sized sack
to store provisions.

His lord, though, was in breast-plate and tunic, and also   24
wore not a soft hat but a glittering helmet of steel.   At his
side hung a sword, swathed to the hilt in gold.   There hung
from his snow-white neck a griffin's claw - but not a whole
claw, only half a cubit long -

```
       qu]e post ad latum uel pre decoratur ad artum
30     ob]rizo mundo, ceruino cinctaque loro,
       no]n ut nix alba tamen ut translucida gemma,
       qu]am dum perflabat tuba quam melius reboabat,
       ul]time dans matri domuique uale simul omni.
       st]at niger ut coruus equus et ceu smigmate lotus,
35     un]dique punctatus hac sub nigredine totus;
       ad] leuam colli complexa iuba iacet illi,
       qu]i faleratus erat ceu summum quemque decebat,
       ad] cuius sellam nil cernitur esse ligatum
       e] corio sutum ni uas mastice perunctum
40     du]lcius ut sapiat potus qui fusus in id sit,
       ex] ostro factum uel ceruical modicellum.
       qu]em super ut saluit equus altius ipse saliuit
       ceu] gaudens domino residenti fortiter illo.
       pre]silit hunc post mox canis in cursu bene uelox,
45     inu]estigator quo non melior fuit alter,
       pre] quo bestiola uel grandis siue minuta
       non abscondere quit se quin hanc mox reperire[t.      M3^r
       ultime fando uale matri famulisque ualete
       perfusa lacrimis facie dabat oscula cunctis.
50     arrepto freno monito calcare poledro
       cursitat in campo cita ceu uolitaret hirundo.
       ast per cancellos post hunc pascebat ocellos
       mater, at in sepes conscendens eius omnis plebs
       post hunc prospiciunt, singultant, flendo gem[iscunt.
55     cum plus non cernunt hunc, planctum multiplicar[unt.
       detersis lacrimis qui tunc lotis faciebus
       consolaturi dominam subeunt cito cuncti,
       que simulando spem premit altum corde dolo[rem;
       consolatur eos male dum se cernit habere.

60     non minor interea natum premit utique cura
       inque uia secum perpendit plurima rerum,
       deseruire domi quod nil ualet emolumenti
       et propter faidas sibi multas undique nactas
```

I.29-63   29 predecoratur *Schmeller, Ford*   35 subnigredine
Schmeller   50 poledro *edd.*: polebro *cod.*

which had later been embellished at the end where it was broad   29
and also where it was narrow with pure gold, and bound tight
with a stag-hide thong.   It was white, but not as snow;   it
was like translucent crystal, and when he blew on it it re-
echoed better than a horn, signalling his final farewell
to his mother and to all his household.

His horse stood there, black as a raven and glossy as if   34
washed with soap, and with speckles showing through from
beneath this blackness all over its body.   Its mane lay in
folds down the left side of its neck;   it was adorned as
befitted a man of the highest rank.   Nothing could be seen
fastened to its saddle save for a bottle sewn of leather and
smeared with resin, so that whatever drink was poured into it
might taste sweeter.   There was also a small pillow made from
purple cloth.   When he mounted up, the horse itself leapt
even higher, as though rejoicing that its master was seated
on its back.

Soon after the horse there came bounding the dog, swift in   44
the chase;   none was better at hunting that he was, and no
beast, whether large or small, could hide before him: he
would soon find them out.

Saying a last 'farewell' to his mother and 'farewell' to   48
his servants, he kissed them all goodbye with tears pouring
down his cheeks.   Then he took the reins, urged his horse
forward, and galloped over the plain as swiftly as a swallow.

But through the lattice his mother gazed with longing after   52
him, while all his folk went down into the fields and gazed
after him, sobbing and wailing as they wept.   When they could
no longer see him they redoubled their crying, then, wiping
away their tears, they all straightaway washed their faces
and went to their mistress to comfort her.   She on the other
hand suppressed the deep grief in her heart, made a pretence
of hope, and comforted them, since she saw that they were
taking it badly.

Meantimes concern pressed down no less heavily on the son,   60
and as he travelled he weighed up many matters in his heart:
the fact that his diligent service at home had brought him no
profit, and that on account of the many feuds which arose
against him everywhere he had to go into exile from his
beloved homeland.

a patria dulci quod debuit exiliari.
65 secum uoluebat se sicubi uile clientet
si fortuna uetus infestaretur ei plus,
esse nouercales omnes inibi sibi fratres,
non meliorasse res sed peius reperisse.
intime suspirans rogat obnixe Dominum flens
70 ut non deseruisset se nolitue perire,   M3^v
sed sibi succurrat erumnas quo superaret.
intranti regnum merenti sic alienum
uenator regis subito tunc fit comes eius,
isque salutat eum resalutaturque per ipsum.
75 exul erat fortis membris facieque uirilis,
uoceque grandiloquus, in responso seriosus.
quem rogat indigena quis et unde sit, ire uelit quo;
quo sibi non dicto dedignanterque sileto
inquisisse piget, uelut est res, menteque tractat
80 'est si legatus, minor est eius comitatus;
dum uenit ad curtem, quis munera, quis gerit ensem?
pauperis est posse, reor, aut uirtutis opime'.
dum satis obticuit demum sibi denuo dixit
'non irascaris de me si plus rogiteris,
85 nam tibi prodesse uolo si possum, nec obesse.
uenator regis sibi carus sumque fidelis,
nec solet audire quemquam clementius ac me.
pro faida grandi patriam si deseruisti,
uis et in hac terra mihi ceu tibimet peregrina
90 quid deseruire causasque tuas superare,
utile consilium tibi tunc do non renuendum,
usum uenandi quoniam bene si didicisti
O quam felicis huc ominis exiliaris!
diligit hanc artem rex hac et in arte peritum.
. . . .   M4^r
95 quisquis habet dare quit: qui non habet, hic dare, dic, quid?
si non cottidie tamen assidue dabit ille,
nunquam sollicitus uictus fueris uel amictus.
cum donantur ei pulchri celeresque caballi,

I.64-98   70 nolit ue *Zeydel*   92 quoniam] quo *Schmeller*

He thought to himself how lowly a vassal he would be anywhere   65
if his fortune of old continued to plague him; there in
exile every stepson would be a brother to him, and he would
have found a worse situation instead of bettering it.

Sighing inwardly and weeping, he prayed resolutely to the
Lord God not to abandon him, nor to desire his death, but
rather to bring help to him so that he might overcome his
troubles.

As he was entering a foreign kingdom in this sorrowful   72
state of mind, a huntsman of the king all of a sudden
joined him on his journey, greeting him and being greeted by
him in return. The stranger had a muscular frame and a
manly face, was firm in speech, and serious when he spoke.
The native of this land asked him who he was, where he was
from, where he wished to go; but when nothing was said in
reply and he met with a disdainful silence, he was ashamed to
have asked, as is often the case, and thought to himself "if
he is an envoy, his company is rather small; if he is on his
way to the court, then for whom does he bring gifts?   And for
whom does he bear the sword?   I think he is poor in power,
or rich in virtue."

When he had been silent long enough, he at last said to him   83
"do not be angry with me if you are asked more questions, for
I wish to assist you if I can, not stand in your way.   I am
the king's huntsman, faithful and dear to him, and he listens
to no-one more kindly than to me.   If you have left your
homeland because of some great feud, and if you wish to do
some service in this land - which is foreign to me, as it
is to you - and to overcome your troubles, then I give you
some useful advice which you should not refuse, since if you
have learnt well the art of hunting, then it is indeed a good
omen that you are in exile here!   Our king is devoted to this
art, and to him who is accomplished in it.

Any may give who has possessions - say, what does the man   95
who has nothing give?   But even if he does not give you
something every day, you shall never be anxious for food or
clothing.   When fine, swift horses are given to him,

nobis prestantur, cursu quo more probentur,
100 qui celer et facilis est nec gyrando rebellis.
est qui maxime tunc opus illi donat et illum.
propter et annonam numquam nummum dabis unum,
nam sine mensura dabitur tibi, dum cupis, illa.
ad mensam comites superexaltans locupletes
105 dum conuiuatur nobiscum fando iocatur.
appositum quicquid melioris erit sibi mittit,
id faciens nobis plus quam mercedis honoris.
si libeat cum me te fidum fedus inire
dando fidem nostras iungamus federe dextras
110 separet ut nil nos dumtaxat amara nisi mors.
simus ubicumque, res alterutrius uterque
sic agat ut proprias, melius siquid queat illas'.
exul tum demum fidens sibi dixit ad illum
'sat mihi domne tuum demonstras uelle benignum,
115 consiliumque tuum non estimo transgrediendum,
namque meas causas, ut sunt, tu coniciebas.
hinc pactum fidei placet inter nos stabiliri'.
dando sibi dextras ibi fiunt moxque sodales
....   M4^V
120 oscula dando sibi firmi statuuntur amici
alterutris dominis famulantes cordibus unis.
dum satis inter se de rebus disposuere
regni metropoli ceperunt appropiare
in qua rex genti legem dedit aduenienti.
125 castris ingressis pueris et equis stabulatis
insimul ad curtem properabant uisere regem.
ut uenatorem rex uidit dixit ad illum
'unde uenis, quid rumoris fers?   dicito nobis.
inuestigasti per siluam quando measti
130 ursum siue suem libeat nos pergere post quem?'
qui non ut domino sed ceu respondit amico
'illorum neutrum sed eorundem domitorem
inuestigaui, reperi, mecum tibi duxi,

I.99-133   101 est cui maxime *m.alt.*:   est cui tunc *m.pr.*
103 dum *cod.*, *Schmeller*: cum *edd. ceteri*   106 quidquid
Seiler, Langosch, Zeydel, Ford   114 demonstras *cod.m.alt.*:
declaras *m.pr.*, *Schmeller*   120 dando...firmi *non habet*
Schmeller

they are offered to us, so that they can be put to the test   99
by being ridden, to see which is fast and easy to handle, and
does not rebel when wheeled about.   The king gives that
horse to whoever is in the greatest need.   More than this,
you will never pay a penny for food, for that will be given
to you without measure whenever you desire it.   At table·   104
he exalts his wealthy barons and joins with us in lighthearted
conversation while we feast.   He sends to us any especial
delicacy that is set before him, and so doing shows us greater
honour than he could with money.   If you are willing to enter
a pact of faith with me, then let us join our right hands in
a pact and plight our faith, that nothing, save only bitter
death, shall come between us.   Let us go everywhere together,
and each so treat the other's property as though it were his
own, or better, if in any way he can."

Then at last the stranger trusted him, and said to him   113
"you have shown me well enough, lord, that you mean well
to me, and I do not think your advice is to be passed over,
for you even guessed the real state of my affairs.   So may
this pact of faith between us be firmly founded from now on."
There, clasping each other's right hand, they quickly became
close companions.   Embracing one another they became firm
friends, each serving the other as his feudal lord with a
single mind.

While they fully explained to one another their situation,   122
they began to come near to the capital city of the kingdom,
in which the king gave his law to approaching people.   Once
in the city, with their squires and horses attended to, they
straightaway hastened to the court to see the king.

When the king saw his huntsman he said to him "where have   127
you come from?   What news do you bring?   Tell it to us.
While you were wandering through the forest did you track down
a bear or a boar which we may go chasing after?"

The huntsman replied, but as though to a friend rather than   131
to his feudal lord, "I have tracked down neither of those, but
rather their tamer, and I have found him and led him with me
to you –

35

scilicet hunc iuuenem tibimet seruire decentem,
135 arte satis catum uenandi satque beatum
ut reor utque suo mihi cernitur in comitatu,
et cum dignaris illum satis ipse probabis;
is sua fert dona tibi parua nec abicienda,
inque clientelam quo suscipias cupit illum.
140 qui precursorem leua tenuit bicolorem
cui fuit aurata collo conexa catena.

I.134-141   141 conexa *cod.*, *Seiler*:   connexa *Schmeller,*
Langosch, Zeydel, Ford

see, this young man who is worthy to serve you, well versed   134
in the art of hunting, and blessed, too - at least so I think,
and so he appeared to me as we rode together.   And when you
have honoured him, you will prove his worth well enough for
yourself.   He brings his own gifts to you;   they are small
but not to be despised, and he wishes you to enlist him in
your retinue."

   With his left hand he held his mottled hound, which had   140
a golden chain fastened to its collar.

illius herbe uim medici dicunt fore talem:
torridula trita cum paruo polline mixta,
hinc pilule facte si fient more fabelle
et iaciantur aquis, quicunque comederet ex his
5   piscis, quod nequeat subtus supra sed aquam net.

inter tres digitos pilulas tornando rotundas
dilapidat stagno, quo pisces agmine magno
conueniunt auide capiendo pilam sibi quisque,
quam qui gustabant, sub aqua plus nare nequibant
10   sed quasi ludendo saltus altos faciendo
undique diffugiunt nec mergere se potuerunt.
ille sed in cimba percurrit remige stagna,
post pisces uirga cogens ad littora sicca,
quos duo cum funda circumcinxere sub unda,
15   cum terram peterent ad aquam resalire nequirent.
sic piscando sibi ludum fecitque sodali.
tunc iussere cocos prunis assare minores,
maiores scuto regi portant ioculando
19   'uenari melius hodie nos non poteramus.'
Rex: 'retibus aut hamis hos cepistis ue sagenis?'
Ven.: 'non sic piscamur' ait incola 'sed dominamur
piscibus, e fundo ueniant ad nos sine grato,
et super stagnum saliendo iocum dare magnum.
dum sub aquam nequeunt satis et saltando fatiscunt,
25   hos tandem uirga facimus requiescere terra.'
'hoc uolo' rex dixit ' speculari copia dum fit.'

Plinius herbarum uires scribens uariarum
laudat buglossam res ad multas nimis aptam.
in ualidum potum dicit qui ponat eandem
30   quantumcunque bibat quod is ebrius haut fore possit.
p]ulueris eiusdem describit Plinius idem

II.1-31

The physicians say that the effect of this herb will be   1
like this: it is ground in a pestle and mixed with fine
flour, and if from this pellets are made, shaped like beans,
and thrown into the water, any fish which eats of them can
no longer stay in the water but swims on the surface.

He rolled the pellets round between fingers and thumb,   6
and threw them into the pond.   The fish gathered there in
a great shoal, each greedily seizing upon a pellet for itself.
As they swallowed them down they became unable to swim in the
water, and made great leaps into the air, as though at play.
They fled everywhere, but they could not submerge themselves.

He on the other hand rowed across the water in a boat,   12
driving the fish to dry land from behind with a stick.   Two
men cut off their escape with a net under the water as they
made for the shore, so that they could not jump back to the
water.   By fishing in this way he made sport for himself and
his companion.

Then they ordered the cooks to roast the smaller ones over   17
the fire, and carried off the larger ones on a shield to the
king, joking the while "we could not have had a better day's
hunting, could we?"   "Did you catch these with nets or hooks"
asked the king "or with seines,"   "We do not fish like that"
said the man from this land, "we rule over the fish, and they
come to us from the deep at no expense, and give us a great
entertainment jumping above the pond; since they can no
longer swim underwater and become exhausted with so much jumping
about, we finally make them rest on dry land with a stick."

"I want to see this" said the king, "when there is an   26
opportunity."

Pliny, discussing the effects of various herbs, praises
buglossa as being very suitable for many purposes.   He says
that a man who puts it into strong drink cannot become drunk,
no matter how much he drinks.   This same Pliny tells how,

q]ui serat in carnem, si forte cani det eandem,
tem]pore quod modico canis obcecetur ab ipso,
e]t quidquid cecum fuerit sine lumine natum
35 hu]ius si gustet quid mox uisum cito perdat.
herbe uenator cuius studiosus amator
i]n siluam pergit, plures hirpos ubi rescit,
c]apram cun fune secum ducente sodale.
q]uam cedunt inibi lato sub tegmine fagi
40 a]bstrahendo cutem cedunt per frustaque carnem,
qu]am super aspergunt cum pulvere, pelle recondunt,
a]mboque scandebant super arbore uel residebant.
e]xul et horribiles hirporum dans ululatus
nun]c ueterum grandes, iuuenum graciles modo uoces
45 ex]primit, ut ueros hirpos ululare putares.
qu]o dum conueniunt hirpi capram repererunt,
q]uam discerpebant in momentoque uorabant,
n]ec procul hinc abeunt ambo quam lumina perdunt.

ta]libus et paribus instat miles peregrinus
50 af]fectans sese cunctis ualet ut studiose,
in] magna pace regnum dum stat uel honore.
al]terius regni marhmanni ualde benigni
nostr]is, a nostris is amor seruatur et ipsis.
al]terutrique meant emptum, quodcunque uolebant,
55 ue]ctigal dantes uectigal et accipientes,
nu]bunt hinc illuc natasque suas dederant huc,
com]patres fiunt uel qui non sunt uocitabant.
hi]c amor inter eos per multos duruit annos,
do]nec peccatis sunt rupta ligamina pacis.
60 ex]osor pacis nostri generalis et hostis
se]men zizanie non cessat multiplicare,
e]st ubicunque fides, ut stet ea non ibi perpes.
q]uo succedente fit grandis uuerra repente.
q]uodam mercato multo populo glomerato,
65 pro] causa uili sunt occisi quia multi...

II.32-65   45 scandebant...residebant *m.alt.*: scandentes
...residentes *m.pr.*   51 regnum dum] dum regnum *Seiler,*
Langosch   55 uetigal *cod.*

if someone puts powdered buglossa onto some meat and then gives   32
this to a dog, the dog is made blind by it in a short time.
And any other animal that was born blind, without sight,
swiftly loses its powers of vision as soon as it tastes any
of this herb.

The huntsman, a great lover of this herb, made his way into   36
the forest, where he knew there were many wolves.   His companion
came too, leading a nanny-goat on a rope.   They killed the goat
there in the shade of a spreading beech, skinned it, and chopped
its flesh into pieces.   They sprinkled this with the powder,
stuffed it back into the skin, and they both climbed up high
into a tree where they sat waiting.   The stranger gave some
horrible wolf-calls and imitated both the deep calls of old
wolves and the lighter calls of young ones, so that you would
have thought they were real wolves howling.   When the wolves
gathered there they found the goat, which they tore apart and
swallowed up in a moment; but they did not get far from there
before they went blind in both eyes.

With these and similar deeds the foreign knight made his   49
mark, eagerly endearing himself to all, as he was well able,
while the kingdom enjoyed a great and praiseworthy peace.
The borderers of the other kingdom were most friendly with our
own, and this mutual love was maintained by our side and by
theirs.   Both journeyed freely to buy whatever they wanted,   54
paying duty abroad and receiving duty at home.   Our men married
their women; they gave their daughters to our sons, became kith
and kin, and called even those who were not so by those terms.
This love between them lasted for many years, until the bonds
of peace were broken by evil deeds.   The hater of peace, the
enemy of us and of all men, does not cease to sow more thickly
the seed of his tares wherever good faith is to be found, so
that it might not stand firm there forever.   He prevailed,
and a great war soon broke out.   A great crowd of people   64
gathered in a certain market-place, bacause many people had
been killed for a trifling reason...

'esse scio regem quia uestrum tam sapientem,   M4b^r
hec quod non iussit, tua stulta superbia suasit:
hinc uideas qualem nunc nanciscaris honorem.
rem peiorasti, cum te famare cupisti:
5   ramo suspendi per suras sat meruisti!'
acclamant cuncti cur hec tardet celerari.
princeps respondit 'rex noster non ita iussit
aut se dedentem uel captum perdere quemquam,
sed si possemus captiuos erueremus
10   cum preda pariter, que fecimus ambo decenter.
uincere uictorem, maiorem uult quis honorem?
sis leo pugnando, par ulciscendo sed agno.
non honor est uobis ulcisci damna doloris.
magnum uindicte genus est si parcitis ire.
15   hinc precor annuite, uestro quo fiat amore,
solus ut iste comes nobiscum uadat inermis,
seu uultis proprio seu quouis uile caballo;
ni placeat uobis, sibi seruiat ut puer unus
qui sibi prendat equum stabulans annonet et ipsum,
20   utque suam gentem uinctam pre se gradientem
cernat in obprobrium duxit uel quale periclum,
ne quicquam temere presumat tale patrare.'
tunc sibi dixere cuncti sua uerba placere,
et iubilo magno patriam repetunt properando
25   et quamuis uideant sua domata qualiter ardent,
non tristabantur dum libertate fruuntur.

signiferi et proceres alii regisque fideles
finipolim subeunt ibi captiuosque reseruant

_____

III.1-28   27 signiferi *cod.*:   signifer *edd. omnes*

42

III

"Because I know that your king is so wise, I know this   1
too, that he did not issue these orders: your stupid pride
has urged them.   Look what sort of honour this has brought
you.   You have made matters worse, though you desired to
exalt yourself - you have done enough to deserve to be hanged
from a tree by the legs."

All cried out, asking why he was slowing up the proceedings. 6
The leader replied, "our king did not give orders that we
should kill anyone surrendering or captured, but rather to
rescue the prisoners if we could, and the plunder as well;
we did both in a proper manner.   Who wants a greater honour
than to conquer a conqueror?   You should be a lion when you
fight, but like a lamb when you take revenge!   It is no honour
to you to avenge your painful loss.   If you spare your anger -
that is a noble kind of vengeance!   Grant then I pray you that 15
by your own good pleasure this man of yours may go with us
alone and unarmed, on a fast horse or on an old hack as you
wish, and if this is not pleasing to you, that one lad may
serve him, to hold his horse for him, stable it and feed it.
Then he may see his own people walking before him in chains,
and also into what shame their rash behaviour has led them,
lest he should presume to attempt any such rash deed."

Then all said that they found his words pleasing, and with   23
great rejoicing they made haste to return to their own country;
and although they saw how their own houses were ablaze they
were not downcast, since they delighted in their freedom.

The standard-bearers, the nobles and the other faithful   27
servants of the king came to the city by the border and there
took back the prisoners.

et numerant socios, sanos habuisseque cunctos
30   intime gaudebant laudemque Deo tribuebant.
missus dirigitur regi qui cuncta loquatur,
quid uelit ut faciant predonibus utque remandet;
qui proper]ando suum poscit sibi ferre caballum,   M4b^v
scutifer] hunc dum fert uirgam de sepe simul dat;
35   quem super] insedit, feriens uolitare coegit,
cepit c]alcare latus obmaculare cruore.
prospicien]s s[axo] regis speculator ab alto
exclamat 'iuuenem uideo nimium properantem:
parua qu]o narret non ab re sic pauitaret.'
40   obueniu]nt illi multi rumoris auari,
comprendu]nt et equum, quid narret eumque requirunt.
dicens] omne bonum nec plus modicum neque multum
dans pue]ro gladium regem properauit ad ipsum
dixit et] 'eternum columen regale tuorum,
45   lete ui]ue, uale, gaude, dignissime laude.'
cui rex] 'dic sodes, nostri sunt ergo fideles
incolum]es aut qui sunt in pugnando perempti?
nobis abl]ata dic si sit preda redempta.'
is tamen] inmensa circumdatus undique turba
50   inclina]ns dixit 'rex a te tale quid absit!
gaude, g]ratorum periit quia nemo tuorum,
cunctaque nunc] preda redit integra, non temerata.
nunc socii que]runt hoc per me uel petierunt
de capti]s quid agant in uincula quos redigebant.
55   trans hoc] commissum nil est mihi, rex, tibi dictum.'
tres marc]as tribui legato rex iubet auri,

III.29-56   33 qui properando *Seiler*: missus quando *Schmeller*
34 scutifer *Seiler*: armiger *Schmeller*   35 quem super *Seiler*
36 coepit *Seiler*   37 prospiciens *Seiler*: aspiciens *Schmeller*
saxo *Laistner*: solio *Schmeller*   39 parua quo *Laistner*: magnum
quo *Seiler*   pauitaret *scripsi* : pauitauit *Seiler, Zeydel*:
pauitabit *Ford*   40 obueniunt *Seiler* : occurrunt *Schmeller*   42
dicens *Seiler*: nuntiat *Schmeller*   43 dans puero *Seiler*   44
dixit et *Seiler*: O rex *Schmeller*   is tamen *scripsi*: nuntius
Schmeller   50 inclinans *Seiler*: respondens *Schmeller*   51
gaude *Seiler*   52 cunctaque nunc *Seiler*   55 trans hoc *Seiler*:
ultra *Schmeller*   mihi] nisi *Schmeller*

They counted up their comrades, rejoiced in their hearts that   29
they had got them all back safe and sound, and gave praise to
God.   An envoy was sent to the king to tell him everything
and to bring back news of what he wished to be done to the
prisoners.   In his haste the messenger asked for his horse
to be brought to him; a squire brought it to him, and at the
same time gave him a wand from the hedge.   He mounted the
horse, and whipping it made it fly high through the air, and
began to spatter its side with blood from his spurs.

Looking down from a high rock, the king's lookout shouted   37
down "I see a young man in a great hurry - no small thing
could make him shake with fear so to tell us his news!"   Many,
greedy for news, went out to meet him.   They took hold of
his horse and asked him what he had to tell them.   He said
that all was well and left it at that, adding nothing, handed
his sword to a page and hurried to see the king himself, to
whom he said "eternal, regal bulwark of your people, may you
live in happiness, be strong, and rejoice, O most worthy of
praise."

The king replied "tell me, pray, are our faithful subjects   46
then safe?   Which of them have fallen in the fighting?   Say,
if the plunder taken from us has been recovered."   The envoy,
surrounded on all sides by a massive crowd, bowed and said "O
king, let any thought like that be far from you!   Rejoice,
because none of your beloved host has perished, and all the
plunder is even now on its way back whole and undefiled.   Now   53
through me my comrades seek to ask this question: what are
they to do about the prisoners whom they are leading back in
chains?   Apart from this errand, O king, nothing has been said
to me to report for you."

The king ordered that three gold marks be given to the envoy.

dicit don]ato misso nimis exhilarato
'care, red]i propere uel ai sociis ita de me:
rex gra]tes dictis uobis demandat et actis,
60 cum uestri]s uinctis sibi quam propere ueniatis.'
tum salie]ns ad equum iuuenis citat ad remeandum.
hora qu]e bina prius iuerat ibat id una:
ad cele]randas res est pernimium bona merces.
ut redi]it socios ueniant iubet insimul omnes;
65 illi cc]nueniunt et in ampla curte steterunt.
tunc] per cancellos legatus dixit ad illos
'uobis in]manes rex iussit dicere grates
non so]llum dictis sed dicta sequentibus actis.
rex uult] uisatis hunc quam citius ualeatis,
70 mandan]s predonum nec dimittatis ut ullum.'

III.57-70 57 dicit donato *Seiler* 61 tum saliens *scripsi*:
inclinans *Strecker*: tunc currens *Seiler* 62 bina *cod. m.alt.*:
gemina *m.pr.* 65 illi conueniunt *Seiler*: illi ueniunt *Schmeller*;
cod. habet ...nueniunt *m.alt.*, ...nuenerunt *m.pr.* 67 inmanes *cod.*
m.alt.: ingentes *m.pr.*

He was overwhelmed by the gift, and the king said to him: 57
"Dear fellow, hurry back to your comrades and tell them
from me 'the king requests that thanks be given to you in
word and deed; may you come to him with all speed, bringing
your prisoners.'"

Then leaping to his horse, the young man hurried on his   61
journey back, and rode in one hour what had taken him two
before; a good reward works wonders in speeding things up.

On his return he ordered all his comrades to come, there   64
and then.   They gathered together and stood in the wide
courtyard.   Then from the balcony the envoy said to them
"his majesty orders me to express his immeasurable thanks to
you not only in words, but in actions which follow them up.
His majesty wishes that you should come to see him as quickly
as you are able, and further instructs you not to set free
any of the plunderers."

'nunc est consilio nobis opus inueniendo   M5^{r}
qualiter illius pietati gratificemus
non solis uerbis, quorum satis inueniemus,
sed quid donorum mittamus ei uariorum,
5   est ut equis frenis auro compte faleratis,
pelliciis crisis uaricosis siue crusennis,
ad quod quid mihi quis dicat uelit auxiliari.'
respondent pariter quod agant id ualde libenter.
grates egit eis rex et post hec ait illis:
10   'quid respondendum sit missis dicite primum.'
est ibi philosophus cunctis sapientior unus,
quem timor aut amor a recto diuertere quoquo
non in iudicio faciendo preualet ullo,
dicere quem pro se dicunt debere petuntque.
15   in regis uelle qui dicens maxime stare
eius consilium solum monet esse sequendum.
rex 'mihi consilium quoniam sinitis tribuendum,
restat ut huc ueniant legati dictaque dicant
utque sciatis ab his si credere neue uelitis.'
20   post hos direxit.   ueniunt quando sibi dixit
'en regis, uestri domini nostri uel amici,
dulcia narraui legamina plena fidei,
quam pie tractauit, merito quos perdere quiuit,
reddere uel sanos mihi contra se nece dignos.
25   clementer nobis demandauit sat honoris.
quod deseruire communiter hos decet et me,
si sic persoluet, per uos uelut ipse spopondit.'
dixit legatus 'non est sic morigeratus

IV.1-28   7 quid *Seiler*: quo *Schmeller*   20 direxit *cod. m.alt.*:
diremit *m.pr.*   22 legamina plena fidei *scripsi*: fidei legamina
plena *cod.*   25 *om. m.pr., add. m.alt. in margine; ponit post v.*
26 Schmeller

IV

"Now needs must we take counsel to see how we may give   1
thanks to that king's godly action, not just with words (we
shall find plenty of those), but to see what variety of gifts
we should send to him, say, horses finely shod and with
bridles of gold, or cloaks of the finest mottled squirrel-
skins.   Let him speak to this matter who wishes to assist me."
They replied with unanimity that they should most willingly   8
act thus.   The king thanked them and then addressed them as
follows: "tell me first what reply we should give to the
messengers."   There was there a certain philosopher, wiser
than all men, whom neither fear nor love could deflect in any
way from the right path in making any judgement.   They all
said that he ought to speak on their behalf, and sent for him.
He said that he was absolutely in accord with the king's
wishes, and advised that his counsel alone ought to be
followed.   The king said "since you permit me to make the   17
decision, it remains for the envoys to come here and speak
their message, so that you may know from this whether or not
you wish to believe them."
He sent someone to fetch them.   When they came, he said   20
to them "behold, I have told of the attractive and wholly
faithful terms set out by the king, your lord and my friend,
how devoutly he treated those whom he might deservedly have
executed, preferring to return to me in full health men who
by their action against him deserved death.   He has mercifully
bestowed enough honour on me.   And so it behoves both them and
me to offer him homage, if he will truly hand them over, as he
has himself sworn through you."   The envoy said "it is not   28
his custom

                ut quid uerborum soleat mutare suorum.
30   est quod ait uerum, dictum sibi uult fore uerum.'
            rex ait 'id quando uel ubi fore possit, ai tu.'
            'hoc' ait 'est uestri iuris, rex, induciari.'
            'tu tamen inque locum quo conueniamus in unum,   M5^V
            ut pax inter nos firmetur mille per annos.'
35   missus ait 'si uis dominis et si placet istis
            non tam nosco locum uestris conuentibus aptum
            campus ut est ille quo nos pugnauimus ante,
            inter clausuras nostri uestrique gemellas,
            sunt ut ubi uicti uestri nostrique redempti
40   dimittantur ibi nobiscum pacificati.'
            omnibus ille locus est uisus ad hoc satis aptus,
            regibus ambobus conuenturis spaciosus;
            induciasque trium laudant ad id ebdomadarum.
            post hec rex surgit sic conciliumque diremit
45   inque caminatam cum paucis it requietum.
            missis ualde bona dantur regalia dona,
            qui regem repetunt dignas gratesque sibi dant,
            quis miscere iubet summi uini quod habebat.
            legati surgunt deturque licentia poscunt.
50   rex ait 'audite mihi dilectique notate
            que uobis dico, que dicite non ut amico
            sed ueluti patri meliora malis referenti:
            "qualis es in corde te talem prodis in ore,
            que nobis uenit tua quod legatio pandit,
55   que spondendo reis ueniam spem dando salutis
            mirum uelle satis docet ultronee pietatis,
            contra que grates non sufficimus dare dignas,
            sed tibi subiecti sumus in pugnando subacti
            semper et omnigeni seruiminis intime prompti.
60   ut demandasti quo uis sumus ire parati,
            est quod laudatum ternarum septimanarum
            ad spacium: uestris est uisum sic uti nostris:
            in campo primus es quo tu consiliatus."
            oblitus si quid sum uestra fides at id implet.'   M6^r

---

IV.29-64   35 uis et dominis *Schmeller*   49 detur que licentia
Zeydel

to be in the habit of changing any of his words.   What he   29
says is true, and he wishes what will be said to him to be
true."   The king said "then you say when or where this may
take place."   "O king," he replied, "it is in your power to
conclude this."   "But you name a place where we can meet face
to face, so that a peace may be affirmed between us for a
thousand years."   The messenger said "if you desire, and if
it pleases these your lords, I know no place so suitable for
your coming together as is that plain where we fought before,
between the twin frontiers of your land and ours, so that in
that place where your men were defeated and ours were redeemed,
they may be set at peace with us, and released."   This spot   41
seemed admirably fitting for the coming together of both kings,
and they declared a truce of three weeks for the purpose.
After this, the king arose and thus dismissed his counsel,
retiring to his chamber with a few attendants. to rest.

Truly regal gifts were given to the messengers, who returned   46
to the king and gave him thanks and praise.   He ordered some
of the finest wine he had to be mixed for them.   The envoys
stood up and asked the king's permission to depart.   The king 50
said: "listen to me, my beloved men, and mark well what I say
to you.   Say this, not as if to a friend, but as if to a
father bringing better things to evil men: 'such as you are
in your heart, so you prove yourself in speech;   your legation
which came to us has shown this by promising mercy to the
guilty and giving the hope of salvation, and demonstrates well
enough your wonderful desire to be merciful of your own volition,
for which we cannot give you sufficient thanks;   but we were   58
defeated by you in the fighting, and are your subjects, and
always ready and willing to serve you in any way.   As you
requested, we are prepared to go to the place you wish in three
weeks' time, as was decided - it seemed fitting to your side
and to ours - in the plain you first proposed.'   If I have
forgotten anything, your good faith will include it."

```
65    respondent pariter 'meruisti sufficienter
      nos seruire tibi semper cum corde fideli.'
      tunc inclinabant cum rite 'ualete' recedunt.
      inde petunt summum, uelut est dignum, uicedomnum,
      a quo donati sunt ualde 'uale' benefacti.
70    ex iussu regis prouisorem dedit illis
      qui procuraret quod opus sit eis ut haberent,
      quod studio summo compleuit cordeque fido
      donec pacifice uel eos perduxit honeste
      extra clausuram fines regni dirimentem;
75    quem bene donatum uel uerbis gratificatum
      poscunt inclinet regi, 'faciam' quibus inquit.
      a se diuisi sunt ad patriamque reuersi.
      utque domum redeunt regem properando reuisunt.
      ut primum uidet bene quos suscepit et inquit
80    'dicite rumoris nunc quid nobis referatis?'
      respondit missus 'quia clemens est tibi Christus,
      quod reges alii nisi grandi non superant ui
      dat Deus id sponte tibi clemens absque labore,
      nam per contigua tibi que sunt undique regna
85    crederis esse leo uigilanti semper ocello;
      quin agnellina pietate tuaque sophia
      tu uincis melius gladius quam uincat alius:
      namque deo teste quo mittebar modo de te
      nescio plus ab eis adameris seu uerearis.
90    cum rex audisset, summatum grex et adesset,
      que demandasti sibi uel plebi simul omni,
      primo seruimen post fidi cordis amorem,
      sublata cydare surgens inclinat honeste,
      tunc residens tacuit donec rem pleniter audit,       M6ᵛ
95    quantum nostrates disceptabantque suates
      atque sui nostros offendentes inopinos
      occidunt spoliant captiuatosque cremabant,
      qualiter et nostri sunt illorum dominati,
      captiuos redimunt captiuantesque ligabant;
100   quos tibi cum referunt perituros seque putarent,
```

IV.65-100   67 recedunt *cod. m.alt.*:   rediebant *m.pr.*: rededunt
Ford   69 bene facti *Zeydel*   70 regis qui prouisorem *cod. m.pr.*
79 utprimum *Zeydel*   97 captiuatosque]captiuantesque *cod. m.pr.*

They replied for their part "you have deserved enough for us   65
to serve you always with a faithful heart."   Then they bowed,
and with a polite "farewell" they departed.

Next they sought out the king's viceroy, as was proper,   68
by whom they were given many gifts and fiefs as he wished them
"farewell."   By order of the king he gave them an agent,
who would see to it that they had whatever they needed, a
task he zealously carried out with a faithful heart until he
brought them in peace and with due honour over the boundary
which divided the borders of the kingdom.   They rewarded him
richly, thanked him politely, and asked him to bow to his
king (for them).   "I will do this," he said to them.   Then
they left him and returned to their homeland.

As soon as they reached home, they went to the king with   78
all speed.   As soon as he saw them he received them well and
said "tell me, what news do you bring to me now?"   The
messenger replied, "because Christ is merciful towards you, what
other kings could achieve only with a massive force, God grants
to you in his mercy, and with no effort on your part, for
throughout the neighbouring kingdoms which surround you, you
are held to be a lion whose eye is ever watchful; yet you are
more victorious with your lamb-like gentleness and your wisdom
than any other's weapon could be.   For as God is witness, I do   88
not know whether you are more loved or feared by the people
of that land where you so recently sent me.   When the king
had heard (and his company of lords was present) what you
asked of him and of all his people - first, their feudal
service, and then faithful, heartfelt love - he removed his
crown, stood up and bowed graciously.   Then he sat down in   94
silence until he had heard all the matter through: how much
our side and his had been in dispute, and how his people
provoked ours without warning, killing, looting, and burning
prisoners; how our men then overcame them, freed the captives
and tied up the captors, who when our men brought them to you
thought they were doomed to die;

quam clementer eis adimendo metum misereris,
illos absoluens consolans et bene tractans
presulibus ducibus locupletibus [atque patronis
ipsos seruandum dederis uel equos ad alendum:
105 non, ut sunt meriti, sub carcere compedis aut ui
nec tractent illos deceat quam regis amicos,
ut dum reddantur super his ne forte querantur.
quin ipsum comitem scelus hoc inmane patrantem
nulli conmisit, super hunc nulli bene fidit,
110 sed sibimet seruit gladium persepeque portat
ut nullus noceat quem rex sic glorificabat.
nolle recordari te sed postquam sibi dixi
dedecus inmensum uel inedicibile damnum
quod tibi fecerunt sub iure tuo modo qui sunt,
115 quos inpunitos quamuis meritos inimicos,
reddere laudares in nulla re nichilatos,
si uelit in plebe pax ut reparetur utrimque.
sic dicens silui uel rege nuente resedi.
in cras induciat his ut responsa rependat.
120 in summo mane curtem cuncti petiere,
plures rumoris cupidi quam regis honoris.
intromittuntur qui quid prodesse uidentur,
regi consilium pro tali re tribuendum;
ualue clauduntur, nescitur quid loquerentur.   M7^r
125 est breue colloquium pro consensu sapientum.
nobis interea data prandia sunt sat opima.
dum pranderemus et adhuc uinum biberemus
mittitur. et post nos tres omnes ut ueniamus.
fecimus ut iussit.   cum pre se uenimus inquit
130 "O nostri domini missi summique patroni,
si respondere bene sciremus uel honeste
demandaminibus clementibus atque paternis,
est ut promeritus nimium, prompte faceremus.
dicite nunc illi de me de plebe uel omni,
135 de summis mediis imis mihi iure subactis
fidum uel promptum subiectorum famulamen.

IV.101-136   103 atque patronis *scripsi*:   abbatibusque *Zeydel*
117 ut firmetur *cod. m.pr.*   129 cum prestamus is inquit *cod.*
m.pr.

54

how you in your grace showed mercy to them, removing their   101
fear, freeing them, comforting them and treating them well.
You gave them over to the bishops, lords and wealthy margraves
to keep them and feed their horses; you did not fetter them
forcibly in a dungeon, as they deserved.   Nor did your men
treat them other than as befits the friends of a king, so that
when they were sent back they might have no cause for complaint
about their treatment.   As for the count who had taken this   108
wicked action, the king gave him over to no-one and trusted
no-one on his account, but kept him to himself, and very often
bore his sword to prevent anyone from harming him whom he had
so honoured.

    After this I said to him that you did not wish to recall   112
the terrible dishonour and unspeakable sin that they had done
to you, they who were now in your power, and that it was your
pleasure to render them up unpunished and unharmed in any way,
though they were deservedly your enemies, if he wished it, so
that peace might be re-established between both peoples.
I said this much, then was silent, and at the king's bidding
I sat down.   The king adjourned the meeting to the following
day, to think over a reply to our message.

    Early in the morning everyone made their way to the court.   120
Many were more greedy for news than for the king's honour;
those were admitted who seemed able to make a useful contrib-
ution in offering cousel to the king on this matter.   The
doors were shut, and it was not known what was said; there
was a brief discussion to ascertain the general opinion of
the wise men.   In the meantime some very fine fare was set
before us.   While we were still eating and drinking, we three
were sent for and all ordered to come to the court.   We did
as the king ordered.   When we had come before him, he said:
"O messengers of our lord and mighty protector, if we knew how   130
to respond in a fitting and proper manner to his merciful and
fatherly requests as he has truly deserved, we should do so
straightaway.   Now report to him from me and from all my
people, 'from the highest to the lowest of those under my
rule, my subjects offer their faithful and ready service.

uirtus mira tua, pietas tua magna, sophia,
intus ut adimplent te sic foris undique comunt.
scimus inequales re militibusque tibi nos,
140   si uelles, posse nos pro meritis nichilasse.
reddere pro prauis bona stat satis ultio grandis,
nam quo rescitur faciens plus inde veretur.
grande tuum posse uel inequiperabile uelle
sunt tibi pro muro per nullum deiciendo.
145   Iesum ledenti ueniam miserendo precari.
nonne deizare nobis merito uideare
indulgens sponte peccantibus absque petente?
econtra nil nos simile prebere ualemus
retribuat sed ut is rex post quem sic imitaris
150   nos exorare debemus corde uel ore
utque diu uiuas ualeas regnes et abundes,
nobis et cunctis affinibus undique regnis
est exoptandum communiter atque precandum,
nam columen nostri tu solus es in uice Christi
155   atque superstite te bene possumus imperitare
sub uestre fidei scuto diutissime tuti.
et nunc O domine non dedignare uenire   M7^{v}
ad loca laudata quando sunt induciata;
uobis congredimur de nostris ac famulamur."
160   sic ait et donis ditauit nos sat opimis,
pelliciis uel equis faleratis siue chrusennis.
post poscit uinum, Gerdrudis amore quod haustum
participat nos tres.   postremo basia figens
quando uale dixit post nos gemit et benedixit.
165   hinc rediebamus uicedomnum postque uidemus,
qui nos condonans prouisorem simul et dans
oscula fert more, grandi nos liquit amore,
tam tibi deuotum mandans ut hero famulatum.
sic datur a cunctis sat amica licentia nobis.
170   disciplinate noster ductor uel honeste
seruiuit nobis in simplicitateque cordis
huius dum regni confinia uidimus ampli.'
talis rumoris rex talis ouans et honoris
subridens modicum nil protulit ore superbum,

IV.137-174   142 inde timetur *cod. m.pr.*   149 rex *om.m.pr.*
151 dum uiuas *Schmeller*

Your remarkable virtue, your great devotion to God and your   137
wisdom grace you outwardly just as they perfect you inwardly.
We know that we are unequal to you in soldiers and equipment,
and that you could if you wished annihilate us with all justification.   To return good things for evil is truly noble
revenge;   as (a man's) actions make known his character, so
he is the more feared.   Your mighty strength and your incomparable will are like a wall for you which no-one can throw
down.   That the injured party should pray in pity for the
injurer, for forgiveness!   Is it any wonder that you seem
to be a god to us, freely showing kindness to sinners without
their asking?   For our part we are able to proffer nothing
'like this, but must pray with heart and voice that that king
whose example you follow may later pay us back in like manner;
it behoves us, and all the kingdoms round about, to hope and   151
pray together that you may live long in good health, and reign
in properity, for you are in Christ's stead our only support,
and while you yet live we may rule securely, safe for ages under
the protecting shield of your good faith.
     And now, O lord, do not scorn to come to the appointed   157
places when they are decided upon;   for our part we shall come
to you and be your servants.'   He said these words, and
rewarded us with very generous gifts, furs, horses with their
trappings, and cloaks.   After this he asked for wine, so we
three could share in a draught for the love of St. Gertrude.
Then as he bid us farewell he kissed us, wept after us and
blessed us.   We departed from there, and next went to see
the viceroy, who gave us leave to go and supplied us with an
agent;   he embraced us in his usual way, and left us with a
deep expression of love, sending his devoted service to you
as though to his master.   Thus was friendly permission to
depart given to us by everyone.
     Our guide served us in purity of heart, with all proper   170
and upright conduct, until we saw the frontiers of this broad
kingdom."
     The king rejoiced at this report of the honour shown to him   173
and smiled a little, though he spoke no haughty words;

175 susspiciens laudat Dominum quo dante triumphat,
nil reputando sibi sed ei dans omnia dixit
'inducie quo sunt laudate, quandoue, dic, sunt?'
'ebdomade cum pretereunt tres inducie sunt
hac in planicie qua concertauimus ante,
180 soluentes nostros in uincla redegimus hostes,
sunt ubi tristati quo fiant letificati.
sic de te regi tunc induciando spopondi.'
rex ait 'hoc laudo promissorum neque fraudo.
dum fueras at ibi, quid agendum, dic, habuisti?'
185 respondit 'summus mihi clemens fit uicedomnus
procurans multum, defectum ne paterer quem.
scachorum ludo temptat me uincere crebro
nec potuit ludo ni sponte dato sibi solo.   M8^r
quinque dies sic me non siuerat ante uenire;
190 explorare cupit meus aduentus quid eo sit.
inuestigare nulla quod dum ualet arte,
post me rex misit, sibi que dixi satis audit,
in cras responso, dixi uelut, induciato.
rex poscens tabulam iubet opponi sibi sellam
195 et me contra se iubet in fulchro residere
ut secum ludam, quod ego nimium renuebam,
dicens "terribile, miserum, conludere rege."
et dum me uidi sibi non audere reniti
ludere laudaui cupiens ab eo superari,
200 "uinci de rege" dicens "quid obest miserum me?
sed timeo domine, quod mox irasceris in me,
si fortuna iuuet mihi quod uictoria constet."
rex subridendo dixit uelut atque iocando
"non opus est, care, super hac re quid uereare.
205 si nunquam uincam, commocior haut ego fiam,
sed quam districte noscas ludas uolo cum me,
nam quos ignotos facies uolo discere tractus."
statim rex et ego studiose traximus ambo,
et, sibi gratia sit, mihi ter uictoria cessit,
210 multis principibus nimis id mirantibus eius.

IV.175-210   176 sibi]tibi *m.pr.*   178 tres]ait *m.pr.*   187
temptans *m.pr.*

but looking up (to heaven) he praised the Lord God, by whose   175
grace he was victorious, and reckoning nothing to himself,
but giving Him all the glory, said "say, when and where has
the meeting been arranged?"   "After three weeks have passed,   178
the meeting is in that plain where we did battle before, freed
our own men and cast our enemies in chains, where those who
had been downcast were made to rejoice.   This is the arrangement I promised to the king on your behalf."

The king said: "I praise this promise you have made, and   183
shall not break it.   But while you were there, tell me, what
did you have to do?"   "The most high viceroy became kind to
me", he replied, "and took great care of me to see that I lacked
for nothing; he tried to beat me repeatedly in games of chess,
but could only do so when I let him win one game.   And so
for five days he did not allow me to come before (the king).
He wanted to find out the purpose of my coming there.   When   190
he could not fathom it out by any means, the king sent for
me, and listened carefully to what I had to say.   He decided
he would reply on the following day, as I have said.   The king
asked for a table and ordered a chair to be brought for him,
and then ordered me to sit down on the bench opposite him, to
play with him.   I declined firmly, saying that "it is fearful   197
and lamentable to play against a king."   Then when I saw that
I dared not withstand him, I determined to play, hoping to be
beaten by him - I said "poor me!   How can being beaten by the
king hurt me?   But, my lord, I am afraid that you will soon
be angry with me, if fortune is pleased to give the victory
to me."   The king smiled and said as if in a jest "my dear
fellow, there is no need for you to have any fears in this
matter.   I shall not be roused to anger if I never win, but
I want you to play with me as intently as you can; you see,
I want to learn the moves you make which I am ignorant of."

At once the king and I began to play eagerly, and, thanks be   208
to him, the victory fell to me three times; many of his nobles
were utterly astounded at this.

is mihi deponit, sibi me deponere nil uult
et dat que posuit pisa quod non una remansit.
plures succedunt, hunc ulcisci uoluerunt,
pignora prebentes, mea pignora despicientes,
215   perdere nil certi, dubie fisi bene sorti.
alterutrumque iuuant nimiumque iuuando nocebant:
prepediebantur uarie dum consiliantur,
inter litigium cito uincebam quod eorum
hoc tribus et uicibus, uolui nam ludere non plus.
220   que deponebant mihi mox donare uolebant.
primo respueram, uitiosum namque putabam   M8^{V}
sic me ditari uel eos per me tenuari.
dixi "non sueui quicquam ludendo lucrari."
dicunt "inter nos dum sis tu uiue uelut nos.
225   quando domum uenias ibi uiuere quis ueluti uis."
cum sat lorifregi que porrexere recepi,
commoda cum laude mihi fortuna tribuente.'
rex ait 'hunc ludum tibi censeo semper amandum,
quo sunt sarcita tua tam bene calciamenta.
230   nunc grates habeas causas quod agis bene nostras.'
misit et ad quosque qui captiuos habuere
hos ut uestirent ad honorem uel sibi reddant,
ipsis quos pedites misit, reddant ut equestres,
insuper armatos uelut ad noua bella paratos.
235   uestiuit comitem uelut ex summatibus unum
binis pelliciis preciosis totque chrusennis,
coccineam tunicam gemmis auroque micantem
dat sibi, qua regi preberet pocula uini,
dat uel equum fortem celerem nimis equipedantem,
240   auratum frenum pulchram faleramque gerentem,
et dat loricam tutus ualeat fore per quam
in quouis bello communi siue duello,

IV.211-242   211 de ponit *Zeydel*   212 *super* posuit *add. m.alt.*
quod   223 dixi non sueui]numquam consueui *m.pr.*   224 cum sis
Ford   donec inter nos sis fac uel uiue uelut nos *m.pr.*   234
post hunc v. add. m.alt. alterum v., et inde delevit;
quem Schmeller inclusit ut suum v.235, ...plumque...
simul....

He laid a wager against me, but wanted me to wager nothing   211
against him, and he gave me what he had put down, because he
didn't have a pea left.   Many took his place, wanting to
avenge him.   They put forward their own stakes but looked
askance at mine, for they were sure that they would lose
nothing, having firm trust in fickle chance.   They helped
one another, but made matters worse by helping too much:
they got in each other's way as they gave conflicting advice,
and while they were quarrelling I swiftly won the game -
three times, in fact, for I wanted to play no more than this.
Then they wanted to give me what they had wagered.   At first   220
I would have none of it, for I thought it sinful to enrich
myself in this way, and weaken them through my action.   I
said "I am not in the habit of winning anything by playing
games."   They replied, "while you are amongst us, you live
as we do!   When you get back home, then you can live as
you like."   I refused what they held out to me for a time,
and then took them.   Fortune gave me presents as well as
praise!"

    The king said "I think that you should always love this   228
game - it's by it that you are so well-heeled!   Now receive
our thanks for handling our affairs so well."

    He also sent word to each man who had brought back prisoners 231
to clothe them as was their due and return them to him, and
to those he had sent out as infantry, to return them as cavalry,
and fully armed at that, as if ready for war.   He fitted out
the count as though he were one of his own nobles, with a
pair of precious fur coats and also a pair of cloaks.   He
gave him a scarlet tunic that glittered with gold and precious
stones, to wear when he served goblets of wine to the king;
and he gave him a swift, strong horse, a well-formed creature
that bore a golden bridle and was beautifully adorned.   He
also gave him a breastplate, in which he would be safe in
any warfare or combat,

ensem uel galeam sibi lanceolam dat acutam.
qui famulantur ei donantur utrique clienti
245 uestes ualde bone semperque domi sibi rare;
insuper ad bella sibi congrua prestitit arma.
misit precones satrapas comitesque uocandos,
ad curtem ueniant quo regis quam bene possint,
et secum ferrent sibi que uel equis opus essent
250 ad tres ebdomadas secum seu plus remanendas.
illuc pontifices inuitantur sapientes
abbatesque pii scioli bene consiliari.

IV.243-252   248 quam bene possint]quo optime possint *Schmeller;*
iuxta hunc v. est glossa quo optime posint pro cooperant

a sword, a helmet, and a sharp lance.   To both those who   243
served him were given superb outfits, such as they rarely
saw at home, and the king furthermore provided them with
weapons like their master's, for fighting in war.   The king
sent heralds to summon his dukes and counts to come to his
court as soon as they could, and to bring with them whatever
they and their horses needed for a stay of three weeks or
more with him.   The wise bishops were invited there, along   251
with the abbots and the wise clerks who gave good counsel.

militibus lata] curtis fuit amphiprehensa,   M9^r
in med]io uacua, scenis foris undique septa,
qua cum presulibus abbatibus et duodenis
posset prandere cenareue sat spaciose.
5   curti contiguum stat tentorium satis amplum
solis ad exortum, de quo posuere podismum,
cuius ad extremum fixerunt papilionem
in quo stans mensa uestita fuit uelut ara,
quam super est posita regis crux et diadema,
10 qua misse regi solet officium celebrari,
matutinalis et uespertina sinaxis
cursibus inmixtis aliis de more diurnis.
quo dum rex uenit missam properantius audit
et per legatum regi demandat eundem
15 qui fuerat rerum prius internuncius harum,
primitus ut uideant sese quam prandia sumant.
quem rex ut uidit bene subridendo recepit
oscula datque sibi 'quid narras' post ait illi
'omne bonum dici tibi de me sat meruisti.'
20 'ad te me misit rex et tibi dicere iussit
ne prandere uelis prius illum quam tuearis.
obuius ad pontem uenit is tibi nos dirimentem.
pax ibi firmatur, res omnis et adbreuiatur,
capti redduntur captos se neue queruntur,
25 nam meliorati redeunt non attenuati.'
rex 'ita fiat' ait, ad herum missus remeauit.

dum conuenerunt reges ubi constituerunt

V.1-27   1 militibus lata *scripsi*: cancellis lata *Ford*: hic reg?
lata *Strecker*: iam regione rata *Laistner*: congregium lata
Schmeller   2 in medio *Seiler*: quae medio *Schmeller*

The king's wide court was surrounded front and rear with   1
knights, open in the centre and hedged around the outside
with lodges, where he could take breakfast or dinner in
comfort with a dozen barons and abbots.   Adjoining the court
on the eastern side stood a large tent, from which they had
measured out a path, at the end of which they had placed a
pavilion in which stood a table bedecked like an altar.   On
this were placed the king's cross and diadem, which were used
when the office of mass was celebrated for him, and also at
mattins and vespers, along with the various customary daily
services.

When the king came there, he heard mass more hurriedly   13
than usual, and then, via the same envoy who had before been
the go-between in this business, sent word to the other king
that they should see one another first before they ate.

When the other king saw him, he received him with a broad   17
smile, embraced him, and then said to him "what news do you
bring?   You fully deserve that I should wish you well."

"My king has sent me to you and ordered me to say to you   20
that it should please you not to eat before you have seen him.
He is coming to meet you at the bridge which separates us from
you.   The peace will be sworn there, and the whole affair
brought to a close.   The prisoners will be handed over, and
they do not grieve at being captives, for they return enriched,
not impoverished."   "Let it be so" said the king.   The
messenger made his way back to his master.

When the kings came together at the place they had decided,   27

nil penitus dicunt sibi quam prius oscula figunt.
noster pontifices ut idem facerent iubet omnes,
30   et post abbates ex ordine basiat omnes;
eius presulibus tunc prebitus est amor ipsus.
reges pontifices abbates clerus et omnis
assumptis ducibus uel summis alterutrius   M9^v
dum resident pariter, rex maior ait sapienter
35   'O nimium nobis rex dilectissime cunctis,
sicut laudaui tibi demandansque spopondi
quicquid stulticie plebs nostra patrauit utrimque
hoc dimittamus et eosdem pacificemus
ut sint inter se concordantes sine fraude.
40   nemo recordetur aduersi quid pateretur,
obliuiscatur ulcisci nec meditetur,
nam mala malo bono quam reddere uincere prauo.'
alter rex surgens huic dignas dicere grates
a nostro uetitus residet, tamen est ita fatus:
45   'pro tot uel tantis impensis nos benefactis
reddere condignas non sufficimus tibi grates.
in cuius parma uictricia tu geris arma,
ille tibi laudis sat prestat et omnis honoris.
non opus est hinc te laudare uel amplificare;
50   uirtus et pietas nimis et tua larga uoluntas
omnibus inuitis cumulant tibi premia laudis.
ipsemet atque mei tibi debemus famulari
ut bello uicti sub uexilloque subacti.'
rex ait 'hoc absit, ego dum uiuam neque fiet,
55   ut tibi quid iuris aut adminuatur honoris:
es rex sicut ego, tibi me preponere nolo.
eiusdem iuris es cuius sum uel honoris.
ob quod uenimus huc modo perficiamus id istuc:
tuque tuos recipe, sed non sine quouis honore.'
60   sic dicens comitem regali ueste nitentem
reddidit armatum ueluti bellare paratum.
sic nongentorum nullum reddebat eorum
quin foret armatus uel ueste decenter amictus.

V.28-63   53 sub *om. Schmeller*   58 istuc *scripsi*: istic *cod.*
62 sic nongentorum] sicut captorum *Schmeller*

they embraced one another before exchanging a single word.   28
Our king ordered all the bishops to do the same, and after
this he embraced all the abbots according to their rank;
then finally his own special affection was shown to his   31
barons.   When the kings, bishops, abbots and all the clergy
were alike seated, along with the dukes and nobles admitted
from either side, the greater king said these wise words:
"O king, most greatly beloved of all of us!   Just as I have
decided, and promised you by my order, let us set aside
whatever stupid thing our people have done on either side
and set them at peace, so that they may be of one mind, with
no deceit between them.   Let no-one recall any harm he has
suffered - let him forget it, and not think about revenge.
I would rather repay bad things with good that conquer through
evil."

The other king rose up to offer the thanks this speech   43
deserved, but he was forbidden by our king, and sat down
again.   Even so, he said these words: "for so many
enormous blessings expended on us, we are not capable of
giving you the thanks you have merited.   He, beneath whose
shield you bear victorious arms, He shows you praise enough,
and every honour too.   So there is no need for us to praise
or extol you: even if we refused to, your courage, your
great devotion to God and the liberality of your wishes heap
up the rewards of praise for you.   I myself and my people
ought to be your servants, as those vanquished in war, and
driven beneath your banner."

"Away with this idea!" said our king, "and let it never   54
happen so long as I live that your power and rank should be
lessened in the slightest: you are a king, as I am, and I
refuse to set myself above you.   You are of the same power
and rank as I am.   Now let us see through this business of
ours, on account of which we have come here.   You take back
your men, and with such honour as you desire."   So saying,   60
he handed over the count, dazzling in his royal robes, and
armed as if ready to do battle.   Likewise he handed over
none of those nine hundred captives without their being armed
or dressed in clothes worthy of them.

post ait 'hi rex sunt quos uiuere fata sinebant,   M10^r
65   qui· non humane dum nobis preualuere
non tractant igne preda uel cede maligne.
qualiter econtra tractarem quos uice uersa
precipe, quo dicant tibi quando domum remearint.
nunc se concordent et sint uelut ante fuerunt,
70   firmi compatres posthac fidique sodales.'
quo facto nempe pax firmabatur utrimque
per iuramentum neutrim penitus temerandum.
tunc ambo reges redeunt ad papiliones
cumque suis prandent.   ibi grandia gaudia fiunt,
75   gaudet quisque suus saluus rediit quod amicus.
mensa sublata dosponit plurima dona
que regi dentur uel eis hunc qui comitentur,
auri quingenta regi donanda talenta,
insuper argentum multum uel pallia centum,
80   centum lorice totidem galee chalibine,
inter equos muli decapenta bis falerati
et bis quindeni onagri totidemque cameli
atque leopardi gemini binique leones
et pariles ursi qui fratres sunt uterini,
85   omnino niuei gambis pedibusque nigelli,
qui uas tollebant ut homo bipedesque gerebant.
mimi quando fides digitis tangunt modulantes
illi saltabant neumas pedibus uariabant,
interdum saliunt seseque superiaciebant,
90   alterutrum dorso se portabant residendo,
amplexando se luctando deiciunt se.
cum plebs altisonam fecit girando choream
accurrunt et se mulieribus applicuere
que gracili uoce cecinerunt deliciose
95   conse]rtisque suis harum manibus speciosis   M10^v
erecti calcant pedetemptim, murmure trinsant,
ut mirarentur ibi circum qui graderentur.

V.64-97   74 ibi] et *m.pr.*   76 disponunt *Schmeller*   81 mulos
m.pr.   faleratos *m.pr.*   82 quindenos *m.pr.*   onagros *m.pr.*
camelos *m.pr.*   83 leopardos *m.pr.* geminos *m.pr.* binosque *m.pr.*
87 digitis] manibus *m.pr.*   95 consertisque *scripsi*: insertisque
Schmeller

After this he said "these, O king, are those whom the fates   64
have allowed to live.   When they had the upper hand over us
they treated us inhumanely, burning, looting, and killing
brutally.   Learn from what they tell you when they arrive
back home how I treated them in turn, however.   Now let them
be reunited, and let them be as they were before, our
steadfast friends, and after this our faithful companions."

This done, peace was assuredly affirmed by both sides, by   71
an oath never to be violated by either party.   Then both
kings returned to their pavilions and ate breakfast with
their men;   there was great rejoicing there.   Each man was
happy because his friends had come back safely.

When the table was removed, the king laid out many gifts,   76
which were to be given to the (great) king or to those who
accompanied him: five hundred talents of gold to be given
to the king, over and above this a mass of silver, a hundred
cloaks, a hundred breastplates, and the same number of steel
helmets, horses, thirty mules decked out, thirty wild asses
and likewise thirty camels;   twin leopards, a pair of lions,
and a pair too of bears that were brothers from the womb, and
were white all over but with black legs and feet.   They would
pick up a cup like a man, and carry it standing on their hind
legs;   and when the minstrels played, plucking their lyres with
their fingers, they would dance, matching the melody with their
steps.   Now and then they would leap in the air and throw themselves over one another, one carrying the other seated   90
on his back;   then, embracing one another, they would wrestle
and throw each other to the floor.   When the people sang out
loudly as they danced around, the bears would rush up and
join themselves to those women who were singing sweetly with
an attractive voice, taking their lovely hands in their own
paws.   Then they stood up straight and stamped very carefully,
growling very softly, which amazed those who were dancing
around them there.

non irascantur quodcunque mali paterentur.
insuper et lincum de uulpe lupoque creatum
100 addiderat donis, expers quod non sit honoris,
eius ab urina quia crescit lucida gemma,
ardens ligurius carbunculus ut preciosus.
qualiter is fiat libeat quem discere discat:
ex ferro clauos tibi fac fabricare quaternos,
105 in lata butina quos fige bis in loca bina
fortiter inpellens, euellere quis queat haut quos,
in medio butine terebello facque foramen.
in quam pone feram licet inuitam ue rebellem
ad clauosque pedes uincire sibi bene cures
110 et circa collum nexam suspende catenam
inclinando caput, ne uincula soluere possit.
ad manducandum sibi sat da siue bibendum,
quod bibat at uinum ualidum sit, dulce bibendum.
ebrius exinde dum uult nequeat retinere,
115 exeat urina, sed ut ignorante retenta,
et fluat in peluim cito per butinam terebratam,
quam dum non poterit dispergere, uiuere claudit.
si non emittat tamen hanc moriensque retentet
abstracta pelle uel aperto cautius aluo
120 tollito uesicam uel acu transpunge minutim
et sic urinam nimis in puram preme peluim;
inque modum pise per cuprea uascula funde
maiorisue nucis ad grossum fundito uasis.
suffodiens terra que uasa dies decapenta
125 esse sinas, post effodiens; exinde resumas
guttas in gemmas concretas cernis et omnes,
que similes prunis lucent caligine noctis,
quas decet imponi reginarum digitali,
regis at impone magnas aptando corone.

130 adduntur donis licet illis nil sit honoris,   M11^{r}
simia nare breui nate nuda murcaque cauda,
uoceque miluina cute crisa catta marina,
in quibus ambabus nil cernitur utilitatis.

V.98-133   115 *hunc v. om. m.pr.*   133 *hunc v. om. m.pr.*

They were not roused to anger, whatever kind of harm they   98
suffered.   As well as this, he added to the gifts a lynx,
born from a vixen and a wolf.   This was not lacking in
esteem, because from its urine is formed a glittering stone,
like a glowing jacinth or a precious turquoise.   He who
wishes to learn how this is done may learn it now.

Have yourself made four nails from iron, and knock two   104
each into two places in a large barrel, firmly, so no-one
can pull them out.   Make an opening in the middle of the
barrel with a drill: then put the wild beast in the barrel
(it may be unwilling, and resist);   take good care to tie   109
its feet securely to the nails, and hang a restraining chain
around its neck, bending its head down so it cannot free
itself from its bonds.   Give it enough to eat and drink,
but let what it drinks be strong wine, sweet to the taste.
It will get drunk from this, and though it wishes to hold
its water, it will not be able to.

Let its urine come out (though in its ignorance it thinks   115
it has held it back) and let it flow into a basin through
the pierced barrel.   If the lynx cannot rid itself of its
urine, it dies;   but if it does not pass water, but holds it
even in death, tear back its skin, open up its belly carefully,
take its bladder and pierce it slightly with a needle;   in
this way, squeeze the urine into a very clean basin;   pour it   121
into pea-sized copper vessels or into cups the size of
largish nuts.   Bury these cups and let them stay in the
ground for fifteen days, and then unearth them;   when you take
them up you will see that all the drops have hardened into
stones which glow like live coals in the darkness of night.
They are worthy to be placed on the fingers of queens, though
the large ones you should have mounted on a king's crown.

To these gifts were added, even though they were without   130
value, a monkey with a snub nose, a bare rump and a cropped
tail, and a baboon with a strident voice and grey skin.
No function whatever could be seen for either of these.

ex genealogia uol[ucrum] regalia dona
135 auxit cum psitachis binis coruisque gemellis,
monedulis, sturnis doctis garrire loquelis,
quicquid et audierint imi[tari q]ue studuerunt.

pontifici cuique sua dona reponit honeste.
loricis galeis ducibus scutis ....alatis
140 munerat, atque tubis auro pre post decoratis,
presidibus, pulchris madris crisisue poledris,
militibus summis seu pelliciisue chrusennis.
his ita dispositis modicum requiescere uult is.
explorare iubet alter rex quando resurgat.
145 post uigilans surgit mulum falerareque iussit
cumque quibus uoluit ad regem tunc equitauit.
plures occurrunt et ei seruire studebant.
quem bene suscepit rex atque sedere rogauit,
qui dixit 'domine, mecum dignare uenire
150 et non abnuito que munera parua tibi do,
quicquid summatum sit et hic, ueniant, rogo, tecum.'
rex ait 'id fiat.   rex alter doma reuisat.'
conuocat iste suos summates conueniendos.
qui dum conueniunt uel coram rege sederunt
155 ut mos eius erat semper rogitando iubebat
quo suus esset honor cuiuis quam munera maior
et nihil acciperet sibi si que rex dare uellet,
'ne sit opus census uobis uideatur ut eius.
mecum nunc ite, quod ego faciam facitote.'
160 ibant cum rege suscepti sunt et honeste.
dum consederunt ter miscendoque biberunt,
rex regem duxit secum quos ireque iussit   M11^v
in curtem latam [canc]ellis amphiprehensam,
in qua stant mense uario censu cumulate,
165 in qua stant et equi decet ut regem falerati,
stant etiam muli stant enormesque cameli
stant et ter deni mites onagri domitique

V.134-167   134 uolucrum *Seiler*: nobili *Schmeller*   137 imitari
que *Seiler*: imitari qui *Schmeller*   139 ....alatis *cod.*:
retalatis *Seiler*   141 crisisque *Schmeller*   144 alius rex *m.pr.*
150 parca *Schmeller*   158 nobis *Schmeller*   163 cancellis *Seiler*

From the family of birds, he augmented the royal gifts with   134
a pair of parrots and twin ravens, jackdaws, and talkative
starlings taught to chatter, which tried to imitate whatever
they heard.

Nobly he laid out his gifts for each bishop. He endowed   138
the dukes with breastplates, helmets, shields and........, and
with trumpets decorated all over with gold; the guards, with
fine brown and grey colts, and the highest-ranking soldiers
with cloaks and furs. When he had done all this, the king
wished to lie down a little. He gave orders to find out when
the other king got up. After he himself had awoken, he arose
and ordered a mule to be got ready, and then rode over to the   146
other king with those he wished to accompany him. Many ran
to meet him and eagerly waited upon him. The king received
him well, and asked him to sit down. He replied 'my lord,'
please deign to come with me, and do not shun the little
gifts I give you. I beg that whatever nobles you have here
should come with you too." Our king said "let it be so; let   152
your majesty return to his tent." He called for his nobles
to gather together. When they had assembled and were seated
before the king, he asked and ordered them, as was always his
custom, to remember that each man's honour was greater than
any gift, and to accept nothing, if the king wished to give
him anything, "lest it appears that you have need of his
wealth; now come with me, and do as I do."

They went with the king and were received courteously.   160
When they were seated together and shared in a drink three
times, the king took the other king with him, along with
those he had ordered to go with him, to a broad courtyard
surrounded by lattices, in which stood tables piled high with
all sorts of riches, along with the horses equipped as befitted
a king, and the mules, the massive camels, the sixty wild
asses, gentle since they had been tamed,

```
        stant et terribiles leopardi siue leones,
        stas et inaurata connexus, lince, catena,
170     simia cum catta stat ibique marina ligata,
        stant ursi gemini multo uariamine ludi;
        quin ibi sunt et aues hominum sermone fruentes,
        psitachus et coruus monedula picaue sturnus.
        tunc ait 'hec dona tua sint, rex optime, cuncta,
175     presulibus sint hec horumque fidelibus istec.'
        auri ter denas uni placuit dare libras
        inque capellanos quinquaginta tribuendas
        argenti libras, totidemque per officiales,
        inter scutiferos uilesque ministeriales
180     uiginti libras nummorum distribuendas;
        nec superexaltat lixas quin hos quoque donet:
        inter eos denas dispergendas quoque libras
        det duodenorum tantundem cuiuis eorum,
        post ducibus galeas loricas ponit et enses,
185     auratas parmas, lituos ad bella canoros
        inque suos libras sexaginta tribuendas,
        et post presidibus det equos faleris redimitos
        atque suis denas cunctis libras tribuendas;
        postremo cunctis abbatibus his duodenis
190     se det in oramen spondendo suum famulamen,
        illorum cuiuis confratribus hosque secutis
        libras triginta puerorum cuiuis et unam;
        mittat et ad claustra monachis libras decapenta.
        regis simnistis aliisque fidelibus eius           M12ʳ
195     eius seruicio qui sunt in cottidiano
        qui ueluti glandes semper flant regis ad aures
        et pro mercedis succurrunt pondere cuiuis
        bona dat eximia census ad mille talenta.
        inter quos illum uenatorem peregrinum
200     munerat uberius, sic collegam facit eius,
        missi qui fuerant ad se pacemque patrabant.
        munera dum uidit ea rex multumque probauit,
        dixit ad equiuocum 'tua munera sunt bona multum.
```

V.168-203   175 sint hec *cod. m.tert.*: istec *m.pr.*: ast hec *m.
sec.*   180 *hunc v. om. m.pr.*   183 dat *m.pr.*   184 ponit] ponet
m.pr.: donet *Schmeller*   187 dat *m.pr.*   190 dat *m.pr.* s. det
moramen *Schmeller*   193 misit et *m.pr.*

the fearful leopards and lions - there you were too, lynx,   168
fastened up with a golden chain.   The monkeys were there,
tied up with the baboons, and also the twin bears with their
great and varied repertoire.   And there also were the birds,
rich in human speech - the parrot, the raven, the jackdaw,
the magpie and the starling.   Then he said "O most high king,   174
let all these gifts be yours;   let these be for your lords,
and these here for their faithful men."   He wished to give
thirty pounds of gold to the king alone, and had fifty pounds
of silver to be given to his chaplains, the same amount for
his officers, and twenty pounds of pennies to be shared
among the squires and lesser officials.   Nor was he so
superior to the menial servants that he did not give gifts
to them also: he gave them ten pounds to divide between
them, and the same amount to each of the twelve bishops and
abbots.   After this he set forth the helmets and swords for   184
the dukes, the gilded shields, the trumpets which sing out the
summons to war, and sixty pounds to give out to their men.
Next he gave horses equipped with full tack to the captains,
and ten pounds to give out to all their men;   and finally he
gave himself to these twelve abbots, to pray, and promised
his service to them.   He also gave to each of them and to
the brothers who had come with them thirty pounds, and one
pound to each of the boys.   He sent fifteen pounds to the
monasteries, for the monks.
    To the king's counsellors and to his other faithful men who   194
wait upon him every day, who are always blasting their advice
in the king's ear and will lend assistance to anyone for a
weighty reward, he gave excellent goods, to the value of a
thousand talents.   Out of them he rewarded that foreign
huntsman more richly, and also his companion;   these were the
two who had been sent to him and had worked out the peace
settlement.
    When our king saw those gifts, he praised them greatly, and   202
said to his peer "your gifts are exceedingly good;

             ne tamen a nobis tantum donando graueris
205   pro donis uotum decernimus accipiendum.
             tam bene ludentes ursos hos tollo gemellos
             atque mee nate picam sturnumque do de te
             et grates habeas tantas ceu cuncta dedisses.
             nec uolo presulibus ducibus quid presidibus des.
210   quod cenobitis dabis aut abbatibus istis
             non contra dico quia redditur id tibi uero;
             hi sunt assidui famulares omnipotenti
             orant et pro te studiose nocte dieque
             et quod das illis pariet tibi gaudia lucis.
215   inter summates nolo plus muneris ut des.'
             gratis an oblitus reticeret is officiales;
             hi bene donantur secretim siue beantur.
             hoc super edictum non ausus est dare cuiquam
             grande uel exiguum, nec desiderat quis eorum.
220   reges inter se quando dixere 'ualete'
             oscula dando sibi placet his patriando reuerti.

             ita domum redeunt iuris propriique fiebant.   M12ᵛ
             Ruodlieb dilecte matris cernens inopine
             ad sese missum quendam bene suscipit illum.
225   ad quem sic dixit 'mea mater, sospes, ai, sit?'
             respondit 'uiuit ualet et bene uel tibi misit
             istas litterulas melius quibus ac mihi credas.'
             susceptaque dice sciolum facit hanc recitare.
             quam super ut legit ait 'arbitror hec breuis inquit
230   "ergo tui domini cuncti tibi ualde benigni
             ut redeas petimus, nam te caruisse dolemus
             temporibus tantis propter quos exiliaris
             et faidas in te non cessabas cumulare,
             donec e patria fugiens petis extera regna,
235   scimus ubi multos te sustinuisse labores.
             quod lamentamur nos quandocumque gregamur
             ad placitum uel ad inducias quacunque statutas;

V.204-237   221 his *om. m.pr.*   222 ita] cumque *m.pr.*   223
Ruodlieb *hoc verbum scriptum est m.alt. super m.pr.*

76

but so that you are not burdened by us, by giving so much,   204
we judge that we should accept your prayer instead of your
gifts. I will take these twin bears that play so well, and
I give to my daughter from you the magpie and the starling,
and you shall receive such thanks from us as though you have
given us everything.   I do not want you to give anything to
my lords, dukes or captains.   I say nought against your
giving anything to the monks or to these abbots, because in
truth it will be returned to you: these men are zealous
servants of the almighty; they pray eagerly for you day and
night, and what you give to them will bring forth the joys of
light for you.   But I do not wish you to give more gifts
among the nobles." He made no mention of the officials,   216
whether from kindness or forgetfulness; they were well
rewarded and blessed with gifts in secret.   After this
edict, no-one dared to give to anyone, and none of them
wished for anything, great or small.   When the kings said   220
"farewell" to one another they embraced each other, and they
cheerfully decided to travel back to their own land.   Thus
they returned home and came into their own territory.
   Ruodlieb saw a certain man sent to him unexpectedly by   223
his dear mother, and gave him a warm welcome.   He said to
him "tell me, is my mother well?"   He replied "she lives in
good health and strength, and sends to you these letters:
you may believe them better than me."   He picked them up
and had a clerk read them out.   As he read it over he said
"I think that the message says this: 'inasmuch as all of us   230
your lords look on you with favour, we ask that you return:
for we grieve at having been without you for such a long time,
we on whose account you are in exile and did not cease from
piling up hostility against yourself, until, fleeing your
homeland, you sought out foreign kingdoms, where we know you
have endured many great endeavours.   We weep for this whenever we assemble in a council, and in negotiations anywhere,

tunc in consilio dando par est tibi nemo
qui uel tam iuste ius dicat tam uel honeste
240 et qui sic uiduas defendat siue pupillos,
propter auariciam cum damnabantur iniquam,
qui lamentantur nimium cum quando premuntur.
ergo tui cuncti cum sunt hostes nihilati,
partim defuncti partim membris mutilati,
245 illorum nulli tibi quod plus sunt nocituri,
kare, redi citius quia quo uenias inhiamus,
inprimis ut nos bene tecum pacificemus
prestita dando tibi sepissime que meruisti
non parcens proprie pro nobis utique uite."
250 ast in fine breuis huius stat epistola matris: M13^{r}
"mi fili care, misere matris memorare
quam sicut nosti discedens deseruisti
inconsolatam, bina [causa] uiduatam,
in genitore tuo simul in te nate secundo.
255 dum fueras mecum mala cuncta mihi releuabas,
cum discessisti gemitus mihi multiplicasti.
sed tamen utcumque decernebam tolerare
secure miseram dum posses ducere uitam
pre tot tam ualidis tibi tam diris inimicis.
260 qui quia sunt cuncti mutilati siue perempti
fili kare redi, luctus finem dato matri
aduentuque tuo consanguineos hylarato
non solumque tuos sed omnes compatriotas."'
omnibus auditis miles nimis exhilaratur,
265 pro sola matre lacrimis perfunditur ore.
id resciscente populi rumore sodale
ultra credibile nimium fit mentis acerbe,
illeque non solum quin quod fuit apparitorum;
stant ubi uel resident simul intime condoluerunt:
270 dicunt quod nunquam uidissent huic similem quem

V.238-270   242 cum *Schmeller*: mihi *Zeydel*   245 plus] non *m.pr.*
247 *post* tecum *posuit et delevit* paci *m.alt.*   249 utique *m.tert.*,
m.pr.: denique *m.sec.*, *Schmeller*   253 bona *Schmeller*   causa
Seiler   255 mecum *om. m.pr.* mecum fueras *Schmeller, Seiler, Ford*
258 miseram] uitam *m.pr.*   260 qui] quia *m.pr.*   269 hunc *v. om.*
m.pr.

for in giving advice there is no-one equal to you, who can   238
say what is right so justly or so nobly, and who defends as
you do the widow and the orphan when they are hurt by cruel
greed, and who weep bitterly whenever they are oppressed.
Inasmuch as all your enemies are brought to nought - some are   243
slain, and some grievously wounded - and none of them shall
cause you any more trouble, O beloved, come back swiftly,
because we sigh for your coming, above all so that we can
make ourselves to be at peace with you by discharging to you
the obligations which you have most frequently deserved, not
even sparing your own life on our behalf.'
    But at the end of the message there is this letter from your   250
mother: 'my dear son, remember your poor mother, whom you
abandoned unconsoled on your departure, as you know, and
widowed twice over - first of your father, and now too of you,
my son.   While you were with me you used to take away all
my pain, but when you left, you redoubled my tears.   Yet
I decided to put up with it in any way I could, so long as
you could live your poor life in safety, before all those
mighty enemies who meant so much harm to you.   But since they
are all disabled or dead, my dear son, come home, put an end
to your mother's grief and by your arrival make your brethren   261
rejoice - not just you own family, but all your countrymen
too.'"
    The knight was utterly thrilled when he heard all this, and   264
wet his cheeks with tears for his mother alone.   When his
companion learned of it - it was on everyone's lips -
he grieved bitterly in his heart, beyond all believing, and
not only him but all the officials who were there, whatever
they were engaged in, at once felt sad at heart; they said
that they had never seen his like

moris honestate fidei uel in integritate
quod nec obest ulli sed ubi quit profuit omni.
at qui seruimen eius nouere diurnum
dicunt 'quid mirum sibi si nunc est onerosum
275   nil deseruisse ni pauper uiuere posse,
uictum uel uestem nullum plus emolumentum,
huius cum regni columen speciale sit omnis.'
qui sibi dilectum secum sumendo sodalem
ad regem graditur, pre quo sic fando precatur:
280   si rex auderem tibi uel fore non graue scirem,
quod nimis angit me tibi uellem notificare.'
rex ait 'eloquere, clemente potiris ad id me.'
ille pedes regis amplectitur oscula dans his
postque resurgendo uix protulit ista gemendo: M13^v
285   'quid mihi cause sit melius rex ipse uidebit'
sic ait inque manus dat litterulas sibi missas.
rex ait his lectis 'nunc compatior satis istis.
que tibi promittunt domini si sic ea soluunt
consilior uideas uenias quin neue relinquas.
290   atque tue matris nimis est legatio suauis;
hinc omnino tibi modo nolo reconsiliari,
quin uadas ad eam uel consoleris eandem
contribulesque tuos uisendi te sat auaros.
quando uelis ito, nobiscum sed tamen esto
295   istius ebdomade spacium; noli prius ire
quam pertractemus quid mercedis tibi demus.
nobis seruisti quam deuotissime scisti:
non obliuisci decet id nos sed reminisci
et tibi prodesse te sepe neci tribuisse
300   pro me pro populo pro cuncto denique regno.'
exul at inclinat regem meminisseque gaudet
eius seruicii paucis respondit et illi:
'quod tibi seruiui mihi quam bene retribuisti.
huc postquam ueni pie rex tibi meque subegi
305   pascha fuit tecum mihi semper cottidianum

V.271-305   271 maris *Ford*   277 speciale *Seiler*: speciali
cod. m.alt.: specialis *m.pr., Schmeller*   288 que] quod *m.pr.*
ea *om. Zeydel*   292 uel consoleris] consoleris et *m.pr.*   301
hunc v. posuit m.alt. super m.pr.

for his upright conduct or the integrity of his good faith,   271
because he never harmed anyone, but where he could, acted for
their good.   But those who knew what his daily duties were
said "it is no surprise if he now finds it burdensome to have
earned nothing except to be able to live like a pauper, with
food and clothing but no other reward, expecially since he
is the mainstay of the whole kingdom."

He took with him his own beloved companion and went to the   278
king, before whom he spoke this request: "O king, if I dared,
or if I knew that it would not be serious to you, I should
wish to inform you of what it is that distresses me so much."
The king said "tell me, for you will find me gracious in this
matter."   He hugged the king's feet and kissed them, and
then stood up and could barely speak these words through his
tears: "the king will better see for himself what my predic-
ament is" and so saying he placed in his hands the letters   286
he had been sent.   When they had been read the king said
"truly now I have pity for your situation; if the lords do
discharge what they have promised to you, I advise you to see
them and to go to them, even - but do not leave the matter
unattended.

And the message from you mother is indeed delightful;   290
I do not wish to advise you further on this at all, except
to say go to her and comfort her and your brethren who hunger
to see you so.   You may go when you wish, but stay with us
for this week, and do not go before we have decided what
reward we should give you.   You have served us with all the
affection you could muster; we ought not to forget it, but
to remember that you often exposed yourself to death for me,
for my people and all my kingdom, and to treat you well."
The exile bowed his head, happy that the king had recalled   301
his service, and replied in these few words: "because I
have been your servant, you have repaid me exceedingly well.
After I came here, godly king, and became your vassal, every
day with you was always like Easter to me,

semper habens multum uel honorum siue bonorum
a te non solum sed ab unoquoque tuorum.'

rex iubet interea fiant argentea uasa,
ut grandes lances per circuitum cubitales,
310 non nisi bis bina duo plana tot atque profunda,
quando coaptentur ceu panes sint uideantur
extra speltina si sint perfusa farina.
quorum uasorum rex unum denariorum
replet, bizantes quos dicunt aurificantes,
315 et sic coniunctim suppingere quod nequit unum
plus cum martello, ne clangant forte mouendo.
quando domum ueniat res inde suas meli[oret   M14^r
atque suos dominos faciat sibi dando benignos
ut sibi promissa dent prestita mente benigna.
320 altera diuiditur lanx in duo sicque repletur.
ex una parte lancis nummos posuere
ex auro factos et in igne sat examinatos,
a pole bizanto quibus agnomen tribuere,
est quibus insculpta grece circum titulata;
325 istac maiestas illac regisque potestas
imponendo manum stans quem signat benedi[ctum;
quos det dilectis consanguineis et amicis
ad congaudendum, mos est uelut, hunc fore sal[uum
exilioque graui non illum degenerasse
330 sed profecisse uel honore domum rediisse.
citra mazeriam lancis nummis ita fartam
bis sex armillas imponit rex operosas,
ex quibus octone solide sunt non recauate,
plumbo replete, ceu serpentes capitate
335 oscula que sibi dant sic se nec amando noce[bant,
quarum queque meri graue pondus gesserat au[ri.
bis gemine relique gyrando fuere recur[ue
queque librans marcam uelut epaticam sper[ulatam;
non in iis decori plus quam studet utilita[ti.
340 et super additur his regine fibula grandis,

V.306-340   310 tot atque *posuit m.alt. super m.pr.*   311 panis
m.pr.   329 illum] hunc *m.pr.*

82

for I always had many honours and favours, not only from you   306
but from each one of your men."

The king ordered that in the meantime silver vessels should
be made, like great dishes a cubit round, and four in number,
two flat and two deep, so that they looked like lóaves of
bread when they were put together and spelt flour was shaken
on the outside.   The king filled one of these vessels with
coins, which goldsmiths call bezants, packed in so tightly
that one could not knock another one in with a hammer, in
order that they did not chink together.   With them he might
better his circumstances when he arrived home, and make his
lords favourable towards him by giving them gifts, so that
they discharged their promises to him in a kindly spirit.

The other dish was fashioned in two parts and filled as   320
follows.   On the one side of the dish they placed pennies
made of gold and well tried in the fire, which men name after
the city of Byzantium, and around which is engraved a Greek
inscription; on one side is depicted majesty, and on the other,
royal power, which stands with its hand on him and gives him
its blessing.   These he might give to his beloved relations
and friends, to make them rejoice, as is the custom, that
he was safe, and had not become worse in his harsh exile but
was successful, and came home with honour.

Outside the bowl-shaped part of the dish, crammed with   331
coins, the king placed a dozen finely-wrought bracelets, eight
of them solid, not hollowed out and filled with lead, shaped
like snakes with large heads which embrace one another and
yet do not hurt each other in their loving.   Each of them
weighed heavily, being pure gold.   The other four were twisted
into a circle; each one weighed as much as a round yellow   338
mark; they were no less useful than they were beautiful.

On top of these was added a splendid brooch for a queen,

in limo fusa non malleolis fabricata
fabrili nullo compactaue machinamento,
per totum solida non omninoque dolata,
in medio cuius aquile stat imago uolantis
345   eius et in rostro pila stat christallina su[mmo,
in qua motari uisuntur tres uolucelli,
essent ceu uiui gestire uolare[que prompti.
aureu]s hanc aqu[ilam] per girum circulus ambit   M14^V
que t]am lata fuit sibi pectus quod bene texit.
350   non erat in]merito sic auri fusa talento.
dat fibula]s alias in pensando leuiores
quauis] et in quarum gemmarum multigenarum
fulgor] erat uarius, uelut inspiceres ibi sydus,
quarum] queque libre quadrantem ponderat eque.
355   non gran]di boga gracili pendendo catena
addidit] his modicam, quam pretendendo diatim
lacern]am cum qua configat ne stet aperta
pectora] ne possint cerni maiuscula si sint.
ex aur]o lunam solidam super addidit unam
360   pensan]tem libram, faber in qua protulit artem.
in cur]uatura sunt inque recircuitura
imposi]ti lapides generosi cuncticolores
orti de] cocleis in maio mense marinis
rorum co]nmixtis auro de more reclusis.
365   sunt in p]lanicie graciles sperule uariate,
conser]itur uitro uitrum, discernitur auro,
compo]nens nodos uel folia uel uolucellos.

V.341-367   343 omninoque] omnino *m.pr.*   345 in] a *m.pr.*   350
non erat inmerito *Zeydel*: non legit inmerito *Laistner*: lata
fuit merito *Seiler*   351 dat fibulas *Ford*: addidit *Seiler*
352 quauis *Seiler*   353 fulgor *Seiler*   354 quarum *Seiler*   355
non grandi *Laistner*: cum grandi *Zeydel*   356 addidit *Ford*: et
super *Zeydel*: insuper *Laistner*   357 lacernam *Zeydel*: inter-
ulam *Ford*: non bogam *Laistner*   358 pectora *Ford*: ossaue
Zeydel: uilli *Laistner*   359 ex auro *Seiler*   361 in curuatura
Laistner: nam curuatura *Seiler*   362 impositi *Seiler*   363 orti
de *Laistner*: inuenti *Seiler*: collectis *Schmeller*   364 rorum
Laistner: rerum *Schmeller*: lectis *Seiler*   365 sunt in *Seiler*
366 conseritur *Laistner*: attrahitur *Seiler*   367 componens
Seiler

cast in a clay mould, not shaped with hammers or struck by a   341
workman's tool, solid right through and not chiselled in any
way.   In the centre of it was pictured a flying eagle, in
the end of whose beak there was a crystal ball in which three
little birds could be seen to be moved round as though they
were alive, and quick in their animated flight.   A golden
chaplet encircled this eagle, which was so broad that it
covered one's breast very well.   But this was only proper,
for it was cast from a talent of gold.

He gave other brooches which weighed less.   The sparkle   350
of their multiplicity of precious stones differed in each
case, as if you were gazing on a star there;   each of them
weighed at least a quarter-pound.   He added to these a
smaller one, with a little bracelet suspended on a delicate
chain;   with it a lady might fasten up her robe at the front
during the day so that it did not gape open, and thus her
breasts might not be seen, if they were amply proportioned.

He added a single solid gold crescent a pound in weight,   359
in which the craftsman had employed great skill: along the
rounded curve of the piece were set fine stones of every hue,
gathered from sea-shells in the month of May, and set fast,
as is the custom, mixed with drops of gold.   The little balls
became variegated on the surface, as glass is drawn to glass
and is repelled by gold, forming knots or leaves or little
birds.

ignibus h]irsuta primo fiunt, tuberosa
cum sput]o uel aqua poliuntur cote scabrosa.
370   id ge]nus electrum fabrile uocatur honestum.
ast in sple]ndente post gemmas margine lune
dant b]ulle dulcem se conlidendo fragorem.
hanc lun]am lanci caute rex precipit addi,
qui post] octonas in lancem ponit inaures.
375   quatt]uor ex illis compte fulsere lapillis
et gemmis] uariis ametistis atque berillis,
quatt]uor ast alie non sunt gemmis redimite,
nexus] delecti mirisue modis uariati
sicut pincillo quis uitrum pingeret au[ro;   M15^r
380   bulle cum bacis clangunt cum se mouet auri[s.
tandem ter denos fabricare iubet digit[ales
ex auro puro reperitur non melius quo.
in quorum quemque iubet includendo locare
ligurium uel iacinctum pulchrumue berillum,
385   quorum tres sponse dandi sunt accipiende,
non grandes, graciles, quos ferre decet m[ulieres.
lancibus impletis his donis imperiosis
atque coaptatis clauis firme capitatis
has iubet obduci rex glutine ualde tena[ci
390   polline commixto multo tribulamine [ficto
ut non abradi nec aqua queat hoc aboleri.

quando dies uenit ad quam rex inducia[uit
quod deberet ei pie respondere clienti,
dixit principibus 'noster miles peregrinus
395   uult remeare domum carta reuocatus h[erorum
pro quorum causa patria caret, ut patet, ipsa.
en hic est carta: nunc uos audite quid illa
dicat.' sic inquit et eam sciolus recitauit.

V.368-398   368 ignibus hirsuta *Laistner*:   que tamen hirsuta
Seiler   369 cum sputo *Laistner*:   mox uino *Seiler*   371 ast in
splendente *Seiler*   372 dant bulle *Seiler*   373 hanc lunam
Seiler   374 qui post *Seiler*   376 et gemmis *Seiler*:   nobilibus
Laistner   378 nexus *Seiler*   mirisue modis *scripsi*:   miris nodis
edd. ceteri: miris...odis *cod.*   390 ficto *scripsi*:   trito *Seiler*

When they are first made in the fire they are coarse, and the   368
bumps are smoothed out with a rough stone and spittle or
water.   This lovely type of manufacture is called 'artificial
amber.' Along the glittering edge of the crescent, behind the
stones, little spheres tinkled together with a sweet sound.
The king ordered this crescent to be placed carefully in the
dish, and then he put eight earrings into it.   Four of these
shone with various stones and gems set in them, amethysts and
beryls, whereas the other four were not encircled with stones;
they were lovely twisted shapes, decorated in amazing ways,
as when an artist paints glass with a brushful of gold.   As
the ear moved, so little baubles tinkled against berries on
it.

    Finally he ordered them to make thirty rings from pure   381
gold - better ones could not be found.   He ordered them to
set on each ring a hyacinth stone or a jacinth or a resplendent
beryl.   Three of them were to be given to his future bride;
they were not large, but slender, the sort that women ought
to wear.

    When the dishes were filled with these regal gifts and   387
firmly fitted together with broad-headed pins, the king
ordered them to be smeared with very strong glue mixed with
very finely ground flour, so that this could not be rubbed
off or washed away by water.

    When the day came on which the king had decided he ought   392
to give a proper response to his vassal, he said to his
nobles: "our foreign knight wishes to journey home, summoned
by a missive from those lords on whose account he is absent
from his homeland, as is plain.   See, here is the missive;
now you listen to what it says."   He said this, and the
scribe read it out loud.

```
          carta perlecta fiunt ibi tristia corda,
400       compare tam fido tam miti tamque ben[igno
          tali tyrone regem seseque carere,
          et regi suadent hunc ui prece seu reti[neret,
          uxorem sibi det et honoribus hunc locupl[etet,
          dicentes dignum comitatu quouis eund[em.
405       rex ait 'absit ut is de me tribuletur [amicus,
          a quo sum numquam minimam commotus in [iram,
          quin irascentem me mitem reddit ut ag[num,
          totius fidei plenum se prebet in omni.
          iam nimis] exilii grauis est sibi sarcina longi,      M15ᵛ
410       qualiter i]n quoquam non hoc sentire ualebam.
          nunc di]mittamus et eum patriare sinamus.
          has habeat gra]tes, si post sua sic ueniat res,
          quod non esse do]mi queat huc bene posse reuerti,
          inueniat u]eteres ut apud nos commoditates.'
415       sic ait et p]uerum iubet ad se quo uocet illum.
          is curren]s uocat hunc, ad regem uenit is illuc.
          dum modicum] siluit, clementer rex sibi dixit
          'te nimis in]uite mi kare reliquero de me.
          semper prom]ptus eras et in omni morigerebas.
420       hinc hab]eo grates tibi dilectissime grandes.
          inuidus] es nulli sed plebi karus es omni.
          nunc mih]i dic uerum, karissime cunctigenorum,
          detur uis t]ibi peccunia, malisne sophia?'
          is reputa]ns mente sibi quid respondeat apte
425       'non cupi]o quod' ait 'componderat usus honori.
          census hab]et multos, ubi noscitur, insidiantes.
```

V.399-426   405 amicus *Zeydel*: in istis *Schmeller*: sodalis *Ford*
409 iam nimis *Schmeller*: nam sic *Seiler*   410 qualiter *Seiler*
411 nunc dimittamus *Seiler*   412 has habeat grates *Seiler*   413
quod non esse *Seiler*   414 inueniat *Seiler*   415 sic ait et
Seiler   416 is currens *Seiler*   417 dum modicum *Seiler*   418
te nimis inuite *Seiler*: ...inuite *Schmeller*   419 semper *Seiler*
omni] omnibus *m.pr.*   420 hinc habeo *Seiler*   421 inuidus *Seiler*
422 nunc mihi *Seiler*   423 detur uis *scripsi*: premia dem *Seiler*
peccunia *scripsi cum cod. m.pr.*: peccunna *cod.m.alt., edd.*
ceteri   424 is reputans *Seiler*: is uoluens *Schmeller*   425
non cupio *Laistner*: id cupio *Seiler*   426 census habet *Seiler*

The missive was read through, and it made them sad at heart   399
that the king and they themselves would be without such a
faithful, mild and kindly comrade, and such a great young
soldier. They urged the king to keep him there, whether
by force or by entreaty, to give him a wife and to enrich
him with honours, pointing out that he was worthy to enter
any man's company. The king said "far be it from me that   405
this man should be troubled by me; he has never provoked me
to the slightest anger - indeed, when I have been furious he
has made me as gentle as a lamb, and he shows himself to be
entirely faithful to every man. The burden of long exile
now weighs heavily on him in a way that I have not been able
to feel in anyone. Now let us dismiss him and let him go   411
home, and let him have these expressions of our gratitude,
so that if it happens that his circumstances so turn out
that he cannot remain at home, he may well return here and
find with us all the benefits of old." He said this, and
ordered his page to summon the man to him.

The boy ran off and called him, and he came there to the   416
king. He was silent for a short while, so the king said to
him in a kindly voice "I release you from my service, my
beloved, though I do not wish to at all: you were always eager
to serve me and pleased me in every way. Because of this
I am enormously grateful to you, my most loved servant. You   421
are inimical to no man, but are dear to all my people. Now,
tell me the truth, O dearest of any men, do you wish a reward
of money to be given you, or do you prefer wisdom?"

He pondered in his mind what he might fittingly reply. "I   424
have no desire" he said "for what is commonly given equal weight
to honour. When wealth becomes known it has many who lie in
wait for it.

pauperies mis]eros cogit plures fore fures,
in consanguineo]s parit inuidiam uel amicos,
uel fratrem] stimulat fidei quo federa rumpat.
430 est meliu]s censu careat quis quam quoque sensu,
et quicum]que pia satagit florere sophia,
ille uel arge]nti semper sat habebit et auri,
que uult] expugnat quia telis intus abundat.
at memini] multos uidisse creberrime stultos,
435 qui cunctis opibu]s per stulticiam nichilatis
uiuebant in]opes uitiose degenerantes,
quos non iuuis]se sed opes patuit nocuisse.
unde potes facile me uerbum tale docere,   M16^r
quod si seruabo quod id ipsum non temerabo
440 tam karum quod erit ceu pondo decem mihi quis det.
nemo mihi rapit id inimicaturue nec odit
propter id et latro me non occidet in arto.
in camera regis census decet ut sit opimus,
pauper homo sat habet si ui ualet arteque pollet.
445 non uolo peccuniam, sitio gustare sophiam.'
hoc rex audito 'mecum' surgens ait 'ito'
in pentralque pedant nullum secumque sinebant.
rex residens pro se tunc exule stante cliente
dixerat in primis 'nunc audi cordis ab imis
450 que tibi predico ceu uerus amicus amico.

non tibi sit rufus umquam specialis amicus.
si fit is iratus non est fidei memoratus,
nam uehemens dira sibi stat durabilis ira.
tam bonus haut fuerit aliqua fraus quin in eo sit
455 quam uitare nequis quin ex hac commaculeris,
nam tangendo picem uix expurgaris ad unguem.

quamuis cenosa per uillam sit uia trita
numquam deuites callem quo per sata pergas

V.427-458   428 in consanguineos *Seiler*   429 uel fratrem *Seiler*
431 pie *m.pr.* sophie *m.pr.*   432 ille uel *Seiler*   433 que uult
Seiler   434 at memini *Seiler*   435 qui cunctis opibus *Seiler*:
qui opibus cunctis *Ford*: qui tot diuitiis *Laistner*   436
uiuebant inopes *Seiler*   437 quos non iuuisse *Seiler*

90

Poverty forces many a poor fellow to be a thief, it gives   427
birth to envy in a man's family and friends, or even eggs
his brother on to break the bonds of good faith.   It is
better for a man to be without wealth than to lose all
feeling, and whoever is busy at prospering in godly wisdom
will always have enough of silver and gold.   He conquers
whatever he wishes, because he is well-armed within.   But
I remember having seen many who were absolutely stupid, who
squandered all their riches through their stupidity and lived
in abject poverty, and brought themselves low in their error.
Riches did not help them - clearly, they harmed them.   So   438
then you can easily teach me such a word of wisdom that, if
I follow it and do not treat it rashly, it will be as dear to
me as if a man were to give me ten pounds.   No-one can steal   441
that from me, or plot against me and hate me because of it,
and no robber will kill me in some narrow place.   Wealth
belongs in a king's chamber if it is very precious, whereas
a poor man has enough if he has his strength and skill.   I
do not want money, but I thirst for the taste of wisdom."
    The king listened to this, and then, getting up, said   446
"come with me" and they walked into the inner chamber, allowing
no-one to go with them.   The king took his seat, with the
exile, his vassal, standing before him, and then began to
speak: "now listen with all your heart to what I say to you,
as a true friend speaks to a friend.
    Never let a redheaded man be a close friend to you.   If   451
he becomes angry, he does not remember good faith, for his
anger is terribly fierce and long-lasting.   He will never
be so good that there is no deceit in him, and you cannot
avoid it - you will be stained by it yourself, for you will
never be clean to your fingertips if you put them into pitch.
    No matter how muddy the road has been trodden through a   457
village, never leave the path and go across the fields,

ne male tracteris careasque tuis ibi frenis
correptus per quem responso dando superbum.

quo uideas iuuenem quod habet senior mulierem
hospicium tribui tibi non poscas iteranti:
in te nam magnam facis insons suspicionem.
hic timet hec sperat fors inter eos ita uersat.
465 ast ubi uir uiduam iuuenis teneat ueteranam
hospitium posce; non hic timet hec nec amat te
tu[nc] ibi secure dormis sine suspicione.

poscit ad occandum si te conciuis agellum   M16^v
ut prestatur equa generandi tempore feta
470 noli prestare ni uis hanc degenerare,
nam perdet pullum si planificabit agellum.

non tibi tam karus sit contribulis tuus ullus
quatinus hunc sepe soleas uisendo grauare
plusque solet rarum quam continuum fore karum:
475 nam cito uilescit homini quodcumque frequens fit.

ancillam propriam quamuis nimium speciosam
non uelut uxorem facias tibi consocialem
ne contemnat te tibi respondendo superbe
neue reatur se domui debere preesse
480 si pernoctabit ad mensam siue sedebit.
tecum manducans pernox tecumue repausans
continuo domina cunctorum uult fore summa,
talia famosum faciunt ignominiosum.

si libet uxorem traducere nobiliorem
485 causa karorum generandorum liberorum
tunc cognoscibilem conquire tibi mulierem
et nusquam mater tibi ni quo consilietur.
quam dum quesieris decet omnimodis et honores
tractes clementer; illi tamen esto magister
490 litigium cum te ne quod presumat habere,

V.459-490   467 tunc *Seiler*: tuque *Schmeller*   469 feta *edd.*:
foeta *cod.*   481 tecum repausans *Schmeller*   488 docet
Schmeller

lest you are badly treated and lose your reins when someone   459
snatches them, giving you a cheeky reply.

Wherever you see that an old man has a young wife, do not   461
ask for accommodation for you on your journey;   for though
you are innocent, you will bring great suspicion on yourself.
It may turn out that his fears will be raised , and her hopes;
but ask for accommodation where a young man has an old widow
for his wife: he will not fear, and she will not love you,
and there you may sleep safely without suspicion.

If a neighbour asks you to lend him your mare to harrow his   468
field, and it is pregnant and close to foaling, do not lend
it, unless you want it to become ill, for if it levels the
field it will lose its foal.

Do not let any kinsman be so dear to you that you become   472
a burden to him by seeing him so often: you see, whatever
happens frequently soon becomes wearisome to a man.

Never make your maidservant - even if she is very pretty -   476
your consort, as if she were your wife, lest she despises
you and answers you back haughtily, and lest she thinks she
ought to be mistress of your household because she sleeps
with you and sits at table with you.   As she eats with you
and lies with you at night, she will want to be the highest
lady over all straightaway.   Such happenings make a noble
man a disgrace.

If you wish to marry a more noble wife in order to have   484
children dear to you, then look for a woman whom you can
know of - and nowhere except where your mother advises you!
When you woo her, you should honour her in every way, and
treat her gently, but be masterful to her, lest she should
presume to have any quarrel with you;

nam uitium nullum maius ualet esse uirorum
quam si subiecti sint quis debent dominari,
et licet in cunctis bene concordet tibi rebus
numquam uelle tuum debes sibi pandere totum,
495   a te correpta si post pro re uitiosa
improperare uelit ut nil tibi dicere possit
unde pudor uel amor inter uos quid minuatur.

nulla repentina tibi tam grauis ingruat ira   M17^r
quin pernoctare uindictam perpetiare,
500   maxime cum dubia res est non ut tibi dicta,
forsan cras gaudes animi quod frena tenebas.

nunquam cum domino tibi lis sit siue magistro,
namque potestate si non iuste superant te.
nec quid eis prestes ueraciter id quia perdes.
505   cum rogat ut prestes est tunc melius sibi quo des
inueniet culpam quia, tantundem tibi per quam
tollat; utrumque perit nec grates nec bona reddet.
"grates" dicet "habe" cum despoliaberis a se,
tunc inclinabis Dominum laudans quod abibis
510   sanus cum uita nihili pensans tua damna.

et numquam sit iter quoquam tibi tam properanter
ut pretermittas quin ecclesias ubi cernas
sanctis committas illis te uel benedicas.
sicubi pulsetur aut quo si missa canatur
515   descendas ab equo currens uelocius illo
kattholice paci quo possis participari.
hoc iter haut longat penitus tibi quin breuiabit
tutius et uadis hostem minus atque timebis.

abnuito numquam si te cogens homo quisquam
520   oret amore pii ieiunia frangere Christi:
non ea nam frangis sua sed mandata replebis.

si tibi sint segetes prope plateas generales
non facias fossas progressus ulteriores
in sata ne fiant, nam fossas circumeundo

V.491-524   492 queis *Schmeller*   511 tam *om. m.pr.*

94

for there is no greater fault in men than when they are 491
subjects of those whom they ought to govern. And even if
she is of one mind with you on every subject, you must
never reveal all your wishes to her, so that afterwards
if she is reproved by you for doing wrong, and wishes to
taunt you, she may have nothing to say which will diminish
love and respect between you.

Let no sudden anger weigh so heavily on you that you 498
cannot bear to pass the night without revenge, especially
when the matter is doubtful, and not as related to you.
You may well be glad the next day that you bridled your
temper.

Never go to law with your lord or your master: even 502
if they do not defeat you justly, they will do so by force;
and do not lend them anything, because in truth you will
lose it. When he asks you to lend him anything, then it
is better that you give it to him, for he will find some
fault for which he will take just as much from you: so
both will be lost to you, and he will repay neither goods
nor gratitude. He will say "receive my thanks" when you
are robbed by him, and you will bow your head to the Lord
God and praise him that you have got away with your life,
counting your losses as nought.

Furthermore, never let your journey to any place be in 511
such haste that when you see a church, you pass on by
without commending yourself to its saints and blessing them.
Wherever bells are rung or mass is sung, get down from your
horse and run there quickly, so that you may share in the
catholic peace. This will not make your journey longer,
but will rather shorten it for you, and you shall travel
more safely and in less fear of an enemy.

Never refuse any man who begs you earnestly to break 519
your fast for the godly love of Christ, for you do not
break it, but fulfil his commands.

If you have crops planted near to public highways, do 522
not dig ditches in them, lest people encroach onto the
fields later on; for, in avoiding the ditches,

525 strata fit utrimque per siccum gente meante.
  si non fodisses damnum minus hinc habuisses.'

  dum rex conticuit sapientia uerbaque finit   M17^v
  ambo prodibant, rex inque throno residebat
  et laudat cunctis uirtutem militis eius,
530 econtra murmur laudantum multiplicatur,
  qui grates regi populo referebat et omni.
  rex ait 'ito domum cunctorum plenus honorum
  atque uide matrem totamque tuam pariter rem,
  si potes in patria tamen esse tua uelut ista
535 soluere sique uelint domini que polliciti sunt.
  qui si fallant te decet ut fallantur et a te
  nec famuleris eis totiens delusus ab illis,
  nulli seruitio parco nimis aut inhonesto.
  si tibi contingat animus tuus unde uacillet
540 tedeat ut patrie proprie te si repetis me
  eiusdem uelle contra te repperies me
  quo nunc te linquo, dubium non huius habeto.'
  post nuerat digito pre se stanti paranimpho
  et sibi secretim de more susurrat in aurem
545 illuc ut peras camerarius afferat illas
  in quibus hi panes fuerant intus locupletes,
  polline perfusi foris intus pecuniosi.
  allatis peris rex inquit 'mi bone sodes
  hos geminos panes numquam, karissime, frangas
550 primitus ad matrem uenias quam tam tibi karam,
  cuius in aspectu solius frange minorem.
  cum sedeas nuptum cum sponsa frange secundum.
  hinc et dilectis quantum uis detur amicis
  ut sapiant qualis noster soleat fore panis,'
555 atque ualedicens rex oscula ter sibi figens
  cum gemitu liquit. miles lacrimando recessit,
  quem sequitur cunctus ad equum populus gemebundus,
  cumque ualedicunt sibi flentes oscula figunt.
  inde recedente solo comitante sodali,   M18^r
560 scutifer enthecam qui uexit eo modicel[lam,
  traxit sagmarium uariis opibus oneratum.

V.525-561 534 *hunc v. om. m.pr. add. m.alt. in margine* 542
dubius *m.pr.* 560 entecam *m.pr.*

96

a path will be made on the dry land on both sides by the   525
people passing by, and you would not have had this trouble
if you had not dug the path up."

When the king had fallen silent and put an end to his   527
wise words, both of them came out. The king sat down on
his throne and praised the qualities of the knight in every
way.   From the opposite side the murmur of those praising
him grew louder, and he returned thanks to the king and to
all the people. The king said "go home replete with every
honour; see how your mother is, and all your affairs, too,
whether you can remain in your own land as you can in this
one, and whether your lords will fulfil what they have
promised. If they trick you, it is proper that they should
be tricked by you, and that you should not serve them, having
been deceived by them so often. Serve no man who is very   538
mean or dishonest. If ever anything happens to you to make
you insecure in your mind, and you grow weary of your own
land and come back to me, you shall find me disposed towards
you exactly as I now leave you: be in no doubt about this."

Then he beckoned with his hand to his chamberlain, who   543
was standing in front of him, and, as was his custom, whispered
some words secretly in his ear, to have the servant bring
that baggage which contained those precious loaves, covered
with flour outside, but inside full of money. When the bags
were brought, the king said "my good companion, my dearest
one, never break these two loaves until first you come to
your mother, who is dear to you. Break open the smaller one
in her presence alone; break the second one when you are
married and sitting with your wife. Let as much as you
wish be given to your close friends, so that they can taste
what sort of bread ours is." Then, bidding him farewell,   555
the king embraced him three times, and left him, weeping.
The knight withdrew with tears in his eyes. All the people
followed him to his horse, crying, and they wept as they
embraced him and bade him farewell.

Then as he departed, accompanied only by one companion, his   559
squire, who had carried just a little pack to that place,
led a pack-horse laden with riches of various kinds.

inter dilectos fit magna querela sodales,
tam breue tunc tempus quod ouarent alterut[rius,
nam non ni triduo simul ibant sermocin[ando.
565   ad noctem mediam prolongant sumere cen[am,
post mensam demptis ambobus calciamen[tis
postquam dormitum decernunt uisere lect[um
auersi flebant taciti, lacrimando ge[mebant.
ut puer ille magis flet se quatiendo soda[lis,
570   a sibi!   tam fido quod disiungendus amic[o.
nescit an hunc umquam fuerit uisurus in [euum.
peruigil insomnem uellet flens ducere noct[em
ni cito quod somnus cor merens opprimit eius.
cumque diescebat ambo simul euigilab[ant,
575   surgunt, induerant se prandent et fa[lerabant,
insimul et pergunt donec confinia cern[unt
alterius regni qua sunt postremo dire[mpti,
exul et ut potuit pre fletu uix sibi dix[it
'kare meo domino de uero corde ue s[ancto
580   dic, precor, oramen uel deuotum famula[men
omnibus atque suis mihi ceu cor semper am[andis.'
basia dum sibi dant ambo nimis inti.[me flebant
alterutrimque 'uale' dicebatur sat abun[de.
discedunt a se sic in sua mestus u[terque.

585   utque sue patrie iam cepit repropi[are
rufus eum uidit ac currens se sibi i[ungit.
quando salutauit hunc un[de m]eet r[ogitauit
ireue quo uellet [c]omes [eius si] fore [posset.
sat dedignanter respondit ei sapienter
590   'est uia] communis, quo uultis pergere quitis.'   M18^V
rufus] parabolas incepit dicere multas
quamquam res]ponsum de milite non capit ullum.

V.562-592   573 cito quod] citius *Schmeller*   quod *om.m.pr.*   575
falerabant *Seiler*:   falerant se *Schmeller*   579 sancto *Seiler*:
uerendo *Schmeller*   582 intime flebant *Seiler*:   intimi amici
Schmeller   587 unde meet *Seiler*:   quaue uia *Schmeller*   588
comes eius si fore posse   *Seiler*]   miles...ferebat *Schmeller*   592
quamquam *Seiler*:   quamuis *Schmeller*

There was great sadness between the two close companions,   562
because they could rejoice in each other's company for so
short a time then, for they could talk as they travelled
together for barely three days.   They put off eating the
evening meal until the middle of the night; and after the
meal, when they had taken off their boots and when they had
decided to lie down and sleep, they turned away from one
another and cried silently, sobbing through their tears.
The companion wept more, trembling like a little child,   569
because, poor fellow, he was going to be separated from his
faithful friend; he did not know if he was ever going
to see him again.   He would have wished to stay awake
all night, keeping a vigil of tears, but sleep quickly
subdued his grieving heart.
    When dawn broke, they woke up together, got up and dressed,   574
ate, saddled their horses together, and set off until they
saw the frontiers of the other kingdom, where they finally
parted, and the exile, who could barely speak because of his
weeping, said to him "my dear friend, tell my lord, I pray
you, that with true and pious feeling I shall pray for him
and serve him with devotion, and shall always love all his   580
people as I do my own heart."   While they embraced one
another, both wept with deep emotion, and "farewell" was
said by both of them a good many times.   And so they left
one another each to his own grief.
    As he was beginning to draw near to his own fatherland,   585
a redheaded man saw him and hastened to join him; when he
greeted him, he asked him where he was journeying from,
where he wished to go, and if he could accompany him.   (The
exile) replied wisely, in a fairly disdainful manner: "this
is a public highway, you may go where you wish."   The redhead
began to tell many stories, although he got no real response
from the knight.

increscen]te die cum ferre suam nequit in se
ad sellam po]st se cappam solet ille ligare.

595 rufus ut a]cquirat hanc tota mente uolutat.
pergeban]t, ueniunt ad aquam uel equos adaquabant;
mulcendo] tergum ceu detergendo caballum
ad se cor]rigiam furtim rapit indeque cappam,
hancque s]ub ascella tenet usque recessit ab unda,

600 tunc salien]s ab equo citat hanc intrudere sacco
cum remor]aretur post hunc uelut experiatur
ungula queque] pedum clauos an haberet eorum.
tunc ad se c]urrit et adulando sibi dixit
'antea no]nne, bone, mihi cernebaris habere

605 in sella ca]ppam?   miror quod non uideo quam.'
cui miles] dixit 'est mirum me sed ubi sit.'
rufus ait] 'sub aqua quid nescio diffluitabat,
sic ub]i potamus ibi forsan perdideramus.
ergo reu]ertamur hanc si reperire queamus.'

610 'absit' m]iles ait simulans sibi ceu nihili sit.
uespere tunc] uille ceperunt appropiare
per quam pl]atea uadit sat lata lutosa.
haut in e]quo quiuis ualet his exire lacunis
nec tran]sire uia prope sepes tam lutulenta

615 quisque pe]dans posset ni pons artissumus esset
quem sa]t temptando sepemque manu retinendo
uix deui]taret in cenum ne cecidisset.
trames] at [est ar]tus e campo per sata tritus.

V.593-618   594 ad sellam *Seiler*: miles tum *Schmeller*   596
pergebant *Seiler*   597 mulcendo *Seiler*: uertendo *Schmeller*
598 ad se *Seiler*: rufus *Schmeller*   600 tunc saliens *Seiler*:
exsiliens *Schmeller*   601 cum remorarentur *Seiler*   602 ungula
queque *Seiler*: quiuis sterni *Laistner*: quouis sterni *Zeydel*
603 tunc ad se *Seiler*   accurrit *Schmeller*   604 antea *Seiler*
605 in sella *Seiler*: post tergum *Schmeller*   606 cui miles
Seiler   me] mihi *Schmeller*   607 rufus ait *Seiler*   608 **sic**
Seiler   609 ergo *Seiler*   612 per quam *Seiler*: per illam
Schmeller   613 haut in equo *Laistner*   614 nec *Laistner*   615
quisque pedans *Laistner*   616 quem sat *Laistner*   617 uix
deuitaret *Laistner*   618 trames *Laistner*   est artus *Laistner*

It was the latter's custom to fasten his hood behind him   593
on his saddle as the day grew hotter and he could no longer
bear to keep it on.   The redhead turned his whole attention
to getting it for himself.   They rode on, came to some
water, and let the horses drink.   Lightly stroking the
horse's back, as though brushing it down, he secretly
snatched the saddle-strap and then the hood, thrust it
under his armpit, and went up from the water.   Then jumping
down from his horse he made haste to thrust it into his bag,
while he remained standing behind it, as though looking to
see if the hooves of its feet had their nails.   Then he   602
ran to him and, fawning over him, said "my good fellow,
I'm sure that before you seemed to have a hood on your
saddle?   I'm amazed that I can't see it."   The knight   606
said to him "it's beyond me where it can be."   The redhead
said, "something was floating about under the water;
perhaps we lost it there, where we stopped to drink.   Let
us turn back, to see if we can find it."   "Never mind"
said the knight, pretending that it was nothing to him.
   Then in the evening they began to draw near to a village,   611
through which led a broad, muddy track.   No-one could get
out of the potholes on horseback, or cross over such a
muddy road on foot near the fence if there were not a very
narrow duckboard there; by feeling his way along this and
keeping a grip on the fence, a man might just avoid falling
in the mud.   There was also a narrow path worn across arable
fields from the open,

per siccum] callem rufus suadebat eundum,
620   dicens il]luuie ceni non posse meare,
        nosse uiam n]ullam tam cenosam uel aquosam.

V.619-621   619 per siccum *scripsi*:   nunc facilem *Zeydel*:
qui dat iter *Laistner*   eundum *Hall*: eundem *cod*.   620
dicens illuuie *Seiler*   621 nosse uiam nullam *Seiler*

and the redhead urged that they take this dry path, saying   619
he could not travel through this filthy mud, and knew no
road as muddy and wet as this.

'posthac cum peccas noceas cui non ma[ledicas,   M19^r
est quia ualde graue duplex damnum tol[erare,
perdere quemque suum super hocque pati maledict[um.'
e regione minas rufus satis egit inanes,
5   non pernoctari dicens quam sint mutilati
insultantes, hos] quia uult incendere cun[ctos.
miles subrisit sibi quid peius fore nam scit.
ad uillam propiant ubi pernoctare uolebant.
sol petit oceanum monet hospitiumque pete[ndum:
10   rufus pastorem uocat unum conueniend]um,
illuc qui uenit, quem rufus mox rogitauit
'dic uicinorum mihi nomina precipuorum.
est hic quis diues nostri fore qui queat hospes?'
pastor ait 'multi sunt hic quos non stupefir[i
15   sat scio si centum scutis comes appetat [unum,
quin his seruire possint omni sub honore.
esset homo pauper, nequeat qui sufficienter
uobis seruire uestros et equos stabulare.
multi sint soliti licet hospitibus famu[lari,
20   inter eos omnes non suscipit aduenientes
tam bene ceu iuuenis ueluti uetu[la uidualis.'
rufus ait 'uiduam quid habet iuuenis ueteranam?
uir uetus uxorem deberet habere uetern[am.'
pastor ait 'nusquam melius nupsisset ad ull[am.
25   pauper erat nimium prius is quam duxerat [illam,
nunc dominatur ei, seruiuit cui uice ser[ui,

VI.1-26   2 tolerare *Seiler*   6 insultantes hos *scripsi*:
insectans numeros *Zeydel*: insculus n...mos *Seiler*   21
uetula uidualis *scripsi*: uetus uxor illius *Zeydel*: uetus
uxor *Seiler*: uetus uxor eius *Schmeller*   25 illam *Seiler*:
istam *Schmeller*   26 uice serui] prius ipsi *Schmeller* serui
Seiler

"After this when you sin against anyone and harm him, do not 1
curse him as well, because it is very hard for a man to endure a
twofold injury, losing his property and suffering a curse to
boot." The redhead on the other hand made many empty threats,
saying that the night would not pass without those who had mocked
him being mangled, because he wanted to burn the lot of them.
The knight smiled, for he know that this would turn out the
worse for him.

They hurried on to the village, where they wanted to spend 8
the night. The sun sank in the West, warning them to seek
shelter. The redhead called a shepherd to come to them.
He came over there, and the redhead asked him briskly "tell
me the names of the local gentry: is there a rich man here
who could be our host?" The shepherd said " there are many
here whom I know very well would not be so staggered if a
count were to seek out one of them with a hundred armed men,
that they could not give them honourable service. He would 16
be a poor man who could not give ample hospitality to you and
stable your horses! Although there are many who are used to
taking in guests, among them all none receives visitors so
well as does a young man or as his little old widow-woman."

The redhead said "what's a young man doing with an old 22
widow? It's an old man who ought to have an old wife."

The shepherd said "nowhere could he have found a better 24
one to marry. He was a very poor man before he married
her. Now he is her master, he who once waited on her as a
servant,

ac] ueluti dignus, est nam pius atque benignus,
gratia sitque Deo qui sic miseretur ege[no.'
tunc dixit miles 'que te rogo dic mihi sodes,
30   qualiter acciderit inopi locuples quia nups[it.'
tunc ait i]s 'domne dic audieris mihi nonne   M19^v
"agna uetu]s cupide uas lingit salis amore?"
.................................ralta
quem] prius hec habuit, secum dirissime uixit,
35   nam fuit i[ngra]tus, parcus, rarissime letus,
numquam ridentem uiderunt neue iocantem.
quid] dix[it] pecorum uel apum fuerit uel equorum
uix] numerum nescit, quantum cuiusque sibi sit,
rar]o tamen carnis proprie saturatur uteruis:
40   cas]eolos comedunt duros serumque biberunt.
qui]cquid habent uendunt precium cauteque recondunt.
sua]uis is huc ueniens iuuenis nudus uel egenus
uad]it ad hunc primo panem mendicat ab illo,
qui] sibi buccellam sigalinam uix dedit unam.
45   han]c dum suscepit reuerenter stabat et edit.
mensa sublata properat sustollere uasa
ne m]ingat catta catulusue coinquinet illa,
sed]ulus ac lauit, post in toreuma reponit.
cocl]ear in disco curat seruare magistro,
50   ut] sibi preponat cum prandit quandoue cenet
app]osito cultro cum sale ue cum cocleari
si be]ne conditum quid non sit condiat hinc id,
seu] sit holus seu sorbicium seu quidque ciborum.
hec] notat in corde senior si non ait ore.
55   nil] pretermisit iuuenis quod opus fore uidit,
bou]es sicut oues adaquat procos ue capellas,

VI.27-56   29 miles que] miles hunc que *m.pr.*   30 quia nupsit]
mulier sit *Schmeller*   31 tunc ait is *Seiler*   32 agna uetus
Laistner: quod uel ouis *Seiler*: omnis ouis *Schmeller*   34
dirissime] laetissime *Schmeller*   35 ingratus *Seiler*   37 quid
dixit *Seiler*   38 uix *Seiler*   39 raro *Seiler*: neue *Schmeller*
proprie] horum *m.pr.*   42 suauis *Seiler*: tunc uis *Schmeller*
43 uadit *Seiler*: currit *Schmeller*   45 hanc *Seiler*: hic
Schmeller   53 seu *Seiler*   54 hec *Schmeller*: id *Zeydel*

and he fully deserves it, for he is a kind and godly man.   27
Thanks be to God, who has shown such pity on a poor man."
     Then the knight said "tell me what I ask you, good
fellow, how it happened that a rich woman married a poor
man."
     Then he replied "my lord, surely you have heard that 'an   31
old ewe likes to lick the trough because it loves the salt'?
.... The first husband she had lived a very
hard life with her, for he was disagreeable, mean, and very
rarely happy; men never saw him smiling or joking.   He could
scarcely tell what cattle, bees or horses he had: he had
no idea how many he had of each, yet both of them seldom fed
on their own meat; they ate hard cheese, and drank whey.
They sold whatever they had, and stashed the money away   41
carefully.   That charming young man came their way poor
and naked; he went to this man, and first begged him for
some bread.   He gave him hardly a mouthful of rye bread;
he took this, stood there politely, and ate it.   When the
table was removed, he made haste to take the dishes away so
that a cat could not foul them or a dog dirty them, washed
them scrupulously and then put them back in the cupboard.
He made sure to set aside a spoon in a dish for the master,
to set before him when he took his early or evening meal,   50
and set down a knife and some salt with a spoon.   If anything
happened not to be well seasoned, he seasoned it with this,
whether it was cabbage, or broth, or any kind of food.   The
old man made a mental note of this, even if he said nothing.
The young man left out nothing he saw a need for.   He
watered the cattle and sheep, the pigs and the goats,

app]ortat fenum quibus annonat parafredis,
que] fecit sponte sibi nemine precipiente.
si quid] alius erat opus id studiosius egit
60 et c]um per triduum mansisset sic apud illum
is n]isi buccellam sibi nil dedit ad comedendum,
cumque diutius esuriem sufferre nequiret   M20^r
inclinabat ei cupiens alio proficisci.
ille sibi dixit hunc cum secedere uidit
65 "nunc hic esto dies binos tantummodo uel tres
alterutrum nostros mores donec uideamus."
consensit iuuenis, mox augetur sibi panis,
quadrans mane datur sibi sero dabatur et alter.
interea rogat hunc si quam cognouerit artem.
70 "artem quam possem cognoscere dic meliorem
quam quod nosco cibos lautos confingere pl[ures
uilibus ex causis, ex herbis siue farinis,
ad que nil nisi lac posco modicumue sagi[men
et tantum salis detur ut dulcedo sapori.
75 est aliud, domine, nobis omnino necesse.
quod non irasci debes de me tibi dici."
"dic" ait "id quid sit, non irascor." puer inquit
"en uelut es cunctis diues satis esse uideris
et tuus est panis solaminis omnis inanis,
80 furfuribus plenus fuscus lolio uel amarus.
si presentare mihi uis cuiusque farine
uel modium uel dimidium panes faciendum
tot bene cribratos presentabo tibi panes
semine conditos apii uel sale respersos
85 et p[icmen]turas aliquas lardo superunctas
atque coronellas [pane]s ali[o]s uti menclas.
hec faciens numerum [non multiplico] tibi [panum.
quicquid et ex cribr[o cautissime uase recondo
atque tuis pullis dabo siue strepentibus au[cis.
90 in pueros panem si fregero distribuendum

VI.57-90   58 que *Seiler*:   omne *Schmeller*   82 panes] ad panes
Schmeller   85 pictmenturas *Laistner*:   placenturas *Ford*:   pir-
aturas *Seiler*   86 panes alios *Ford*:   alias aliis *Laistner*:
mixtis aliis *Seiler*   87 non multiplico *scripsi*:   non deminuo
Ford: rerum minuo *Zeydel*   numerum] merum *Schmeller*   panum
Ford: paruum *Zeydel*   89 cautissime uase recondo *Seiler*

he brought fodder to feed the horses, and did this all of him-   58
self - no-one gave him orders to.   If anything else needed
doing, he did it quite energetically, and when he had stayed
with him like this for three days, the old fellow had given
him nothing but a mouthful of bread to eat, and since he
couldn't stand the hunger any longer, he bowed to him, for
he wanted to leave for some other place.   When he saw that
he wanted to leave, this chap said to him "stay here just two
or three days now, till we can see what each other's habits
are."

The young chap agreed, and soon his bread ration got bigger: 67
a quarter-loaf was given him in the morning, and another
quarter in the evening.   In the meantime, the old chap asked
him if he knew any trade.   "Tell me if I could know a better
trade than the one I do know, how to make many excellent
dishes from cheap ingredients, herbs, or flour, and apart
from these I ask only for milk, a little lard, and as much
salt as will bring out the flavour.   And there is one other
thing, my lord, which it is imperative we have, and which you
must not be annoyed about if it is told you by me."   "Speak,"
he said, "I shall not be angry, whatever it is."   The lad said   77
"look at you, you seem wealthy to everyone, and your bread
is utterly without taste.   It's full of bran, dark, and
bitter with darnel-weed.   If you want to let me have a measure,
or half, of any flour, to make some loaves, I shall present
you with very many well-sifted loaves seasoned with parsley-
seed and sprinkled with salt, some cakes smeared on top with
lard, and other loaves, coronet-shaped and long straight ones.
In making these, I shall not increase the number of loaves   87
you have, and I shall most carefully put whatever falls out
of the sieve in a bowl and I'll give it to your hens and
your cackling geese.   If ever I break bread and share it
among the boys,

non ita [do] se[ru]is ut eis lenis uidearis.
hec faciendo domum totam tibi promptifi[cabo,
inspiciens] cuncta presens sta, nitere furca."   M20^v
esset quod] iuuenis multum sapiens homo cernens

95   procura]nda sua commisit ei bona cuncta,
res ut pro]uideat puerosque suos uti uellet.
tali cau]tela facit hoc tali quoque cura
ut domi]no nil deficeret nulliue suorum.
ultra pre]bendam sibi nil tulit ille statutam,

100   sepe l]aborabat quo se uestire ualeret,
sic fam]ulando fide domino summa sine fraude
tempus] nescio quod posthec moritur scelus illud;
sordidio]r nemo uixit uel amarior illo.
a paucis] fletur propriorum dum tumulatur.

105   nil obst]at uidua iuueni tunc fiat amica
corde te]nus, sed ad ecclesiam simul ire uidemus,
"ad me]nsam resident simul ad lectum simul ibunt."
"matrem"] iam dominam uocat hanc ast hunc ea "natum."
mox famuli famule "patrem" suescunt uocitare,

110   ille su]os "liberos" econtra nominat illos.
numqu]am maiorem nos cernebamus amorem
nec co]nectales sibi tam bene conuenientes.
ianua] que uiduis prius est et clausa pupillis,
hec nu]nc diuitibus semper patet atque misellis.

115   illic] hospitium si uultis habebitis aptum:
stat uel] in ingressu uille grandis domus horum.'

VI.91-116   91 do seruis *Ford*: seiris *Seiler*   92
promptificabo *Schmeller*: promptificabis *Seiler*   93
inspiciens *Seiler*   95 procuranda *Seiler*: iamque regenda
Schmeller   100 sepe *Seiler*: ipse *Schmeller*   101 sic
Seiler: ac *Schmeller*   102 tempus *Schmeller*: uixit *Seiler*
105 nil obstat *scripsi*: nemo uetat *Seiler*: quis dubitat
Schmeller   106 corde ténus *Seiler*: protinus *Schmeller*   108
matrem *Seiler*: illeque *Schmeller*   116 stat uel *Seiler*: est
et *Schmeller*

I shall not give it to the servants in such a way as to make you 91
look oft-hearted to them.   In doing this I shall smarten up your
whole house.   You just stand there yourself, leaning on your
fork and looking everything over."
    Seeing that the young man was very wise, this fellow gave him 94
charge over all his property, to provide for his servants
however he wished.   He took such precautions and such care,
too, that his master and his household lacked for nothing.
He never took more for himself than the wages they had agreed
on, and toiled often just to have clothes to wear.   He
served his lord in this way with the greatest of faith and
without deceit for I don't know how long.   Then that old
villain died: no-one lived who was more unpleasant and sour
than him.   He was wept for at his burial by a few of his
relations.   Nothing stood against them then, and the widow   105
became the lover of the young man.   They kept it to themselves, but we saw them go to church together, and 'they
who eat together will soon be in bed together.'   By this
time he was calling his lady 'mother' and she called him
'son'.   The menservants and maidservants soon got used to
calling him 'father', and he for his part called them
'children'.   We never saw a greater love, nor a couple so   111
suited to one another.   Their door, which before was shut
to widows and orphans, is now always open wide to both rich
and poor.   You'll find suitable accommodation there if you
want it, their home is large, it stands at the entrance to
the village."

tunc a]it et rufus uanus nimiumque superbus
'est uet]us hic aliquis cui sit pulcherrima coniunx?'
hic a]it 'est senior multum bona cui fuit uxor.
120   pro d]olor, ah moritur, is nupsit denuo nuper
et duxit iuuenem stultam nimiumque procacem.
censet] pro nihilo contemnit eum quia crebro
huncce procis] stultis ludens inhonestius illis.

VI.117-123   119 hic *Seiler*: ille *Schmeller*   121 stultam
edd.: stulta *cod.*   122 censet *Seiler*: censens *Schmeller*
123 huncce procis *Laistner*: cum moechis *Schmeller*

Then the foolish, overweening redhead said "is there an
old man here who has a very beautiful wife?"   This man said
"there is an elderly man, who had a very good wife.   Sad to
say, she died; he recently married again, and took himself
a silly young woman, a shameless wench.   She despishes him,
and so thinks it nothing to keep tricking him with her
stupid lovers - but she is more wicked than they are."

panes ille secat et in illos distribuebat,   M21^r
carnes de senis discis quod et accidit illis.
his consolatis letis ad doma reuersis
hospes item dixit 'cum Christus quem mihi mittit
5   tunc est pascha meum mihi uelque meis celebra[ndum,
sicut in hac nocte dum letificabimur a te.
est mihi quod uenit de te Deus ut mihi mittat.'
cui mox de scapula partem mittit quoque sura,
in plures offas quam concidendo minutas
10   pro sacramentis pueros partitur in omnes.
post hec sat cocti domino sat ponitur assi,
potus at in patera summi tuberis nucerina
precipui uini piperati siue medonis
in qua bis bina sunt aurea flumina sculpta;
15   dextra Dei fundo patere confixa stat imo,
quam dum pernoctat ibi quidam summus ei dat.
numquam gustauit tamen ex hac ni sibi mittat
cui seruitur in hac, in opus seruatur at istud.
finita cena postquamque datur sibi lympha
20   fertur ei uinum de quo bibit et sibi misit,
qui dederat domine prius et post ebibit ipse.
de mensa surgit miles modicumque resedit,
sicque iacens tractat hominem qui gratificar[et.
tandem matrone dederat sua pallia prompte,
25   possit ut ecclesiam sic compta reuisere sanctam.

VII.1-25   5 celebrandum Seiler: celebratum Schmeller   17
tamen m.alt.   20 post hunc v. posuit m.alt. cuius in amore
dederat sibi que bibat ipse, deinde cuius in amore sibi
quatinus que bibat ipse, postremo delevit; vide v.21   23
gratificaret Seiler: gratificarat Schmeller

He cut the bread up and shared it out among them, with   1
what meat fell to them from the six dishes.   Refreshed with
these, the poor folk went home rejoicing, and the host said
"whenever Christ sends someone to me, then I and my family
should celebrate our own festival, just as we have been made
glad by you this night.   I consider that whatever comes from
you is sent to me by God."   He handed him a piece off the   8
shoulder and some off the leg, cut it into little pieces
and shared it among all the servants, like the sacraments.
After this, plenty of boiled and roast meat was set before
the lord, and his drink poured into a walnut goblet carved
from the hardest wood, finest spiced wine and mead;   four
golden rivers were carved on it, and the right hand of God
was represented at the very bottom.   A great lord had given
it to him when he had stayed the night there.   He never
tasted of it unless the man who had been served from it
handed it to him;   it was kept for that purpose.
When the meal was over and water had been given to him,   19
wine was brought to him.   He drank some and handed it to
his host;   he gave it to his lady, and afterwards drank
himself.   The knight got up from the table and sat down a
little, and relaxing thus he thought to himself how he could
please the man.   Finally he gave to the old lady his
cloaks, so that she could wear them when she went to the
holy church.

interea rufus quid agat non pretereamus.
miles ut intrauit ubi tot bona repperiebat
rufus cur subeat uetus est ubi simia dixit.
miles ait 'uelles mecum post forsan ouares;
30   quod uolui reperi, sed quod tu queris habebi[s.
asstantes multi rufo sunt consiliati,
deserat haut comitem, diuer[tere tam bene nusquam.
at dedig]nanter discessit ab hoc properanter   M21^v
currit et ad] neptem nil nacturus nisi mortem.
35   inuenit] portam senioris sepe seratam.
stat senio]r curte liberique sui duo pre se.
tunc rufus] pulsat quatiens portam nimis inquit
'iamque for]es aperi uel me prelinquere noli.'
cumque sene]x 'quis sit per sepem prospice' dixit
40   'uir quat]it et frangit portam' currens puer inquit.
rufus] ait 'pande, rogitas quasi nescieris me.'
tunc sunt i]rati iuuenes nimis hinc stomachati.
uim metu]endo mali iubet illi tunc aperiri:
rufus pro]terue nimis incursando superbe
45   in curtem] mitram non deponebat et ensem;
desili]ens ab equo, freni loro sude iacto
strinxit ut] insanus, pre se stetit utque profanus.
sed rufu]s tandem ridens ait ad seniorem
'si uos n]oscatis me miror quod reticetis.'
50   'nescio qu]is sitis' ait is 'stulte satis itis,
nescio qu]is sitis nunc nobis quidue uelitis.'
'est uxor uest]ra mea neptis ualde propinqua;
hanc ut] conueniam solus permittite solam.'
is dixit] 'facite' iubet hanc ad eumque uenire

VII.26-54   30 *post hunc v. ponit v.59 Ford*   32 diuertere tam
bene nusquam *Seiler*   33 at *Seiler*: ast *Schmeller*   34 currit
et ad *Seiler*: iam praeter *Schmeller*   35 inuenit *Seiler*:
irruit in *Schmeller*   36 stat senior *Seiler*: is stetit in
Schmeller   38 iamque fores *scripsi*: quam cito quis *Seiler*
40 uir quatit *Laistner*: iam uenit *Schmeller*   43 uim metuendo
Seiler   45 in curtem *Seiler*: de capite *Schmeller*   47 strinxit
ut *Seiler*: stringens *Schmeller*   48 sed rufus *Schmeller*: et
tunc is *Zeydel*: ad fruges *Seiler* ridens *cod.*: rediens
Schmeller, Seiler, Langosch   54 is dixit *Seiler*: permitto
Schmeller

Let us not pass over what the redhead was doing in the   26
meantime.   When the knight went into that place where he
found so many good things, the redhead asked him why he
was going "where there's a old monkey", as he put it.   The
knight said "perhaps later you'll wish you had come with me.
I have found what I wanted, but you shall get what you are
looking for."

Many bystanders advised the redhead not to leave his   31
companion, for he could not put up so well anywhere.   But
he hurried off and left him with a sneer, and hastened to
see his niece, though he was to find only death.

He found the old man's gate well and truly bolted.   The   35
old man was standing in the yard, with his two children by
him.   Then the redhead knocked, and shaking the gate
fiercely said "someone open the door now, don't leave me
outside."   The old man said "look through the fence, see who
it is."   A boy ran up and said "there's a man shaking the
gate and breaking it."   The redhead said, "open up, you
keep asking as if you didn't know me."   At this the young men
were annoyed and extremely irritated.   Frightened of the
wicked man's strength, he ordered the gate to be opened to
him.   The impudent redhead rode shamelessly into the court-   45
yard, not even laying aside his hat, and drew his sword
like a madman as he jumped down from his horse, and threw
the thong of its reins around a post.   He stood before him
in a very insulting manner.   But gradually the redhead
smiled, and said to the old man "I'm amazed you don't speak,
if you know me."   "I don't know who you are" he said, "you
go about things stupidly enough.   I don't know who you are
or what you want with us."   "Your wife is my niece, and very
close to me; allow me to meet with her alone."   He said
"do it", and ordered her to come to him.

```
55   que uenit;  u]t uidit ardens in corde cupiuit,
     gauden]s arrisit, ea congaudens sibi risit.
     'omne bon]um genitor tibi mandat uel tua mater.
     post dicam] solus ubiuis et quicquid alius.'
     ad portam] tunc stant, ad sepem seque reclinant.
60   rufus ait] 'primo que dico corde notato,
     nostrum col]loquium nam non debet fore longum.
     non fle non ride te contineas seriose
     ne uetu]s ille canis sapiat nostram rationem.
     si mihi] consentis ab eo citius redimeris.
65   est hic n]am iuuenis satur omnigene probitatis,
     haut b]reuis haut longus sed stature mediocris,
     est similagineus totusue genis rubicundus.              M22ʳ
     in toto mundo non est speciosior illo.
     qui dum rescisset tu quam speciosa fuisses
70   et quas erumnas patereris cottidianas
     cordetenus doluit gemebundus uel mihi dixit
     "umquam si fueris mihi fidus kare sodalis
     ito, dic illi mulieri martirizate
     si uelit ut redimam se uel de carcere tollam
75   audierit gracilem cras quando tubam reboantem
     ut dicens nulli sibi tam fide mulieri
     exeat e curte platea stans inopine
     donec accurram cum pluribus hanc rapiendam.
     posthac hec hera sit agat et sibi quodque placebit."
80   nunc sibi demanda quod uis neptis mea cara.'
     disciplinate stans hoc audiuit et omne
     interius gaudens tamen inquit ei quasi merens
     'cuncta libens facio, sis certior, atque fidem do.'
     accepta dextra rufus dubitans nihil ultra
85   'ter mihi succumbas in mercedem uolo laudes.'        R
     'si decies possis fac' inquit 'uel quotiens uis.'    N
     'sicut abire uelim facio, quod tu prohibeto,'        R
```

VII.55-87   55 que uenit ut *Seiler*: que simulac *Schmeller*   57
omne bonum *Seiler*   58 post dicam *Seiler*   59 ad portam *Seiler*:
isti ambo *Schmeller*   *hunc v. posuit post v.30 Ford*   62 *hunc v.*
om. m.pr.   63 ne uetus *Seiler*: ne uelis *Schmeller*   67 totusue]
totus ac *Schmeller*   75 cras] mox *m.pr.*   76 sibi *om.m.pr.*   79
sit] mea *m.pr.*   placebat *m.pr.*

She came; when she saw him she burned with lust for him in   55
her heart, smiled happily at him, and smiled to herself in
her happiness at these things.   "Your father and your mother
send you every good wish.   Later I shall speak to you alone -
where you like - about something of a different kind."
Then they stood by the gate, and leaned against the   60
fence.   The redhead said "note first in your heart what
I tell you, because our conversation must not be a long one:
don't cry, don't laugh, keep a straight face lest that old
dog senses our intentions: if you go along with me, you'll
soon be free from him.   For there is a young man here who   65
is well endowed with every kind of good quality - he's not
too short, not too tall, but of an average stature.   He's
fair-skinned, and his cheeks are all rosy;   there's no-one
more handsome than him in all the world.   When he found out
how beautiful you were and what troubles you endure every
day, he was sad at heart and said to me, weeping, 'if you were
ever faithful to me, dear comrade, go and tell that woman in   73
her torment that if she wishes, I will rescue her and free
her from her prison.   When tomorrow she hears my melodious
horn ring out, without speaking even to a woman whom she can
trust, let her leave the courtyard unexpectedly and stand in
the street until I come with many men to snatch her away.
After this she will be my lady and shall do as she wishes.'
Now send him what message you like, my darling niece."
She stood and listened to all this in a well-bred way,   81
and her heart leapt for joy, but she said to him as though
she was sad "I shall do all this, be assured, and I give
my word."   The redhead took her right hand;   by now his
doubts had vanished.   "For my wages I want you to sleep with
me three times."   "Do it ten times, if you can" she said,
"or as many times as you like."   "I shall make out that I
wish to leave, and you forbid it."

adque senem rediit 'mihi precipitote'que dixit.
ille libens faceret si pre muliere ualeret: H
90 illa rogat multum discedere ne sinat illum.
'si uelit hic maneat, quod nobis sit sibimet sit.'   H
duxerat in stabulum properantius illa caballum,   N
non ea nec rufus reminiscuntur magis eius,
manducet si quid ibi graminis is reperisset.
95 intrantemque domum neptis bene suscipit illum,
insimul assidunt sat sermocinandoque ludunt.
insertos stringunt digitos, sibi basia figunt.
ingreditur senior, quo non seriosior alter,   M22^V
hispidus in facie, poterat quod nemo uidere
100 eius quid uultus, fuerat, quia ualde pilosus,
ni solus nasus curuus fuit et uaricosus.
stant oculi gemini uelut effosi tenebrosi,
hosque retortorum superumbrat silua pilorum
neue foramen ubi sit in os quit quisque uidere
105 sic se barbicia pretendunt longa ue spissa.
ille parare tamen pueris iussit sat edendum.
istorum nimius cum displicuit sibi ludus
inter eos residet natibus disiunxit et ipsos.
ad modicum reticent intersessosque dolebant;
110 pre se curuando fantur per plura iocando.
cum pertedebat mensam uelare iubebat
dixit et uxori 'satis est, iam parce pudori.
non debet mulier sic esse procax, neque sed uir,
et presente uiro ludat decet haut alieno.'
115 sic dicens surgit ad latrinam uelut iret,
respiciebat eo terebelli perque foramen.
rufus et in solium salit infeliciter ipsum,
una manus mammas tractabat et altera gambas,
quod celabat ea super expandendo crusenna.
120 hoc totum ceu fur rimans senior speculatur.
quando redit sibi non cedit, nam non ea siuit.
tuncque sedens solio nimis indignando supremo
sepe monet dominam quo precipiat dare cenam,

VII.88-123   100 fuerat *edd. omnes*: qui erat *cod.*   106 pueros
m.pr.   iussit sat] precepit *m.pr.*   107 illorum *m.pr.*   109
reticent [se] *Schmeller*   115 ad latrinam] ad secretum *m.pr.*,
Seiler, Zeydel, Ford

He went back to the old man, and said "give me your   88
counsel (to go)."   He would willingly have done this, had
he any authority over his wife.   She asked him loudly not
to let him depart.   "Let him stay if he wants, and let him
have whatever is ours!"   She led his horse into the stable
in a great hurry, and neither she nor the redhead gave it
another thought: it could eat any grass it could find there.

The niece received him well as he entered the house.   95
They sat down together straightaway and talked together very
playfully, entwined their fingers together, and gave one
another kisses.

The old man came in - no other was more serious than he -   98
his face was all shaggy, and no-one was able to see what
expression he wore because he was so very hairy, except for
his nose, which was hooked and deeply-veined.   His
two eyes were dark, as if they had been dug out, and a forest
of twisted hair overshadowed them.   No-one could see where
he had an opening in his face, his whiskers hung so long and
thick.   He ordered the servants to prepare enough for them   106
to eat.   Since their playing was distasteful to him, he
sat between them and kept them apart with his own backside.
They grew quiet a little, and were sad that he had sat
between them.   They leaned in front of him and talked,
making many jokes.   When he grew tired of this, he ordered   110
the table to be laid, and said to his wife "that's enough:
now show some decency.   A woman should not be forward like
this, and nor should a man.   It isn't proper for her to
flirt with a stranger in front of her husband."

He said this and got up as though going to the privy, and   115
watched there through an auger-hole.   The wretched redhead
jumped into the master's chair, one hand caressed her breasts
and the other her thighs, and she hid all this by spreading her
fur cloak over her.   The old man watched all this, peeping
like a thief.   When he came back, the man did not make way
for him, for she would not permit it.   He sat very angrily
at the head of the table, and frequently urged his lady to
hurry up and have the meal served.

que subsannando cenam differt ioculando.
125　is rogitat cena pueros essetne parata,
'quam cito uos uultis' dicunt 'cenare ualetis.'
'nunc, hera, cenemus requiescendumque meemus.
pauset et est tempus ut uester karus amicus,
satque fatigastis hunc, nunc pausare sinatis.'

VII.124-129

She mocked him, and laughingly delayed the dinner. He asked 124
the servants if the dinner was ready.   "You can eat as soon
as you like," they said.   "Now my lady, let us eat and go
and lie down.   It is time too that your dear friend had a
rest; you've worn him out enough, now let him be."

uenit is atque fidem sibi uult predicere sanctam. M23^r
non ualet is 'credo' gemebundus ait nisi crebro.
peniteat uel eum rogitat mala que faciebat;
nutibus et uerbis se penituisse docebat,
5   per domini corpus fit ab omni crimine mundus.
exhalans animam Domino commiserat illam
dicens 'Christe pie mihi ualde reo miserere,
his et dimitte mihi uiuere qui rapuere,
inspiresque meis ut idem faciant rogo natis.'
10   sic dicens siluit.   cito post hec uiuere clausit.

aurorante die populus conuenit ubique,
ante fit ecclesiam multus conuentus et ipsam
et uicinorum maiorum siue minorum.
rector eo uenit, scelus ut miserabile rescit,
15   utque resederunt ibi quos residere decebat
'hic' ait 'est' rector 'miserabilis utique rumor
quod sit percussus quo non melior fuit ullus.'
flentes dicebant omnes ibi qui residebant
'ulciscatur ni rescimus par iterari.'
20   misit post liberos, post mordritas simul ipsos.
qui dum uenerunt coram rectore steterunt,
rufus ridendo, terram rea conspiciendo.
rector dum uidit quod risit 'pessime' dixit
'rides,   cum cunctos hic flentes cum uideas nos.
25   quid succensebas quod eum sic martirizabas?'
rufus   ait 'dentes mihi dempserat anteriores
ob nullam caus[am] n[i] quod sedi prope neptem.'
dixit et 'ancilla tua neptis si fuit illa,

VIII.1-28   9 inspiraque *m.pr.*   faciat *m.pr.*   27 ni
Seiler: nisi *Schmeller*   neptim *Schmeller*

(The priest) came and wanted to declare the holy faith   1
to him.   He had only the strength to groan over and over
again "I believe."   He asked him if he was sorry for all
the sins he had committed.   He made it plain through nods
and single words that he was sorry, and was then cleansed of
all sin through the holy sacrament.   With a sigh he committed his soul to the Lord, saying "Holy Christ have mercy
on me, a great sinner;   forgive these people who have taken
my life from me, and enable my children to do the same, I
pray."   He said this and no more, and soon afterwards he
breathed his last.
When morning came the people assembled everywhere, and   11
in front of the church itself there was a massive throng
of the greater and lesser people of the region.   The
governor came when he had learned about the despicable crime,
and when all those worthy to be seated had taken their seats,
the governor said "here is terrible news: a man than whom
there was none better has been struck down dead."   Those
sitting there wept and said "unless he is avenged, we know
the same thing will happen again."   He sent for the   20
children and for the murderers themselves.   When they arrived
they stood in the governor's presence, the redhead grinning,
the guilty woman gazing at the ground.   When the governor
saw him smiling he said "it is a very bad thing that you
should smile when you see us all weeping here.   What kind
of anger possessed you, to put him to death like that?"   The   25
redhead said, "he knocked my front teeth out for no other
reason than that I sat down near my niece."   He said "if
that young girl is your niece,

	cur hanc stuprabas, sceleri scelus adiciebas?'
30	rufus ait 'cur me fur hec attraxerat ad se?
	cur [feci, queras?] facerem non ni peteret me!'
	que tantum fleuit riuus lacrimis ibi quod fit,
	ex oculis sanguis posthec fluxit sibi grandis.
	postquam conualuit quod quid fari ualet inquit
35	"O nimis infide cur sic mentire super me?
	exemplaris Adam qui culpam uertit in Euam.
	non post te misi, non te prius impie uidi.
	me cum promissis mendosis decipiebas.
	non ego defendo quod feci, sed mage damno
40	quod tu fecisti, me consiliante patrasti.
	non ego, confiteor, ulcisci me super opto.
	iudicium, rector, fieri differto parumper,
	donec accusem memet donec quoque damnem.
	en mea iudex sto quia ualde libens tolerabo.
45	si me suspendi uultis super arbore grandi
	radite cesariem mihi, longam plectite funem,
	stranguler ut per eam per quam rea sepe fiebam.
	sed rogo post triduum corpus tollatis ut ipsum
	et comburatis, in aquam cinerem iaciatis,
50	ne iubar abscondat sol aut aer neget imbrem,
	ne per me grando dicatur ledere mundo.
	inclusam uase uultis submergere si me,
	deforis in uase quod feci notificate,
	inueniant qui me ne presumant sepelire;
55	tantum uas rumpant in aquam uel reiciant me,
	piscibus ut citius uorer aut diris cocodrillis.
	uultis in ignitum fumosum trudere furnum,
	ingrediar sponte, quo non cremer igne gehenne.
	ut caream uita si uultis mersa cloaca,
60	sum nimis inmunda, tali dignissima pena,
	incidero prompte quia tali gaudeo fine,
	tartareus fetor mihi post ne perpetuetur.
	quicquid supplicii reperitis adhuc grauioris,
	omne libens patiar, multo peiora merebar.'

VIII.29-64   30 fur hec] mulier *coni. Schmeller*   31 feci queras
scripsi: queram facere *Laistner*: misit post me *Seiler*   46
mihi] in *Schmeller*   50, 51 *hos vv. om. m.pr.*   51 per *om. m.
sec.*

why did you ravish her and pile crime on crime?"

The redhead said "why did this wretch pull me towards her? 29
You ask me why I did it?   I wouldn't have if she hadn't
made advances towards me!"   She wept so much that a stream
formed from her tears, and then great drops of blood flowed
from her eyes.   After she regained her strength she stammered 35
out as best she could "O you foul traitor, why do you lie
about me like this?   You are from the same mould as Adam,
who put the blame on Eve.   I made no advances to you, you
villain, I had not seen you before!   You deceived me with
lying promises.   I do not defend what I have done, I
rather condemn what you have done, the exploit you've done
at my behest.   I confess, I do not want to be avenged. 41
Governor, suspend the trial for a little while, while I
accuse myself, while I condemn myself too.   See, I stand
here as my own judge, and will suffer of my own free will.
If you want me to be hanged from a tall tree, shave off my
hair, weave a long rope from it, so that I may be choked by 46
that which often made me guilty.   But I ask that you take my
body down after three days and burn it, and throw the ashes
into some water, lest the sun hides its ray or the air withholds its rain, lest hail is said to bring harm to the earth
because of me.   If you wish to shut me up in a box and drown 52
me, write what I have done on the outside of the box, lest
any who find me presume to give me burial; let them just
break the box open and throw me into the water, so that I may
more swiftly be eaten by fish and fierce crocodiles.   If you
want to thrust me into a burning smoky furnace, I shall step 57
inside willingly, so that I may not be burned by the fires of
hell.   If you wish me to lose my life drowned in a sewer,
for I am filthy through and through, and deserve such a
punishment, I will jump in straightaway, because I would be
happy at such an end, so that afterwards the stink of Tartarus
would not last forever for me.   Whatever even harsher punishment you find, I will willingly suffer it all, I deserved
much worse."

65 que dum conticuit, rector miserans ita dixit:
'iudicat hec semet; uos dicite si sat in hoc sit.'
omnes plorantes nimium sibi compatientes
dicunt 'non opus est rector rogitet super hoc plus.'
dicunt causidici 'uitam decernimus illi
70 donari tantum si peniteat male factum.'
eius priuigni mansuefacti uelut agni
uoluuntur pedibus rectoris dando precatus
ut uitam ueniam sibi concedatque salutem,
esse domus dominam uelut ante fuit sinat illam.
75 quod dum promisit clementer id illa recusat:
'amodo non dominam sed me dicant homicidam.
uiuere si uultis me, sed tamen, oro, salutis
ut mihi tollatis, quo me non debilitatis,
nares truncate quidquid sit et oris utrimque,
80 ut stent horribiles omni sine tegmine dentes,
ut nullum libeat posthac mihi basia quo det,
in crucis atque modum me comburatis in altum,
per geminas buccas rosa ceu tenus hac rutilantes,
nouerit ut quisquam propter scelus hoc mihi factum,
85 et dicat "tibi ue, meruisti tale quid in te?"
ne grandis culpa penitus me sic stet inulta.'
tunc rector liberis hanc commisit senioris,
mater et ut domina sit eis nec ut ante nouerca.
que uestes pulchras ornatus abicit omnes,
90 induitur tunica uelut ex fuligine tincta.
cesariem rasit, hinc resticulos ea plectit
cum quibus et teneras constrinxerat illa mamillas,
restes ui mordent carnes donec putrefiunt.
tegmen pannosum caput omne tegebat et ipsum,
95 sic nil ni nares oculi cernuntur et eius.
psalterium discit anime senis idque canebat.
non manducabat nisi stellam quando uidebat,
tunc siccum panem comedens, atrum, cinerosum,
u[el bi]bit ex limpha tantum coclearia terna.
100 ambulat hec pedibus nudis per frigus et estus,
dormit et in lecto nihilo palea nisi strato

VIII.65-101   68 rector] ?dominus *m.pr.*   79 truncate]
?abscidi *m.pr.*   86 me] mea *vel* mei *m.pr.*

She fell silent, and the governor said with pity in his   65
voice "this woman has judged herself; you say if it is
enough in this case."   All were weeping, and had great
compassion on her.   They said "there is no need for the
governor to ask any more in this instance."   The advocates
said "we decree that her life be given her only if she
repents of this foul deed."   Her step-children were as
gentle as lambs, and fell at the governor's feet, pleading   72
that he should grant her life, pardon, and wholeness of
body, and allow her to be mistress of her household as she
was before.   He promised this mercifully, but she refused
it: "may they not call me mistress now, but rather murderer.
If you wish me to live, I pray, at least take my wholeness
from me.   So that you do not disable me, cut off my nose   78
and face either side, so that my teeth stand out foul and
uncovered, so that afterwards no-one may give me kisses,
and brand me with a cross on my forehead and on my two
cheeks, which up to this glowed red as a rose, so that anyone
will know that this was done to me because of my crime, and
will say 'woe to you, what did you do to deserve that?',   85
so this enormous guilt will not go unpunished in me."   Then
the governor put her in the care of the old man's children,
so that she might be a mother and mistress to them and not,
as before, a step-mother.
    She cast off all her lovely clothes, and dressed in a   89
tunic dyed black as soot.   She shaved her head and plaited
little cords from this, with which she bound her tender breasts,
so that the cords bit into her flesh until it became infected.
A ragged cloth covered up her whole head, too, and so only
her nose and eyes could be seen.   She learned the psalter,
and sang it for the soul of the old man.   She would only eat   97
when she could see a star, and then she ate burnt, black dry
bread, and drank only three spoonfuls of plain water.   She
would walk barefoot through cold and heat, and slept on a bed
covered only in straw

et pro plumacio posito tantummodo ligno.
ante diem surgit, senis ad tumulum u[igila]uit
donec sudauit, donec plus stare nequiuit,
105 tunc ruit in faciem, dum fontem flens ibi fecit.
ningeret aut plueret seu sol torrendo cremaret
uenit ad ecclesiam mox ut pulsatur ad ipsam
et non inde redit dum circumquaque diescit.
ad breue tunc rediit donec faciem sibi lauit
110 presbiter ad missam uel pulsabat celebrandam.
tunc rediit, nonam post hec ibi mansit ad horam,
nilque potestatis sibi uendicat, hanc sinit illis,
quod sibi dant habuit, quod non dant non ea querit.
hec numquam risit, cum nemine postea lusit,
115 cum rident alii fletus dulcis fuit illi.
hanc irascentem rixantem luxuriantem
nemo uidebat eam dum uitam deserit istam.
illa commissa natis ab eisque recepta
rector ait populo 'quid agamus, dicite, rufo,
120 qui scelus hoc geminum patrat inter nos gemebundum?'
rufus iudicii certus necis 'obsecro' dixit
'hic habeo comitem, prius hunc curate uocandum,
quam quid in his culpis ulciscendum rogitetis,
qui cuius generis sim, quit sat dicere uobis.'
125 mittere dum post hunc eius cupidi uoluerunt
militis hospes ait 'quem uos uultis citus asstat.
hac mecum nocte mansit, quod non fuit iste.'
quem dum produxit stantem rector rogitauit
'dic, miles summe, socius tuus iste uir estne?'

VIII.102-129 103 uigilauit *scripsi*: uel adiuit *Ford*:
ueniauit *Schmeller* 128 perduxit *Schmeller*

with just a log there for a pillow.   She got up before   102
daybreak and kept watch at the old man's grave until she
broke into a sweat and could no longer stand up;   then she
fell face down while she made a pool with her tears.
Whether it snowed or rained, or whether the sun burned down
in its heat, she went to that church as soon as the bell was
rung, and did not return from there until it was daylight all
around.   Then she returned for a little while and washed
her face, and the priest rang the bell to celebrate mass.   110
Then she went back and afterwards stayed there until the
ninth hour.   She asked no authority for herself, but
granted it all to the sons.   She had what they gave her,
and what they did not give her she did not ask for.   She
never smiled, played with no-one, and when others were
smiling, weeping was sweet to her.   No-one saw her angry,
quarrelsome, or playful, until she left this life.   When she
had been entrusted to the sons, and had been taken up by
them, the governor said to the people "say, what are we to do
with the redhead, who committed this doubly lamentable crime
amongst us?"

The redhead, sure of the death sentence, said "I beg you,   121
I have here a comrade;   have him called here before you ask
what punishment there should be for these evil deeds.   He
can tell you well enough what kind of man I am."

When, anxious to see him, they wanted to send for him,   125
the knight's host said "the man you want is ready standing
here.   He stayed with me last night, but that fellow
didn't."   They led him out, and the governor asked him as
he stood there, "tell me, noble knight, is this man here a
friend of yours?"

qu... M28^r

'obuiat omnia que [fuerant grandis tibi cure
que cum tempus erit tibi dicere cuncta licebit.
nunc falerare tibi iubeas unique clienti,
5   nam cognoscunt te magis ac me compatriote;
quando uidebunt te deuitabunt penitus me.
debes ire domum si sit tua gratia mecum.'
cui cor mox hylarat, pre leticia quoque flebat.
'desine' miles ait [riuus lacrimis uereor fit.
10   ....
scutiferum uocat ....
....
ambo scutiferi c................................
....
15   qui mox ascen...................................
....
scutiferos dico ....
....
cursu ueloci re..................................
20   ....
quidue uolun.....................................
....
neue seram de ....
....

IX.1-24   2 fuerant grandis tibi cure *Zeydel*   9 riuus
lacrimis uereor fit *Zeydel*

132

IX

....
"He stands against everything which was of great import to   2
you.   When it is time, I will be free to tell you all.
Now, do you order him to saddle a horse for you and for one
of your men, for your countrymen know you more than me;
while they will see you, they will avoid me completely.
You must go home, if your favour is with me."
     His heart soon became happy, and he wept for joy.   "Stop"   8
the knight said.......

He called his squire........

Both the squires............

Who soon mounted up..........   15

I call them squires (?)......

Went at high speed..........

Whatever they wanted........   21

lest they were late (?)......

est ibi secrete prope secessus ....   M28^v
in quo sunt claui plures in pariete fixi,
quis suspendere res potuissent quasque uiantes,
ne noceant mures, cum non timeant ibi fures.
5   cum dominis domina pedat ad solaria celsa,
qua dicebat eis 'multum bene nunc ueniatis.'
dum grates referunt rogat illos ut residerent
atque iocarentur di[uersa dum loquerentur.
    ....
10 et sibi quos uellent pis[cari ....
    ....
moles multigene pis[cum.................
    ....
tantum tres desunt ....
15 ....
miles ait 'nunc piscari [uolo uel sine rete
    ....
puluere buglosse [quo piscabamur et ante
    ....
20 ast in aqua cimba [parua sed ad id satis apta
    ....
assumunt uirgam, p[isces ....
    ....
donec uenerunt pisce[s, pilulas comederunt
25 [buglosse factas in stagno milite iactas]
quas qui gustabant [sub aquam uel nare nequibant
[pisces, e fundo uenientes et sine grato,]

X.1-27   7 dum] qui *m.pr.*   8 diuersa dum loquerentur *Zeydel*
12 piscum *scripsi*   16 uolo uel sine rete *scripsi*   18 quo
piscabamur et ante *Seiler*   20 parua sed ad id satis apta
scripsi   22 pisces *scripsi*   24 pilulas comederunt *Seiler*
25 *scripsi*   26 sub aquam uel nare nequibant *scripsi*: sub
aquam resalire nequibant *Seiler*   27 *scripsi*

There was near there a secret hiding place, in which many   1
nails were driven into the wall.   Travellers could hang
various things on them so that the mice did not damage them,
since they were not afraid of thieves there.   The lady
walked with her lords to the upper room, where she said to
them "you are most welcome here now."   They returned their
thanks, she asked them to sit down, and to be cheerful as they
talked among themselves.

And to him which they wished to angle for........   10

Many heaps of fish........

only three were missing........

the knight said "now I wish to fish, and without a net"

with the buglossa powder, which we used to fish before

there is a boat on the water, small but suitable enough   20

they picked up a rod,.......the fish........

until the fish came and ate all the pellets made of buglossa,   24
which the knight threw into the water.   When they ate them
the fish could not swim in the pond, and came up from the
deep for free,

quos miles uirga perterrens cogit ad arua.
miratur domina dominellarumque caterua,
30 contribulisque suus ouat in uirtutibus eius.
fit nimium risus manuum plaususue cachinnus
accurruntque coci, tollunt properantque parari.
egressus lintre cuncto populo comitante
ad dominam repedat, ea quem bene suscipiebat:
35 'piscator talis est nusquam uos uelut estis.'
tunc iubet exponi pisces in gramine molli,
ut diuersos quot uideat lacus is generaret.
tunc sunt expositi quotquot fuerant ibi capti:
lucius et rufus, qui sunt in piscibus hirpus,
40 pisces namque uorant, illos ubi prendere possunt,
prahsina, lahs, charpho, tinco, barbatulus, oruo,
alnt, naso, qui bini nimis intus sunt acerosi,
rubeta fundicola, truta digena, rufa uel alba,
in capite grandis capito post degener alis,
45 labilis anguilla uel per caput horrida uualra,
asco, rinanch, ambo dulces nimis in comedendo,
ast agapuz ut acus in dorso pungit acutus,
preterea multi pisces mihi non bene noti.
his uisis tolli citius iubet illa parari.
50 mensa parabatur, latis similis cumulatur.
mittit et interea cito quo ueniat sua nata,
post quam mox agiles plures saluere tyrones,
texuit ex auro que bina ligamina sponso,
post quemcumque sibi tribuat clementia Christi.
55 que dum procedit ceu lucida luna reluxit.
quam sollers esset nemo discernere posset,
an uolet an naret an se quocumque moueret;
semper ut auis erat uel se formosa] leuabat.
tunc hera poscit aqua]m quam sumere iussit herilem,
60 et post hospitibus datur, ultime sed sibi post hos.
militibus domine consid]unt insimul ambe,

X.28-61   31 cachinus *m.pr.*   32 parare *Schmeller*   45 walsa
Schmeller   50 lotis *Schmeller*   *post hunc v. sunt* abrasi duo
vv., quos inclusit Schmeller   58 semper ut auis erat uel se
formosa *Zeydel*   59 tunc hera poscit aquam *Seiler*   sed] se
Langosch, Ford   61 militibus domine considunt *scripsi*

and the knight frightened them with the rod and drove them   28
to the dry land.   The lady and the band of young ladies
were astounded, and her kinsman rejoiced in his attainments.
There was much mirth, clapping, and laughing, and the cooks   32
ran up, picked up the fish, and made haste to be ready.   He
got out of the boat and, along with all the people, made his
way back to the lady.   She received him gladly: "nowhere
is there such a fisherman as you are."   Then she ordered
the fish to be placed out on the soft grass, to see how many
different ones that pond had spawned.   As many as had been
caught there were laid out then: the pike and red bass,   41
which are like the wolf in the fish world, for they devour
fish wherever they can catch them; the bream, salmon, carp,
tench, the barbel, the orf, the chub and the nose-fish, both
of which are full of bones; the char, which lives at the
bottom; trout of two kinds, red and white; the bullhead,
with a big head but otherwise slender, the slippery eel and
the catfish with its bristly head, the grayling, the Rhine
trout, both these last two very sweet to eat, and the perch,
which stabs as though it had a sharp knife on its back, and
moreover many fish not well known to me.   When she had seen   48
them she ordered them to be taken and prepared quickly.   The
table was made ready and piled high with white bread.
     In the meantime she sent word that her daughter should   51
come quickly.   Several lively young men stepped lightly
after her; she had wrought a pair of golden bands for her
betrothed, whoever he might be whom Christ's mercy might later
give to her.   When she went out, she shone like the
radiant moon.   She was so graceful that no-one could tell
whether she flew, or swam, or moved herself in any way at
all; she was always beautiful, like a bird, when she stood
up.
     Then·the mistress asked for water, and ordered the young   59
mistress to take some.   Afterwards it was passed to the
guests, and finally, after them, to her.   The two ladies
sat down at the same time as the knights,

maior maiori iunior consedit herili.
cuique bonum sedile uel mensam tunc] iubet apte.
eius contribulis conuiua fiebat herilis:
65　ambobus panis uel lanx etia]m datur una,
pre quibus ille canis stat furti proditor omnis.
qui gannito clamans crebro] faciemque reuertens
cauda blanditur, quid ei, monet, ut tribuatur.
contribulis quicquid sibi sponte d]at ille recepit,
70　excidit at sibi quid casu non id repetiuit.
at si dans dixit gusta 'malus] hoc homo coxit'
nunquam gustauit aut gustatum reuomebat.
militis a sella dapifer calc]aria tollit.
po[stmodo] scutellas dapifer cum posceret illas,
75　porrigat has sibi mox.　cunctis lixis uelut est mos
illum tunc gannito cani]s inspiciens male crebro
insiluit tandem lacerando trahit sibi uestem
atque momordisset ni scutifer eripuisset.　　　　　M29^v
miles ridebat, plebs cetera cuncta stupebat.
80　tunc dixit domina 'res cernitur hec mihi mira.'
miles ait 'furti canis est hic conscius isti.
quod furabaris nisi reddideris, morieris.
uade, fer in medium quod fecisti cito furtum.'
currens absque mora retulit calcaria bina.
85　'hec' ait 'a sella denodaui modo uestra.
tunc ibi nemo fuit uiuentum nemoque uidit
neue canis sciret, a demone ni didicisset.'
miles ait 'sibi da, cernas cui prebeat illa.'
que sibi dum iecit, cuius fuerant ea reddit,
90　hic dixitque cani 'nunc illa referto sodali.'
que dat scutifero caudam persepe mouendo.

X.62-91　63 cumque bonum sedile uel mensam Zeydel　65 ambobus
panis uel lanx etiam scripsi: una sibi patera sibi lanx etiam
Seiler　67 qui gannito clamans crebro Zeydel　69 contribulis
quicquid sibi sponte dat Seiler　71 at si dans dixit gusta
malus coni. Seiler: ille cani dixit malus quod Zeydel　72
reuomebat] reutimebat vel retumebat Schmeller　73 militis a
sella dapifer Zeydel　74 postmodo Laistner: postea Seiler
76 illum tunc gannito Zeydel

the elder knight with the elder lady, the younger with the 62
young mistress.   The lady ordered that a good and suitable
place be arranged for each of them to sit, and the knight's
kinsman was placed at the same table as the young mistress.
A single loaf and serving-dish were set before both of them,
and that hound stood beside them, betrayer of every secret
act.   It barked and growled fiercely, turned its face to
them, and wagged its tail to ask that something be given it. 68
It took whatever the knight's kinsman willingly gave it,
but it did not go after anything that dropped accidentally.
But if he said "a bad man cooked this" as he gave it tit-
bits, it would never taste them - or if it did, would spit
them out.

A waiter took some spurs from the knight's saddle. 73
Afterwards when the waiter collected the plates he held them
out to the hound, as is the custom with all servants.
The hound looked at him, growling fiercely, and then at last
leapt on him, ripped his tunic off, tearing it, and would
have bitten him if the squire had not dragged it off.
The knight smiled; all the rest of the folk were astounded. 79
Then the lady said "this seems an amazing thing to me."
The knight said "this hound is aware of that fellow's
thieving.   Unless you return what you have stolen, you
shall die.   Go and bring into the open what you stole -
quickly!"   He ran off and without delay brought back the
pair of spurs.   "I untied these," he said, "from your saddle
just now; there was nothing near there then, and no-one saw
it, and the dog would not have known if an evil spirit hadn't
told him."

The knight said "give them to it and see who it offers 88
them to."   He threw them to it, and it gave them back to
the man whose they were.   He said to the hound, "now take
them to my companion."   It gave them to the squire, wagging
its tail briskly.

'ante pedes cadite furis ueniamque rogate.'
qui se prostrauit caput inque pedes sibi ponit
et ueluti fleret ueniam poscens ululauit.
95 'nunc tu dic "surge uel amici simus ut ante."'
quod cum dixisset surgens canis exhilarescit,
nunc hunc nunc dominos nunc gratificat residentes.
miles ait 'uestrum sibi quis captando capillum
accipiat baculum, uelut ulciscendo reatum.'
100 quod duo dum faciunt 'cur furabaris?' et aiunt
insiliebat eos canis hunc ab eisque redemit,
mordens in suras illos nimium dolituros -
sic se lusisse, cum quo pre pacificat se.
quidam ridebant, quidam nimis inde stupebant.
105 prandia cum cena sic sat fiunt opulenta.
fercula post multa, post pocula tam numerosa
limpha datur, modicum residetur dum biberetur.
tempus pomorum non tunc fuit ulligenorum,
ni pueri ueniunt de silua fraga ferebant,
110 quedam pars uasis, pars corticibus corilinis,
que singillatim legerunt undique passim.
his esis mensa remouetur, sumitur aqua.

.... it se discaligandum.
ille ligaminibus de Lukka crura coemptis
115 .... .cca sibi fluitaret.
atque super pedules se calceolos sericatos
.... iu]nxit sericosis.
contribulis rubeos soccos sub corduanellis
.... gestans operosis.
120 ambo ligaturis coniunxit crura gemellis
perpuncteque ligatu]re sunt margine cuncte,
a quibus et multe dependent undique bulle.

X.92-122   102 nimium] serio *m.pr.*   112 *duo vv. deletos esse
post hunc v. censuit Schmeller*   117 iunxit *scripsi*   121
perpuncteque ligature *scripsi*

140

"Now lie at the thief's feet and ask his forgiveness."   92
The dog lay down and put its head on his feet, and howled
as though crying and asking for forgiveness.   "Now you say
'get up, and let us be friends as before.'"   When he had
said this the hound got up, happier now, and showed its
delight now to this man, then to the lords, then to those
who were sitting there.   The knight said "let someone take
you by the hair and pick up a stick, as though punishing
your guilt."   When two men did this and said "why did you
steal?", the dog leapt at them and rescued him from them,
biting their ears, which caused them great pain - or so they   103
pretended before they made peace with him.   Some laughed at
this, and some were utterly astounded.
    And so, the meal and banquet were made very rich.   After
many courses and equally numerous cups, water was given to
them and they sat down for a little while they drank.   It   108
was not the season then for any kind of fruit, but some boys
came and brought wild strawberries from the forest, some in
bowls and some in hazel bark, which they had picked one by
one throughout every place.   When these had been eaten the
table was taken away, and water was given them.
.................to take off their shoes.
He bound his legs with bands from Lukka
...............might drape over him
and on top of his slippers he fastened silken puttees with
silk cords.   His kinsman wore red hose beneath his........   118
of finely-worked Cordovan leather.
    He fastened both his thighs with a pair of straps;   the
whole of the straps were pierced along the edge, and many
little balls were hung all along them.

141

              post hec pellicium mox in]duerat uaricosum,
              pre uel post fissum uel circumquaque gulatum,
125   .... crus]inam ponendo profundam
              fibro limbatam lato nimis atque nigello.
              sumpsit herilis quem sibi donauit digitalem
              ad minimum digitum bene uix tum conuenientem.
              deponit tunicam sed et] interulam male lotam,
130   mantel mardrinum senio sudoreque fuscum.
              illos induerant, m]ox ad dominas repedabant,
              quas ad cancellos inuenerunt speculantes.

X.123-132   123 post hec pellicium mox induerat *Seiler*   125
crusinam *Seiler*   129 deponit tunicam sed et *scripsi*   131
illos induerant, mox *scripsi*: uestiti sic erant mox *Zeydel*

After this he quickly put on a mottled fur coat,   123
divided front and back and trimmed with fine fur.......
putting on a long cloak bordered with broad black beaver
fur.   He put on the ring which the young mistress had
given to him: it scarcely fitted on his little finger.
He lay aside his vest, his unwashed shirt, and his marten-
fur cloak, stale with age and sweat.   They put on these
(other) clothes, and hurried back to the ladies, whom they
found looking out at the latticed windows.

tunc sibimet comedunt [satis et] pullis tribuerunt.   Fl^r
cum per aperturas in domate quis sibi micas
prebet, mox illo concurrebant adhiando
captantes auide quod quit contingere cuique.
5   sic consuefacte sunt post modicum cito cuncte;
quin post ostiolum sibi cum fieret patefactum
in manibus resident, quod eis datur accipiebant,
dumque fiunt sature leniendo manuque polite,
doma sua sponte certatim mox subiere
10 et componendo rostris pennas residendo,
sic gaudendo diem quod non siluere per omnem.
oblectamentum fit herili deliciosum,
cum nimis insuaue senibus sit tale quid omne.
pabula nulligena uel limpha stat in domicella   XXXVI
15 sturnorum, sed eos duxere fame domitandos,
ut per aperturas poscant escas sibi dandas,
quod primo ueteres nimium renuere parentes.
cum pullis non dant, has illi deseruerunt,
qui digitum prebent his illi mox adhiabant.
20 eligitur sciola super hos doctura magistra   XXXVII
nostratim fari 'pater' et 'noster' recitare
usque 'qui es in celis' lis lis lis triplicatis,
staza soror, 'canite canite' doceat geminare,
quod pulli discunt ueteres quam discere possent.
25 interea miles consanguineus simul eius   XXXVIII
cum domina uadunt, harpatores ubi ludunt.
miles ut audiuit male quam rithmum modulauit
inter eos summus illius artis alumnus,
ad dominam dixit ibi si plus harpa fuisset.

XI.1-29   1 satis et *Seiler*:   illae et *Schmeller*:   ueteres
Zeydel   4 quod] quid *m.pr.*   7 datum *Schmeller*   8 fiunt]
sunt *m.pr.*   9 subiere *Laistner*:   subierunt *cod.*, *Schmeller*,
Seiler, *Zeydel*   14 limpha] aqua *m.pr.*

Then they ate enough for themselves, and offered some to   1
their chicks.   Whenever anyone held crumbs out to them
through the openings in their little home, they would
swiftly gather there with gaping beaks, and greedily take
whatever each could seize for itself.

After a short while they all soon became used to this,   5
and indeed later, when the little door had been opened for
them, they would sit on people's hands and take what was
given them;   and when they were quite soothed with soft words
and stroking, they were eager swiftly to enter their residence
and sat preening their feathers with their bills, so happy
that they did not fall silent all day.

This was especially delightful to the young mistress,   11
though all this sort of thing is most disagreeable to old folk.
There was no kind of food or drink in the starlings' little
house, but they thought that they ought to be trained by
hunger so that they asked for food to be given them through
the openings, something that the old parent birds refused to
do at first.   When they gave the chicks no food, these
deserted them and soon made for whoever offered them their
finger.   A scholarly bird was chosen to be mistress over them,   20
and to teach them to say the 'Our Father' just like us, and
to recite it as far as "who art in heaven", though with "-ven
-ven -ven" three times over - Sister Starling, who taught them
"O sing O sing" twice over.   The chicks learned to do this,
the older birds learned as best they could.

Meanwhile the knight made his way to the place where the   25
harpers were playing, along with his kinsman and the lady.
When the knight heard how badly the best student of this art
played the tune, he asked the lady if there was another harp
there.

30 'est' ait 'hic harpa melior qua non erit ulla,
in qua dum uixit meus heros simphoniauit,
cuius clangore mea mens languescit amore,
quam nemo tetigit is postquam uiuere finit,
in qua si uultis rithmos modulare ualetis.'
35 quam iubet afferri sibi, quam citat is moderari

....
....
pulsans mox leua] digitis geminis, modo dextra
tangendo chordas dulces reddit nimis odas,
40 multum distincte faciens uariamina queque,
quod pede saltandi manibus neumas uel agendi
nescius omnino citus hec perdisceret ambo.
qui prius audacter chordas pulsant ioculanter
auscultant illi taciti modulare nec ausi.
45 sic tribus insolitis actis dulcissime rithmis
quartum poscit hera faceret petit et sua nata,
eius contribulis quem saltaret uel herilis;
quem per sistema siue diastema dando responsa
dum mirabiliter operareturue decenter
50 surrexit iuuenis, quo contra surgit herilis.
ille uelut falcho se girat et hec ut hirundo,
ast ubi conueniunt, citius se preteriebant.
i]s se mouisse, sed cernitur illa natasse,
neutrum saltasse neumas manibus uariasse
55 nemo corrigere quo posset si uoluisset.
tunc signum dederant ibi multi quod doluerunt,
deponendo manus, finitus sit quia rithmus.
insimul et resident et in alterutrum nimis ardent
lege maritali cupientes consociari,
60 illius id matre fieri nimium cupiente
atque facultante, quod uellent, sermocinare.
hunc dominella rogat quo secum tessere ludat,
annulus ut uicti donetur ter superanti.
tunc is 'qui ludum quem ludamus modo primum

XI.30-64   38 pulsans mox leua *Seiler*   41 neunas *m.pr.*

"There is a harp here" she said "better than any shall ever   30
be, on which my brave husband played when he was alive.   My
heart would grow weak with love at the sound of it.   No-one
has touched it since he departed this life; if you wish,
you may play melodies on it."   She ordered it to be brought
to her, and he made haste to tune it.

Swiftly plucking it with two fingers of his left hand and   38
then of his right, he played on the strings and produced
truly beautiful tunes, playing some improvisations very
clearly.   A man who was totally ignorant of them could
learn very quickly both what steps to dance and where to
clap his hands.   Those who had earlier been bold in plucking   43
carefree strings now listened in silence, and did not dare
to play.   When he had most sweetly played three new tunes
like this, the mistress asked him for a fourth, and her
daughter added her plea, to which his kinsman and the young
mistress could dance.

While he performed it with wonderful grace, and played the   49
variations in harmony, the young man stood up, and the young
mistress rose up opposite him.   He wheeled around like a
falcon, and she like a swallow, and when they came together
they passed by one another quickly.   It seemed that he was
walking, but that she was floating, and that neither danced
or moved their hands in time to the music in such a way as
anyone could have corrected them if he had wished.   Then
they gave a signal by lowering their hands which made many very
sad, because the music had finished.   They sat down again
straight away, burning with love for one another greatly and
desiring to be joined in the bond of marriage.   Her mother
wanted this to happen very much, and gave them leave to talk
about anything they wished.

The young lady asked him to play at dice with her, and   62
that the loser's ring should be given to whoever won three
times.   But then he said "whoever wins the first game we
play

65 acquirat' dixit 'digitalis uterque suus sit.'
hec] ea laudauit ludens et eum superauit,
gratis perdente iuuene gratis sibi dante.
que nimium leta se sic habuisse trophea
ludendo proprium cito perdebat digitalem,
70 quem trahit a digito iaciebat eique rotando.
in cuius medio nodus fuerat cauus intro;
hunc ni laxaret digito non imposuisset.

XI.65-72   66 hec *Haupt*   72 ni] nisi *Schmeller*

shall have both rings."   She liked this, played, and beat
him; the young man was happy to lose, and happy to give
(his ring) to her.   She was very happy to have won a trophy
in this way, and soon lost her own ring in a game.   She took
it from her finger and tossed it, spinning, to him.   It had
a hollow knot in the middle, inside it, and without undoing
this he could not have put it on his finger.

'nunc, hera, nunc matrem quam proxime uideris [ipsam,   M26^r
dic mihi si ualeat, si tranquille sua res stet,
quandoque commater fieret tua, si mihi frater
ex illa sit quem de fonte leuaueris, inque,
anne tuam natam de fonte leuauerit ill[am?'
5   obstupefacta nimis dictis hera militis ist[is
'ah quid dixisti?   quod eam nupsisse putasti
cui fuerat sine te non ipsum uiuere dulce?
nam flendo uisum post te iam perdidit ipsum.
10   illa meam natam de fonte leuauerat istam
et pro natabus propriis nos post habet amb[as,
sepeque nos uisit uel nobis tunc aliquid fert.'
audit ut hoc miles matri compassus ait flens
'an queo septimana reuenire domum uel in ist[a?'
15   'cras' ait 'ad seram matrem quis cernere karam,
sed panem missi penes hanc uolo prima mereri.'
est diuulgatum commatris eum fore natum,
inter mancipia fit leticia cito magna,
congaudent matri reditu pro sospite nati.
20   tunc hera direxit missum quem dicere iussit
commatri natum presente die rediturum.
interea iuuenis pariter ludunt et herilis.
hunc ea ter uicit, hanc is totiens superauit,
alterutrum uicti gaudentes omine pacti,
25   uirginis is quod erat, iuuenis quod uirgo manebat,
non se uicisse sed uictos succubuisse.
hec suus, ille sua uocitabantur uice uersa,
mutato sexu soloecismi scemate facto.
nec iam celarunt se quin ardenter amarent,
30   mater si sineret uel in ipsa nocte coirent.

XII.1-30   1 ipsam *Schmeller*: inque *Seiler*   11 habet]
...erat *m.pr.*

"Now my lady, this mother of mine whom you have recently   1
seen - tell me, is she well, and are her affairs at peace?
And since she has become a godmother to you, do I have a
brother from her, whom you took from the font - tell me -
or was it she who took your daughter from the font?"
        The lady was utterly taken aback by these words from the   5
knight: "ah, what have you said?   Do you think that she
could have married, she to whom life itself was bitter
without you?   Why, after she lost you she lost her very
sight from weeping.   It was she who took my daughter from
the font, and afterwards regarded us both as her own daughters.
She often comes to see us and brings us something."
        When the knight heard this, he had pity on his mother,   13
and said tearfully "may I return home during this week?"
"You may see your dear mother tomorrow in the evening, but
I want to be the first to deserve the messenger's bread
from her."   News spread that he was the son of her godmother, and there was soon great rejoicing among the servants,
who shared the mother's happiness at her son's safe return.
Then the lady sent out a messenger and ordered him to tell
her godmother that her son would come home that very day.
        Meanwhile the young man and the young lady were playing   22
as before.   She beat him three times, and he defeated her
the same number;   no matter who lost, this omen made them
glad to be betrothed, for he was the maiden's and the maiden
remained the young man's: they had not beaten one another,
but had yielded in defeat.   She was wont to be called his
'lad' and he in turn her 'girl', changing their sexes in a
mistaken figure of speech.   They no longer hid the fact that   29
they were passionately in love, and if her mother had
allowed it they would have slept together that very night.

illa tamen sineret sibi si non dedecus esset.
ut prestoletur tunc uirgo uix superatur.

....................lus non dominetur

................qua] uelit ire sinatur

35 ....domino domineque placebat

....................um, domini faciendum

....................s resident quibus illi

....................m]ulta uiando loquentes

............famul]os uidet a matre missos

40 ....omnibus oscula prebet

..................matris amorem

..................um prius intueatur

..................Deus utque remittat

..................debemus famulari

45 ....rediise uidemus

sat locupletatum uel ho]noribus amplificatum.

....................gra]tes uobis et habebo

....................matri bonitatis

..................re]spondent et ouantur

50 ....s accuset apud te

..................i]lli debueramus

..................et ante non uti seruos

..................ius ad hec famulari

..................r non uenere nisi tres

55 ....ectant here nostri

..................endum facientes

..................dans oscula dixit

..................s grandis fit in illis

..................ibi fuit atque bibebant

60 ....herum comitantur ouantes

..................m cum reliqua re

..................q]aliter omnia starent

..................diceret omnia stare

..................d nocuisse suorum

65 ....pe]nitus iacuisset agrorum

..................erat omnipotentem

..................cerasiorum

XII.31-67   34 qua *scripsi*   46 sat locupletatum uel *Seiler*
47 grates *Seiler*   60 ouantque *Schmeller*   65 penitus *scripsi*

She would have allowed it but for the disgrace it would have   31
brought her.   Even then, the maiden was barely persuaded to
wait.
................might not reign   33
................he might be allowed to go where he wished
................pleased the lord and the lady
................master's.....should be done
................where they lived
................talking a great deal as they journeyed
................saw servants sent by his mother
................embraced them all   40
................love of his mother
................before (she?) saw him
................that God might send him back
................we ought to serve him
................we have seen him come home   45
wealthy enough, and laden with honours.
................and I shall be grateful to you"
................of goodness to his mother
................they reply and are praised
................may accuse before you   50
................we had owed to him
................and before not as slaves
................to serve for this?
................only three came
................our kinsmen yesterday   55
................seeing this was done
................kissing him said
................a great (reward?) is given them
................was there, and they drank
................accompanied their master, praising him   60
................with the rest of his belongings
................how everything was placed
................might say that everything was placed
................had harmed his men's
................the...of the fields would totally have been laid waste
................the almighty   66
................of cherries

         sederat hinc speculans pre se pendentia spernens
         ....rantia mora.
70   nunciet ut primus dominus cum uenerit eius
         ....monedula supra
         explorans quid agat, cur cerasiis ita parcat
         quidquid agit uel ait notat ut post] hoc ea prodat.
         ille magis dominum cupit ut uideat equitantem,
75   semper ait pro se 'Ruodlieb her]e curre uenique,'
         idque monedula discit et ad dominam reuolauit
         sic dicens illi 'quod nunc dicam] precor audi.'
         que dixit 'loquere'. 'Ruodlieb here curre uenique.'
         tunc quamuis dominam pueri uider]e gementem,
80   omnes risere uolucrem quid tale notare.
         mater ait 'reuola pu]er et sedeas ubi supra,
         quod dicatque nota si clamet tu quoque clama.'
         tunc reuolat rectaue notat] monedula uerba
         ipsius pueri Ruodlieb uenientis auari;
85   dum dubitet herus unde meet] uel quando ueniret
         prospicit e silua socios emergere densa.
         primo contribulis, iu]xta quem scutifer eius,
         postremo dominus meat officialis et eius
         ....queque suarum.
90   tunc puer exclamat 'dominus, gaudete, propinquat!'

XII.68-90   73 quidquid agit uel ait notat ut post
Seiler   75 semper ait pro se *Seiler*   77 sic dicens illi
quod nunc dicam *Seiler*   79 tunc quamuis dominam pueri uidere
Seiler   81 mater ait reuola puer *Seiler*   83 tunc reuolat
rectaue notat *Zeydel*   85 dum dubitet herus unde meet *scripsi*:
Ruodlieb querit ubi uel esset *Zeydel*   87 primo contribulis
Seiler

154

had sat there looking out in front of him, ignoring the fruit   68
hanging there.
...............myrtle berries, so he might be the first to
announce when his master came.
...............a jackdaw above him, looking at what he was
doing, and why he spared the cherries so.   It took note of
whatever he did and said, so that it could report them later.
He wanted more and more to see his lord riding along, and
kept saying to himself "master Ruodlieb, hurry, come home."
The jackdaw learned this, flew back to its mistress and said
to her "hear what I have to say, I pray you."   She said
"speak then."   "Master Ruodlieb, hurry, come home."   Then
although her pages could see their lady crying they all
laughed that a bird could take heed of such a thing.   His
mother said "fly back and sit above where the boy is, and
take note of whatever he says.   If he cries out, you cry
out too."   Then the jackdaw flew back and took careful note   83
of the words of the boy who was so anxious for Ruodlieb's
homecoming.   While he was wondering where his master might
be coming from and when he might come, he saw the companions
coming out of the thick forest, first the kinsman, the squire
beside him, and finally the master emerged, and his official
.......and each of their..... Then the lad cried out
"hurrah! the master approaches!"

mentum non] scabit quia non pilus unus ibi sit.   M27^r
quod tam nemo uafer sit qui discernere possit
clericus an mulier inberbes an esset alumnus,
est tam iocunde tam uirginee faciei.
5   dum se tondebant sordes limphaque lauabant,
exierant butinam.   lauacralem mox sibi lenam
scutifer imposuit, qua lectum tectus adiuit,
donec siccetur estusque sibi minuatur.
post modicum surgit, sua calciamenta requirit.

10   sic pedat ad mensam comes, insed[it tum ad illam.   F2^r
non tamen in solio uoluit residere supremo,
sed subiectiue matris dextrim uelut hospes
atque libens totum sibi permisit dominatum;
hec quod ei dederat reuerenter suscipiebat.
15   incidens panem turbam partitur in omnem,
transmisit cuiuis discum specialibus escis,
cum uino pateram, mittens aliquando medonem.
Ruotlieb contribulis conuiua fuit socialis,
ex uno pane comedunt una quoque lance,
20   ex uno cyato biberant communiter ambo.
matri conuiua solet esse monedula sola,
cui pilulam mice cum dat capit illa superbe
perspacians mensam transuersim transilit omnem.
fercula post multa post pocula totque secuta
25   tunc hera poscit aquam, camerarius attulit ill[am.
ad mensas quasque summo iubet hanc dare cuique.
posthinc pincerne passim potum tribuere.

XIII.1-27   1 mentum non *scripsi*: barbam non *Zeydel*:
barbiciam *Ford*   quia *Schmeller*: quod *Seiler*   6 exierant e
m.pr.   10 insedit tum ad illam *scripsi*: insedit ad illam
Zeydel   23 perspaciens *m.pr.* 25 illam *Haupt*

XIII

He did not scrape his beard, for there was not a single   1
hair there; there was no-one so cunning as to be able to
tell if he was a clerk, a woman or a beardless youth, he had
such a joyful, girlish face.   When they had shaved themselves and washed off the dirt, they got out of the bath.
Then the squire put a bath-robe on him, and covered with
this he went to the bench until he was dry and had cooled
off.   After a while he stood up and asked for his shoes.
And so the count walked to the table and sat down at it.   10
He did not want to sit in the highest place, however, but
submissively at his mother's right hand, like a guest, and
he willingly granted her all authority over him.   He took
whatever she gave him graciously.   She cut up a loaf and
shared it among all the people there, and handed to each a
plate of finest foods, a dish, some wine, and to some she
gave mead.
Ruodlieb's kinsman was his companion and partner in the   18
feast.   They ate from one loaf and from one plate, and
both drank alike from a single wine-cup.   Only the jackdaw
used to feast with his mother, and when she gave it a little
bit of a crumb it would take it, walk to and fro proudly,
and hop about all over the table.   Then, after many courses   24
and after as many cups of wine had followed them, the
mistress asked for water, and her chamberlain brought it.
She ordered him to give it to the highest in rank on each
table.   After this, the stewards passed drinks round
everywhere.

```
        mensis amotis mensalibus atque plicatis
        leti consurgunt domine gratesque dederunt,
30      dicunt gaudere Ruotlieb sanum rediisse,                      M27^V
        quo consoletur matrem ne plus tribuletur,
        primitus ut sepe dolet illo cum caruisse.
        est diuulgatum cito per totam regionem
        Ruotlieb uenisse locupletatum sat abunde.


35      dum sibi post placuit dum secretumque sibi fit
        intrat conclaue cum dilecta sibi matre
        scutiferumque iubet enthecam quo sibi ferret
        de qua multiplices extraxit opes preciosas,
        in chrusinis in pelliciis census et alius,
40      exul que denis nanciscebatur in annis.
        post poscit peras quas scutifer attulit amb[as.
        extrahat ut panes iubet hunc factos aput Afr[os,
        quos dum produxit matri ioculanter is inquit
        'hos deseruiui tenus hac mater ubi mansi.
45      hos mihi rex dederat m[odo frangere meque sinebat.'
        [mater ait 'famulos nobis reor ante uocandos,]
        quam bene sint sapidi uideant panes Africani.'          F2^V
        is dixit 'melius] puto quo soli uideamus.'
        educens cultrum quo panem dissec[et] unum
50      percipit arge]ntum lancis sub quo fuit aurum.
        pollen ut abrasit iubar argentique reluxit
        clauis coniun]ctos cernens tria per loca lances
        comminuens lima cito clauorum capitella
        dissoluens] lances uidet aureolos ibi nummos
55      tam strictim iunctos quod suppingi nequit unus.
        Ruodlieb exult]at Domino grates et agebat.             LXX
        nec cunctan]s parilem manibus sustollere lancem
        tergendo p]ollen clauos limando minutim
```

XIII.28-58   30 samum *m.pr.*   41 ambas *Haupt*   42 extrahit *m.
pr.*   Afros *Haupt*   45 modo frangere meque sinebat *Laistner*:
nunc frangere meque sinebat *Seiler*   46 *suppl. Seiler*   48 is
dixit melius *Seiler*   49 dissecet *Schmeller*: dissecat *Seiler*
52 clauis coniunctos *Seiler*:   .....disiunctos *Schmeller*   54
dissoluens *Seiler*: recludens *Schmeller*   56 Ruodlieb exultat
Seiler   57 nec cunctans *Seiler*   58 tergendo *Seiler*

When the tables had been taken away and the tablecloths   28
folded up, they got up, glad at heart, and gave thanks to
the lady, saying that they were happy indeed that Ruodlieb
had returned safely so that he could comfort his mother,
and so that she would be tormented no more, as she was at
first, by the pain of losing him.   News swiftly spread
through the whole area that Ruodlieb had come home, and
wealthy enough, too.

Later, when it seemed right to him and when he had the   35
opportunity to speak in private, he went into a chamber with
his beloved mother, and ordered his squire to bring him his
chest.   He took many valuable things from it in the form of
skins and fur cloaks and other kinds of riches which he had
acquired in his ten years as an exile.   Then he asked for   41
the bags, and the squire brought them both.   He ordered him
to take out the loaves made in the Africans' land.   When he
took them out, the knight said jokingly to his mother "I have
earned these where I have been staying up till now, mother.   The
king gave them to me, and permitted me to break them only
now."   His mother said "I think that we ought to summon   46
our servants first, to let them see how well-flavoured
African loaves are."   He said "I think it is better for us
to look at them alone."   He took out a knife to cut open
one of the loaves and noticed the silver of the dish,
beneath which lay the gold.   As he rubbed off the crust and   51
the gleaming silver shone out, he saw the dishes, fastened
together with pins in three places.   He quickly broke off
the heads of the pins with a file, separated the dishes, and
saw the golden coins there packed in so tightly that another
could not be hammered in.   Ruodlieb rejoiced and gave thanks
to the Lord God.   Without delaying he took the other dish
like it in his hands, tore off the bread, broke the pins
into little pieces,

```
          nummis confert]am uario censuque repletam
60        cernit et ob]stupuit.   nimium sua mater ouauit,
          tunc gemitus e]dens in mente sat ast hylarescens
          perfusis] oculis grates Christo dat in altis
          quod tam ditat]um dederat sibi tamque beatum.
          miles humi dat] se terram premit oreque sepe.
65        ceu se pro] regis pedibus domini daret eius.
          tunc nimium plo]rans faciem lacrimandoque tingens
          orabat 'Dom]ine num par tibi quis ualet esse,
          qui clemens] illum miserum dignaris homullum
          sic locuplet]are uel honoribus amplificare,
70        eius nec uitiis] reminiscere quod patereris?
          nunc mihi des, D]omine, quo non moriar precor ante
          quam rursus u]ideam quem pauper egensque petebam,
          qui manda]nte te clementer suscipiens me
          fecit tantar]um consortem deliciarum
75        et miserum d]enos secum retinendo per annos
          amplificaui]t me queo quod posthac sat honeste
          uiuere fi]denter hec si tracto sapienter.'
          Ruodlieb cum m]atre dum sat gaudent super hac re      LXXI
          lances conclu]dunt cautissime quam ualuerunt
80        et prendunt cen]sus secum fert quicquid alius.
          accurrunt] plures proprii serui iuniores.
```

XIII.59-81   59 nummis confertam *Seiler*   60 cernit et ob-
stupuit *Seiler*   61 tunc gemitus edens *Seiler*   62 perfusis
Seiler: lacrimans *Schmeller*   63 quod tam ditatum *scripsi*:
quod locupletatum *Seiler*: quod filium karum *Schmeller*   64
miles humi dat *Seiler*   65 ceu pro se *Seiler*   66 tunc
nimium plorans *Seiler*   67 orabat domine *Seiler*   68 qui clemens
Seiler   69 sic locupletare *Seiler*   70 eius nec uitiis *Seiler*
71 nunc mihi des *Seiler*: condones *Schmeller*   73 qui mandante
Seiler: qui donante *Schmeller*   75 et *Seiler*: me *Schmeller*
76 amplificauit *Seiler*   78 Ruodlieb cum *Seiler*   79 lances
concludunt *Seiler*   80 et prendunt census *Seiler*   81
accurrunt *Seiler*

saw that it was laden with coins and filled with all kinds   59
of riches, and was astonished at it;   his mother was
utterly overjoyed, then began to weep, though she was still
happy in her heart, and with tearful eyes she gave thanks
to Christ on high for giving him to her so enriched and
blessed.   The knight threw himself to the ground and
kissed it often, as though he were prostrating himself at
the feet of his lord's own king.   Then weeping greatly and
with tears coursing down his cheeks, he prayed "Lord,   67
surely no-one can be equal to you?   In your mercy you
have deigned to bestow such wealth on this pitiable wretch
of a man, and to heap honours on him, and you have suffered
not to remember his sins.   Now grant, O Lord, that I may
not die, I pray, before I see once again him whom I sought
out when poor and needy, and who at your behest mercifully
took me up and made me to share in so many great pleasures,
and by keeping this poor man in his service for ten years
raised me up so that after this I may live faithfully and in
all decency, if I handle these things wisely."   While   78
Ruodlieb and his mother were still overjoyed at this matter
they put the dishes together as carefully as they could and
took them away, along with whatever other valuables he had
brought with him.   Several of their own younger servants
ran up to them.

'dicti sunt hodie] pueris, ceu credo, uenire   M30^r
quidam karorum nostri consanguineorum,   •
qui quando ueniant hec dum firmentur ibi sint.
ad uos nunc illam uos inuitate puellam,
5   uestri communes ueniant utrimque fideles.'
que cum uenisset hanc hi circumque stetissent,
curtis amicorum cito plena fit aduenientum.
quos Ruodlieb bene suscepit, quibus oscula prebet
et prandere rogat satis illis et tribuebat.
10   amotis mensis dominabus et inde reuersis
ad sua secreta, precedit eas ea nata,
post illasque pedant sibi qui plumatia portant
et plures alii comitantes his famulari.
his uinum ferri iubet illo pro famulari,
15   dumque bibit quisque sibi uicino dedit usque
pincerne pateram reddebant euacuatam.
inclinant, abeunt Ruodlieb dominosque reuisunt.

tunc Ruodlieb dixit 'quia uos Deus huc glomerauit
nunc audite mihi curate uel auxiliari,
20   conubium quoddam quo fiat nunc stabilitum,
est quod laudatum sic ad nos induciatum,
ad quod presentes mihi uos cupio fore testes.
contigit ut iuuenis meus iste nepos et herilis
mutuo diligerent sese dum t ssere ludunt,
25   lege maritali cupientes consociari.'
dicunt 'hoc cuncti debemus consiliari,
indolis ut tante uir tam uirtutis opime

XIV.1-27   1 dicti sunt hodie *scripsi*: uisi sunt clare *sugg.*
Hall   2 quidam] partim *m.pr.*   4 ad nos *Laistner*   5 nostri
m.pr.   6 qui cum *Schmeller*   19 curate] cupite *Schmeller*   20
iuxta hunc v. legitur in marg. ad quam est quod *(vide v.21)*.

XIV

"Some of our dear relations are said to be on their way   1
today by our pages, as I believe; when they come, they may be
present while these things are made firm.   Now you summon
your daughter to you, and let your faithful comrades on both
sides attend."

When the girl had come and the men were standing round   6
about her, the court quickly filled with friends arriving.
Ruodlieb welcomed them all and embraced them, asked them to
eat and offered them plenty.   When the tables had been
removed, the ladies retired to their chambers and the
daughter went in front of them;   behind them walked those
who carried their cushions, and many others who waited on
them.   She ordered wine to be brought to them to show their
service to him;   each one drank and passed the cup to his
neighbour, until they handed the vessel back empty to the
wine-steward.   They bowed to her and left, returning to
Ruodlieb and the lords.

Then Ruodlieb said "seeing that God has gathered you here,   18
listen to me now and take care to assist me, so that this
marriage which has been decided upon and entrusted to our
care may now be established firmly.   I desire that you here
present should be witnesses to it for me.   It is the case
that this young nephew of mine and the young mistress fell
in love with one another while playing at dice, and desire
to be joined by the bond of matrimony."   They all replied,   26
"we must all consider this, that a man of such great nobility
and wondrous virtue

non dehonestetur citius sed ut eripiatur
a scorto turpi digne satis igne cremari'
30   et laudant Dominum quod in hoc cosmo fuit usquam
femina que magicam de se diuelleret ipsam.
tunc surgit iuuenis, grates dabat omnibus illis
quod tam clementes sibi sunt communiter omnes,
inquit et horrere penitus se seque pudere
35   sic dehonestatum per id execrabile scortum.
'nunc opus uxore nimium mihi cernitis esse,
quam quoniam facile nunc.possumus hic reperire,
hanc desponsari desidero uel mihi iungi,
ut sitis testes et ad hoc mihi, queso, libentes,
40   alterutros cum nos dotabimus, est ueluti mos.'
qui dicunt 'prompte tibi subueniemus in hac re.'
Ruodlieb post dominas pariter direxit eas tres,
que cito uenere nata preeunte mo[rose.
contra quas agmen surrexit eis ad honorem.
45   cuncti dum resident spatium breue conticuerunt,
tunc Ruotlieb surgit et ut auscultent sibi poscit.
his post contribulis pactum dixit uel amicis
hic] quod et hec ferueret in alterutrius amorem.
hanc hunc uxorem suimet si uellet haber[e
50   [demandant cuncti. 'sic' inquit is ore uolenti.]   M30ᵛ
illam [tunc pariter dominum retinere libenter
illum si uellet rogitant; parum quoque ridet,
post ait 'an seruum nolim ludo superatum,
tessere quem uici sub talis fenore pacti
55   seu uincat seu succumbat soli mihi nubat?
s]eruiat obnixe uolo quo mihi nocte dieque,
quod quanto melius facit est tanto mihi karus.'
t]unc risus magnus fit ab omnibus atque cachinnus,
tam presumptiue loquitur quod tam uel amice.
60   e]ius at ut matrem cernunt hec non renuentem
e]t genus amborum par posseque diuitiarum
discutiunt caute bene conueniant quod utrimque,
hanc desponsari sibi censent lege iugali.

XIV.28-63   34-49 *hi vv. scripti sunt in marg.*   43 morose
Seiler: modeste *Schmeller*   48 hic *Seiler*   49 habere *Seiler*
50 *suppleui*   51 tunc...libenter *scripsi*: si cupio rogitatis
credite certo *Zeydel*

should not be disgraced, but should be snatched quickly from   28
that shameful harlot, who truly deserves to be burned in the
fire," and they praised the Lord God that in all this world
there was ever a woman who could tear this witch away from
him.

Then the young man stood up and thanked them all for   32
showing such mercy to him, one and all, and said that he
shuddered inwardly at the great shame of having disgraced
himself because of that damnable prostitute.   "Now you see
that I have great need of a wife, and since we may most
easily find her here, I wish this lady to be betrothed to me
as my own, so you may be witnesses to this for me and, I pray,
willing ones, when we exchange dowries, as is the custom."

They replied, "we will gladly assist you in this matter."   41
Then Ruodlieb sent for those three ladies, who hurried there
fretfully, the daughter in front.   The company stood up
before them in their honour.   When all had taken their
seats, they fell silent for a time, and then Ruodlieb stood
up and asked them all to listen to him.   Then he said that
it was agreed by all relations and friends that this youth
and this girl were burning with love for one another.   They
all asked him if he wished to take her as his wife, and with
a smile on his face he replied "I do."   Then they asked her   50
if she for her part wished willingly to take him as her
lord; she too smiled a little, and then said "should I not
want a slave vanquished in a game, whom I beat at dice with
this agreement as our stake, that whether he won or whether
he lost he should marry only me?   I want him to serve me   56
with all his might both night and day, and the better he does
this, the dearer he shall be to me."   Then there was a
tremendous roar of laughter from everyone, because she had
spoken so brazenly and yet in such a friendly way.   When
they saw that her mother did not oppose these things and that
the families of both were well-matched in status and wealth,
they took counsel and decided that they were well suited to
one another, and that she should be betrothed to him in a
lawful bond.

s]ponsus at extraxit ensem ue piramide tersit;
65 anulus in capulo fixus fuit aureus ipso,
affert quem sponse sponsus dicebat et ad se
'anulus ut digitum circumcapit undique totum
sic tibi stringo fidem firmam uel perpetualem,
hanc seruare mihi debes aut decapitari.'
70 que satis astute iuueni respondit et apte
'iudicium parile decet ut patiatur uterque:
cur seruare fidem tibi debeo, dic, meliorem
quam mihi tu debes? dic si defendere possis
si licuisset Ade mecham superaddat ut Eue
75 unam cum costam faceret Deus in mulierem.
quam de se sumptam cum proclamauerat Adam
dic ubi concessas binas sibi legeris Euas?
cum meretricares essem scortum tibi uelles?
absit ut hoc pacto tibi iungar, uade, ualeto
80 et quantumcunque scortare uelis, sine sed me.
tot sunt in mundo tibi ceu quo tam bene nubo.'
sic dicens gladium sibi liquerat et digitalem.
cui dixit iuuenis 'fiat dilecta uelut uis.
umquam si ·faciam tibi que dedero bona perdam,
85 istius capitis abscidendique potens sis.'
que modicum ridens ad eum seseque reuertens
inquit 'ea lege modo iungamur sine fraude.'
huius 'amen' dixit procus et sibi basia fixit.

his ita coniunctis enesis fit maxima plebis,
90 laudantes Dominum cantizabant hymeneum.
Ruotlieb pellicium dederat bene ualde gulatum
sponso uel crusinam limbo terre crepitantem,
dat et equum celerem sibi compte sat faleratum.
munerat et sponse consanguineo sociate;
95 huic tria dat spintra que uelent pectora pulchra,
atque dat armillas sibi bis binas operosas
et pariter sibi tres dat gemmatos digitales
datque superductam cocco crusinam migalinam.
cetera turba sua sibi dant sponsalia magna.
100 qualiter inter se concordent quid mihi cure?

XIV.64-100   88-100 *hi vv. scripti sunt in marg.*

The bridegroom drew his sword and scraped it along the   64
stonework. A gold ring was fixed onto its hilt, and the
bridegroom offered it to his bride, saying to her "as this
ring encircles the whole of your finger all around, so I
bind my faith to you firmly and forever, and you must observe   70
it towards me, or lose your head." She very wittily gave
him the apt reply "it is fitting for both to suffer the same
judgement: why must I keep better faith towards you than
you towards me? Tell me, if you can defend this - was
Adam allowed to have a mistress as well as Eve, since God
made one of his ribs into a woman; when Adam shouted out
that she was taken out from himself, tell me, where do you
read that he was permitted two Eves? When you went off
wenching, would you have liked me to be a whore for you? May it
not be that I should be joined to you on this condition; be
off with you, farewell, you may go wenching as much as you
wish, but not with me. There are plenty in the world whom   81
I can wed as well as you." So saying, she left him his
sword and his ring. The young man said to her "let it
be done as you wish, darling. If I ever do this, let me
lose the goods I gave you, and let you have the right to cut
off this head of mine." A smile passed over her lips as
she turned back to him and said "let us be joined now on
those terms, with no deceit." Her suitor said "amen" to this
and kissed her.
      When they were thus united the people gave a roar of approval 89
and praising God, they sang a wedding hymn. Ruodlieb gave
the groom a leather coat beautifully edged with fur, and a
cloak whose fringe rustled down to the ground. He also gave
him a swift horse well equipped. He gave gifts to the bride
who had wed his kinsman, too: he gave her three brooches,
to wear on her beautiful breast, two pairs of finely-wrought
bangles, and likewise three rings set with jewels. He also
gave her a cloak of ermine lined with scarlet cloth. The
rest of the crowd gave them great wedding gifts of their own.
But why should I worry how they got on together?

'quamuis [nunc ualeas, scito tibi quod manet etas   M25^r
parcere que nescit pariter cunctos domi[tauit.
femina que lune par est in flore iuu[ente
par uetule simie fit post etate senecte.
5   rugis sulcata frons que fuit antea pl[ana,
ante columbini sibi stant oculi te[nebrosi.
deguttat nasus sordes nimium mucul[entus.
dependent bucce quondam pinguedine t[ense.
dentes oblongi moti stant ut ruitur[i,
10   per quos lingua foras pellit locutura fa[bellas
et uerbum profert plenum ceu pollinis o[s sit.
utque recuruatum resupinum stat sibi m[entum,
os et risibile quod plures allicit in se
stat semper patulum populum terrere uel [aptum.
15   stat collum gracile deplumate quasi p[ice,
extantes mamme iam ceu trochi tub[erose
molles ut fungi succi pendent uacu[ati.
et prius usque nates qui crines auricolore[s
pendent discretim dorsum uelando pil[atim,
20   extant horribiles terrentes inspici[entes,
per sepem caput ut anuatim sit sibi t[ractum.
inclinata caput humeris extantibus [umbrat
ut tardus uultur ubi scit iacuisse cad[auer,
et que discincta consueuerat ire iuue[nta
25   alte succingit tunicam ne sordifica[ret,

XV.1-25   1 nunc ualeas...etas *scripsi*: ...senectus *Zeydel*   2
domitauit *Seiler*   6 tenebrosi *Seiler*: uitulini *Schmeller*   11
os sit *Laistner*: ouum *Schmeller*   14 aptum *Ford*: antrum *Schmeller*   16 tuberose *Laistner*: tuberantes *Seiler*   17 uacuati
Seiler   18 qui *censuit Seiler posuisse m.alt.*: sibi *m.pr.*,
Schmeller   19 pilatim *Seiler*: pilosum *Schmeller*   21 tractum
Seiler: tonsum *Schmeller*   22 umbrat *Seiler*: it nunc *Schmeller*
25 sordificaret *Seiler*: sordificarit *Schmeller*

XV

"Although you are still strong, remember that old age waits   1
for you, it knows no pity and rules over all alike.   A woman
who in the flower of her youth is as lovely as the moon later
becomes like a little old ape in her elderly years.   Her
brow is ploughed with furrows, where before it was smooth,
and her eyes, formerly like little doves, are cloudy.   Her
foully snivelling nose drips filth.   Her cheeks, once firm   8
and healthy, sag down.   Her teeth grow long and loose, as
though ready to drop out, and through them her wagging tongue
spits out her tales, and she speaks her words as though her
mouth was full of flour.   Her chin droops down, bent back on
itself, and her cackling mouth, which was attractive to so
many, gapes ever open, and fair frightens the people.   Her   15
lovely neck now looks like a featherless magpie's; her firm
round breasts are now lumpy, and hang down empty and floppy as
dried mushrooms.   And her golden hair, which formerly hung
down as far as her bottom, covering her back in separate
plaits, now sticks out bristly and strikes terror in those
who see it, as through she had been dragged through a hedge
backwards.   Her head is bowed low, overshadowing her bony   22
shoulders like a slothful vulture when it knows where a corpse
lies.   She who as a girl used to go about with her dress
flowing free now gathers it up high so it doesn't get dirty,

calcatura fabas ueluti pultem coquitu[ra.
calciamenta sua que iam fuerant nim[is arta
cum soccis laxa ligo ceu stant, ante sup[ina,
sustollunt luti nimium calcando limo[si.
30   et graciles digiti quondam pinguedine pl[eni
nunc super ossa cutem sucosi, carne care[ntem.
sordent rugosis nimis ex fuligine nod[is,
unguibus incisis longis squalore nige[llis.
sic agilem iuuenem senium domat ut mu[lierem.
35   ....   M25^V
................s sibi celsior est ubi tellus
...........pon]at quis crus sellam super ipsam
...............m suspendat se socialem
...............et girans si sella uacillet
40   ....netum fuerit si forte iumentum
...............dum latum saliens super amnem
conatur b]aculo sese sustollere crebro
...............n post multa leuamina tandem
...............s post se transit tussi quatiente
45   ....eas cernit girare choreas
...............us iuuenis fugitabit amarus
...............bunt cuncti uel ei maledicunt
...............uel in his iuuenilis ouabat
...............idit quid cantent aure notabit
50   ....uit digitis neumas agitabit
...............meros huc huc uertens hilarescens
.........cunct]os ad sese respicientes
...............es optant rediisse priores
...............fieri si posset eundem
55   ....let dum sponte libens obiisset
...............do suspirans intime flendo
...............um dicens sepissime secum
"mors humanorum] finis tu sola malorum
cur mihi ser]a uenis, cur non me carcere soluis?"

XV.26-59   26 ueluti *om.m.pr.*:   uel ut *Schmeller*   27 arcta
Schmeller   28 laxa] arta *m.pr.*   ligo ceu] nimis *m.pr.*   supina
Laistner: superba *Schmeller*   31 sucosi] suco uel *Schmeller*
36 celsior] cliuior *m.pr.*   42 conatur *Zeydel*   44 tussi *om.*
m.pr.   59 cur mihi sera *Laistner*:   cur tam sera *Schmeller*

as though she's about to trample on beans, to cook pottage.   26
She used to wear very tight shoes; now they are loose, with
leggings, and curve up at the front like a hoe; they are
filthy, picking up mud as she walks along. As for her
delicate fingers, once firmly fleshed, now they are skin and
bone; once moist, they now have no flesh at all. Their
wrinkled joints are filthy with soot, and her uncut nails are
long and black with filth. Old age overtakes the sprightly
young man just as it does the woman........................
................for him where the land lies higher   36
................throw his leg right over the saddle
................hangs himself up.....his comrade
................spins round if the saddle wobbles
................if the old mare happens to be   40
................leaping over a broad stream
tries to support himself with a thick stick
................finally after many respites
................crosses over after him with a cough that makes
                              him shudder
................watches (the girls) dancing   45
................the young men will flee away bitterly
................they all curse him
................and as a young man cheered them
................will listen closely to what they are singing
................will play the notes with his fingers   50
................turning here and there, full of happiness
................looking back at themselves
................wish that the former....had come back
................if the same could be done
................when he would happily have chosen to die   55
................sighing and weeping at heart
................often says to himself:
"You, death, are the sole end of human misery:
why do you come late to me? Why do you not set me free from
this prison?

```
60    mors autem parcit nul]li languore, dolore
      quos tolerare manet] licet id sibi uiuere mors sit
      donec, quando] iubet Deus, eius spiritus exit:
      is nam termi]nat omne quod est, uolet ambulet aut net.
      principium quod] habet non quodam fine carebit.'
65    non cessat ma]ter Ruotlieb minitare frequenter
      que sic languis]set et id effugitare nequisset
      ...............et alius nil habuerunt
      ...............quicquam tractare suarum
      ...............fili tua magna sophia
70    ...............e plus quam claresc.........
```

XV.60-70   60 mors autem parcit nulli *scripsi*: debeo nunc
uere uigili languere dolore *uel. sim. sugg. Hall*: mors o
solue me uili *Zeydel*   61 quos tolerare manet *scripsi*: quem
tolerare manet *sugg. Hall*: quos tolerare debet *Zeydel*   62
donec quando *Laistner*   63 is nam terminat *Loewenthal,
Zeydel*: hec nam lex domat *Laistner, Ford*   64 principium
quod *Zeydel*   65 non cessat mater *Laistner*   66 que sic
languisset *Laistner*: cur id fecissent *Seiler*

Death however spares no man from weariness and pain, which he   60
must endure, even when to live is death to him, until his
spirit leaves him at the time God commands.   For He brings
to an end everything that is, whether it flies, walks, or
swims.   Whatever has a beginning shall not lack an end of
some kind."
    Ruodlieb's mother did not cease from warning him that he   65
would grow weary like this, and that he could not escape it.
................and they had nothing else
................to handle anything of his (ladies?)
................my son, your great wisdom
................more than illuminate......

'heres tunc ualeat si filius haut tibi fiat!   M31^r
si sine, dic, liberis, quid erit, fili, morieris?
de nostris rebus erit altercatio grandis.
deficiunt uires omnino mihi iuueni[les,
5   nam denos annos quos tu fueras apud [Afros
cottidie curis angebar in omnibus hor[is
post te merendo pro nostra reque tuenda,
nique reuertisses citius iam ceca fuisse[m;
sed iuuenescebam cum te remeare sciebam,
10   contineo melius et me modo quam mea sit u[is.
uellem si uelles quo nostros congenerales
et nobis fidos nunc conueniamus amicos,
quorum consilio quorumque iuuamine fido
possis in uxorem reperire tibi muliere[m,
15   esse parentele quam noris talis utrimque,
claudicet ut neutrim uestri genitura [uicissim,
per cuius mores tibi nec minuantur hono[res.
quam tibi demonstret clemens Deus ac tibi i[ungat!'
Ruodlieb respondit matri, placidissime [dixit
20   'cras demandemus consanguineis et ami[cis
ut nos conueniant quam uelocissime possi[nt.
quod mihi consilium dant, si censes id agendum,
non pretermittam quod uultis quin ego solu[am.
missis legatis et amicis conglomera[tis
25   ad se dum ueniunt bene suscepti[que sibi sunt
Ruotlieb disposuit sedilia ceu bene [nouit
in quo quisque loco sedeat sibi certificato,
dans geminis unam mensam dominis ad h[abendum,
et matri solium fieri iubet altius un[um,

XVI.1-29   25 ueniant *Zeydel*   susceptique sibi sunt *Seiler*:
suscepti nimium sunt *Zeydel*   28 habendum *Seiler*: habendam
Schmeller

"Farewell to an heir, if you do not have a son!   What   1
will happen, son, if you die without children?   There will
be a terrible dispute over our estates.   I have no youthful
vigour at all, for during the ten years that you spent with   5
the Africans I was afflicted with woes every day and at every
hour, grieving for you and managing our affairs, and if you
had not come back I should soon have gone blind.   But I grew
young again when I knew that you were coming home, and now
I keep a better hold on myself than my strength warrants.
I should like us, if it is your desire too, to summon our
vassals and our faithful friends, by whose counsel and
faithful assistance you may find a woman to be a wife for
you, whom you would know to be of such lineage on both sides
that your offspring are not defective because of either line,
and their behaviour might not lessen your renown.   May God
point her out to you and join her to you!"

Ruodlieb very calmly spoke these words in reply to his   19
mother: "tomorrow we shall inform our relations and friends
that they should come to us as quickly as they can.   I shall
not overlook the counsel that they give me, if you think it
should be done;   I shall rather accomplish what you want."

Messengers were sent and their friends assembled.   When   24
they came to him and were welcomed by him, Ruodlieb arranged
their seats, for he knew well that each should sit in the
place designated to him.   He assigned one table to each two
lords, and commanded one higher chair to be placed for his
mother,

30   ut super aspiceret cunctos ibi qui resi[derent,
    solaque manducet, hera cerni sic fore [posset.
    sic et honorando matrem dominam uel h[abendo
    a populis laudem sed ab omnipotente coronam
    atque diuturnam uitam meruitue bea[tam.
35   dum manducauit, mensas remouere] rogauit   M31^V
    claudunturque] fores quos obseruant duo fortes,
    qui non ire sinun]t intro quem neue foras quem
    donec consili]um diffiniretur id ipsum.
    tunc Ruodlieb] surgens modicum sileant rogat omnes,
40   quo sibi notific]et, propter quod eos glomeraret.
    cum sileant dix]it genetrix sua ceu sibi suasit
    'nunc audite, me]i consanguinei uel amici.
    quanto merore] mea mater quoue labore
    pertulerit m]ulta, patris atque mei uiduata,
45   curando cun]cta, uobis in re patet ipsa.
    nunc se defi]ciunt uires et membra fatiscunt
    nec quidquam facere] ualet amodo quiuit ut ante,
    quod mihi uel cre]bro narrat uel id ipse uidebo.
    hinc mihi sponsa]ri non cessat consiliari.
50   quare nunc ad u]os misi me conueniendos
    ut reputare qu]eat sibi quisque uel hoc mihi dicat;
    nam nimium pauce] mulieres sunt mihi note
    nec ualeo] scire quo me uertam mihi fauste.
    uos mihi dicatis] super hac re quid faciatis,
55   uxorem nobis] si quam reperire queatis,
    que non indecor]et nostrum genus id sed inauret
    moribus ingen]ita uel uite nobilitate.'

XVI.30-57   31 posset *Seiler*: quo quit *Schmeller*   35 dum
manducauit mensas remouere *Seiler*   36 claudunturque *Seiler*
38 donec consilium *Seiler*   39 tunc Ruodlieb *Seiler*   40 quo
sibi notificet *Seiler*   41 cum sileant dixit *Seiler*   42 nunc
audite mei *Seiler*   43 quanto merore *Seiler*   44 pertulerit
multa *Seiler*   45 curando cuncta *Seiler*   46 nunc se *Seiler*
47 nec quidquam facere *Seiler*   48 quod mihi uel crebro *Seiler*
49 hinc mihi sponsari *Seiler*   50 quare nunc ad uos *Seiler*
51 ut reputare queat *Seiler*   52 nam nimium pauce *Seiler*   53
nec ualeo *Seiler*   54 uos mihi dicatis *Seiler*   55 uxorem nobis
Seiler   56 que non indecoret *Seiler*   57 moribus ingenita
Seiler

so that she might look down on all those who were seated   30
there and eat alone, so that in this way she could be seen
to be mistress.   By giving honour to his mother in this
way, and holding her as his liege-lady, he earned praise
from the people, but from the almighty a crown and everlasting
life in heaven.

When she had eaten, he asked them to remove the tables,   35
and the doors were closed.   Two strong men guarded them, and
they did not allow anyone in or out until that deliberation
had come to a close.

Then Ruodlieb stood and asked them to be silent for a   39
little, so that he could inform them for what reason he had
summoned them.   When they were silent he said, as his
mother had persuaded him, "Now listen to me, my relations
and friends!   It is perfectly plain to you what great grief
and what travail have affected my mother in her suffering,
as bereft of my father and of myself she managed all our
affairs.   Now her health fails her, her limbs are weary,
and she has not the strength now to do anything that she could
do before.   She has told me this frequently, and I shall   48
see it for myself.   And so she does not cease from advising
me to take a wife.   For this reason I sent to you to come to
me now, so that each of you can think this over for himself
and speak with me.   Very few women are known to me, nor am
I in a position to know where to turn with a happy outcome.
You tell me what you would do in this matter, if you can find   54
a wife for us who would not disgrace our family, but would
enrich it with her fine manners and the noble breeding of
her behaviour."

```
          respondent p]ariter 'id quam faciemus ouanter,
          ut natum carum d]e te uideamus obortum
60        heredem morum] uirtutum siue bonorum,
          quis dita]uit te Christus et honorificauit.'
          adnuerat quis]que se spondens hec agitare.
          unus at exsurg]ens cui note sunt regiones
          et noti domini bene] qui fuerant ibi summi,
65        is 'dominam' dixit] 'unam scio que tibi par fit
          moris honestate] uirtute ue nobilitate.
          hanc uellem ui]deas, cum uideris ut fatearis
          in mundo] nullam quod uidisses dominellam
          omnem uirtut]em tam strennuiter facientem,
70        talis que fuer]it ut quemque uirum decuisset.'
```

XVI.58-70   59 ut natum carum de *Seiler*   60 heredem morum
Seiler   61 quis ditauit *scripsi*: quibus ditauit *Schmeller*
quis locupletauit *Seiler* Christ *Seiler, Langosch, Zeydel,
Ford*   62 adnuerat quisque *Seiler*   63 unus at exsurgens *Seiler*
64 et noti domini bene *Seiler*   65 is dominam dixit *Seiler*
66 moris honestate *Seiler*   67 hanc uellem uideas *Seiler*   68
in mundo *Seiler*   69 omnem uirtutem *Seiler*   70 talis que
fuerit *Seiler*

They for their part replied "we will willingly do this as   58
best we can, so that we may see a dear son born of your line,
your heir in manners and in the good qualities with which
Christ has enriched and honoured you."   Each one agreed,
and promised to do this.   Then one of them stood up who   63
knew those regions well, and the noble lords who lived there.
He said "I know one lady whose upright behaviour, virtue
and nobility make her a match for you.   I should like you
to see her, so that having seen her you may admit that in all
the world you have seen no young lady who strives so hard to
do every good work, and who is such as would honour any man."

apportans patera nunc ipsamet optima uina   M32^r
auratis uasis dulcorem sepe medonis
stans de uirginibus rogitabat compatrioti[s
cuius sint fame, formose sint an honeste.
5   subridens ille 'scio quod minime rogitas me.
nil minus intromisi me quam tale notare,
quid facerent domine; morem talem sino scurr[e.
sicubi pretereo dominas ubi stare uidebo
illis inclino quo mens est ire uel ibo.
10   quid respondere Ruotlieb nunc uis, hera, per m[e?'
dixit 'dic illi nunc de me corde fideli
tantundem liebes, ueniat quantum modo loub[es,
et uolucrum uuunna quot sint, tot dic sibi m[inna,
graminis et florum quantum sit, dic et honor[um.'
15   qui dubitans minime huic illam nubere p[osse
dum se dimitti petit ut mutus subito fit,
et ueluti stupidus loquitur uix ut gemeb[undus
'qualiter acciderit mihi quam male quam uici[ose
me pudet id fari, peius non contigit ulli,
20   nam sigillata misit tibi xenia parua,'
pixiden e caliga trahit in qua sunt ea dona.
quam dum suscepit ab eo properando recedit
adque fenestellam stans soluit pixiden [illam,
in qua subtilem dum cernebat fore pan[num
25   sigillis cum bis binis suimet digitalis
tam bene munitum, quid sit, mirans ea [multum,
sigillis fractis panni nodisque solutis
dum tam preclarum conuinctum uiderat ostr[um,
id pandens cydarim reperitue ligam[ina crurum,
30   que cedidere sibi dum clericus iungitur i[lli.
hec cum uidisset ubi perderet et memi[nisset

XVII.1-31   13 uuunnt? *m.pr.*

She herself brought some very fine wine in a wine-bowl,   1
and sweet mead in golden cups, and standing before him she
asked about the girls in his homeland, what reputation they
had, whether they were beautiful or virtuous.   He smiled
and said "little do I know what you are asking me.   There
is nothing I have meddled in less than noting this kind of
thing, what ladies do;   I leave such a practice to the
womaniser.   If ever I pass by a place where I see ladies
standing around, I bow to them and go where I intended.
Now, what reply do you wish to make through me to Ruodlieb,
my lady?"

She said "tell him that I send him now with a faithful   11
heart as much love as the leaves which have just come,
and as much passion as there are delights in birds, and as
many honours as there are grasses and flowers."

He had little doubt but that she might well marry him.   15
When he asked for leave to go, he was suddenly struck dumb;
then as if covered in confusion he stammered as though very
upset "What has happened to me?   How awful, how terrible!
I am ashamed to say it: a worse thing never happened to any
man;   for he has sent you some little presents, all sealed
up."   He took from his boot a small box containing these
gifts.   She took it and retreated hastily from him to the
window, where she stood and opened the box.   When she saw   24
that in it there was an exquisite cloth so carefully secured
with a double pair of seals marked with his ring, she
wondered greatly what it could be, broke the seals and undid
the knots in the cloth.   Then when she saw a purple cloth,
tied up, she opened that, and found her headband and garters
which she had dropped while the clerk was making love to her.
When she saw them and remembered where she had lost them,

contremit] et pallet, per totum corpus et alget,   M32^v
ignar]us dubitat quin is sit, qui simulabat,
conspexit modo que]m nimis insipienter agentem.
35   'usque pudicam] me plebes omnes habuere'
tractat; uis an]imi cepit firmata reuerti,
ad missum rem]eat, si sciret eumque requirit
munera quid fu]erint que sic signata fuerunt,
num presens fuerit] in pixide cum posuisset.
40   iurauit nosse] per eum quem nil latet haut se
munera, quidquid s]it, mirans cur id rogitarit,
id sigillatum quia] sit quod erat sibi missum.
tunc ait illa 'tu]o dic contribuli uel amico
usquam si nullus] uir plus foret is nisi solus
45   ille uel in dotem] mihi mundum si daret omnem,
nubere nolo sibi,] dic tu ueraciter illi.'
missus ait domine] qui factus tristis ab hac re
'miror cur in e]am deueni suspicionem.
non ego posse qui]dem uideor tibi soluere fraudem,'
50   illa 'tace cito] nunc' ait 'absque uale modo uade.'
nuntius absced]it, ad Ruodlieb reproperatque.
is simulac uid]it subridens dixit ad illum
'quod bene sis potu]s, scio, tractatus saturatus.
qualiter accept]a sint demandamina narra:
55   num bene suscepta], non hesita, sunt mea dona?'
sic dicens gaudet] sese quatiendo cachinnat.
missus respondit] quod amicum perderet ipsi

XVII.32-57   33 ignarus *scripsi*: nec uerus *Laistner*: nec
penitus *Seiler*   34 conspexit modo quem *Laistner*: conscius
oblitum *Seiler*   35 usque pudicam *Laistner*: notitiam de *Seiler*
36 tractat uis *Laistner*: dixit mox *Seiler*   37 ad missum
remeat *Seiler*   38 munera quid fuerint *Seiler*   39 num presens
fuerit *Seiler*   40 iurauit nosse *Seiler*: iurauit per eum rerum
Schmeller   41 munera quidquid sit *Seiler*   42 id sigillatum
quia *Seiler*   47 missus ait domine *Seiler*   48 miror cur in eam
Seiler   49 non ego posse quidem *scripsi*: certo posse quidem
Zeydel   uideor] uidens *Schmeller*   50 illa tace cito *Seiler*
51 nuntius abscedit *Schmeller*: nuntius remeat *Zeydel*   53
quod bene sis potus *Seiler*   54 qualiter accepta *Seiler*   55
num bene suscepta *Seiler*   56 sic dicens gaudet *Seiler*   57
missus respondit *scripsi*: missus ait sibi *Zeydel*

she shuddered, her whole body grew pale, and she felt a   32
chill.   She doubted that the messenger was unaware of them;
he was putting on a show, and she had just seen him acting
most foolishly.   "All the people have so far thought me a
chaste woman" she mused: then she began to regain her
strength of mind, went over to the envoy, and asked him if
he knew what the gifts were that had been sealed up so, and
if he had been there when Ruodlieb put them in the little
box.   He swore by him from whom no secrets are hidden that
he did not know what the gifts were at all, and was puzzled
why she had asked that;   it had been sealed up when it had
been entrusted to him.

Then she said "tell your relation, your friend, even if   43
there were no man left alive anywhere except him, and even if
he were to give me the whole world for my wedding gift, I do
not wish to marry him: you tell him that truthfully."   The
envoy, who was saddened by this turn of events, said to the
lady "I am amazed as to why I have come under your suspicion.   Do
I not seem able to undo any deceit for you?"   She said
"be quiet now, and be off, without my blessing."

The messenger left and hastened back to Ruodlieb.   As   51
soon as he saw him he said to him with a smile "I know that
you have been well treated, and given food and drink;   now
relate how my requests were received.   My gifts were well
accepted, were they not?   Out with it!"   He said this with   56
a smile, and shook with laughter.   The messenger said to
him that he would lose him as a friend

siue petens iterum] tunc se faceret sibi missum.
talia dum spreuit] Ruodlieb sibi serio dixit
60 'dic nunc contribul]is ea dixisset quid herilis
illi quando] meum magnum narraris amorem?'
'quod demandasti sibi cum plenissime dixi $M33^r$
omnino siluit, mihi prandia summa parauit,
apportans uinum satis et super atque medonem.
65 respondere tibi quid uelit cumque rogaui
dixit "dic illi de me de corde fideli
tantundem liebes quantum ueniat modo loubes,
et uolucrum uuunna quot sunt sibi dic mea minna,
graminis et florum quantum sit dic et honorum."
70 quando licentia quo detur mihi uel rogitaui,
obmutui subito uel ei "quid sit mihi" dico,
oblitum simulans tua non sibi dona dedisse.
que dum suscepit de me iubilando recessit.
post modicum rediit nimis indignanter et inquit
75 "dic mihi si nosti quid sint que dona tulisti."
iuraui per eum qui cuncta scit omnipotentem
numquam uidisse penitus quid sint ea scire,
nam sigillatum patuit mihi scire negatum.
tunc ait illa "tuo dic contribuli uel amico
80 usquam si nullus uir plus foret is nisi solus
ille uel in dotem mihi mundum si daret omnem,
nubere nolo sibi, dic tu ueraciter illi."'
Ruo. 'nunc opus est aliam, reor ut, mihi poscere sponsam,
que non furtiue quem suescat amare super me.'

85 sed Ruodlieb mater quodcumque potest operatur
in Christi miseros uiduas orbos peregrinos,
inde merebatur quod Ruodlieb ualde beatur,
namque reuelat ei uelit hunc quam glorificare.
in somnis geminos uice quadam uiderat apros,
90 hos grandisque suum comitatur dente minacum
turba uelut bellum cum Ruodlieb inire minantum:
ille sed utrique caput apro diripit ense,
quodque suum fuerat ferientum strage cadebat.

XVII.58-93 58 siue petens iterum *Zeydel*   59 talia dum
spreuit *Zeydel*   60 dic nunc contribulis *Seiler*   61 illi
quando *Seiler*

184

if he asked him to be his messenger a second time.   58
Ruodlieb passed over these remarks and said to him in a
serious tone "now tell me, my kinsman, what did that young
mistress say when you recounted my great passion to her?"
"When I had told her most fully what you asked of her, she
was quite speechless, and got ready a great meal for me,
bringing plenty of wine, and mead too.   When I asked her
what she wished to reply to you, she said 'tell him that I   66
send him with a faithful heart as much love as the leaves
which have just come, and as much passion as there are
delights in birds, and as many honours as there are grasses
and flowers.'   When I asked that leave be given me to
depart I fell silent all of a sudden and then said 'what
is the matter with me?' pretending that I had forgotten
something and not given her your gifts.   She took them from
me and went away rejoicing.   After a little while she came
back in a terrible temper and said 'tell me if you knew what   75
these gifts are that you've brought!'   I swore by the
almighty, who knows everything, that I had never looked
inside to see what they were, for it was sealed up, and it
was obvious to me that I was not supposed to know.   Then
she said 'tell your kinsman, your friend, even if there was
ever no man left alive anywhere except him, and he were to
give me the whole world for my wedding gift, I do not wish
to marry him - you tell him that truthfully.'"
   "Now I think I need to ask another's hand" said Ruodlieb,
"a lady who will not have a secret lover besides me."
   But Ruodlieb's mother devoted herself in whatever way she   85
could to Christ's poor, widows, orphans, and pilgrims, and by this
she won a mighty blessing for Ruodlieb, for Christ showed her
that he wished to raise him up.   At a certain time she saw a
pair of boars in her dreams, and a great crowd of swine with
menacing tusks went along with them, as though they threatened
to make war with Ruodlieb: but he cut off the head of each
boar with his sword, and cut down all the swine that attacked
him in a great slaughter.

```
        post mater tiliam latam uidet et nimis altam,
95      in cuius summo residere cacumine fulchro
        Ruodlieb cernebat, circa quem plurima stabat          M33^V
        in ramis turba ueluti bellare parata.
        post modicum niuea uenit speciosa columba
        rostro gemmatam preciosam fertque coronam,
100     inponens capiti Ruodlieb mox assidet illi
        sauia figendo, recipit que non renuendo.
        in uisu mater hec cernens premeditatur
        quid queat hoc omne quod uidit significare.
        et quamuis sciret quod honorem pretitularet,
105     inde superbior haut ea fit sed humillima mansit,
        nil sibi sed Domini dans gratuite pietati
        quicquid tantorum Ruodlieb concedat honorum.
        post triduum narrat Deus illi queque reuelat
        de suibus capita quibus abscidit truculenta
110     et de strage suum geminos apros comitantum,
        qualiter in tilie summo uidet hunc residere
        in ramisque suos sub se uidisset alumnos,
        quodque columba sibi ferat aduolitando coronam
        in manibusque sedens sibi dulcia sauia prebens.
115     'hec dum cernebam subito mox euigilabam
        atque pigebat me nimium sic euigilasse.
        id uigilare scio quia signat me morituram
        esse prius rerum ueniat quam finis earum.
        nate recordare quam sepe sua bonitate
120     te Deus adiuuit et ab ipsa morte redemit,
        et quod in exilio multum tibi subueniendo
        sospes uel locuples patriam dat quod repetebas.
        nunc scio maiores nacturus eris quod honores
        et timeo ualde Dominum sic retribuisse
125     nobis ambobus umquam siquid faceremus
        quod placuisset ei, caueas quod dicere, fili.
        nam quid possemus qui nil nisi quod dat habemus?
        sed bene seu male contingat tibi, da sibi grates.'
```

XVII.94-128   101 suauia *Schmeller*   114 suauia *Schmeller*

Then his mother saw a linden-tree, broad and very high, at   94
whose very top she saw Ruodlieb sitting on a couch, and
around him in the branches stood an army as though ready
for war.   After a while a beautiful snow-white dove came
carrying an ornate, bejewelled crown in its beak, and
putting it on Ruodlieb's head it swiftly perched beside him   100
and gave him loving kisses, which he accepted without
refusal.   His mother saw all these things in a vision
and wondered what all that she had seen could portend.
Although she knew that they pointed to honour, she did not
become more proud because of them, but continued to be
very humble, reckoning nothing to herself, but rather
attributing to the gracious favour of the Lord whatever
great honours he might grant to Ruodlieb.
　　Three days later, she told him what God had revealed to   108
her, about the swine whose fierce heads he cut off, and
about the carnage of the swine that accompanied those twin
boars, how she saw him sitting at the top of a linden-tree,
and his followers beneath him in the branches, and that the
dove had flown to him carrying a crown, and sitting in his
hands had offered him sweet kisses of love.   "While I   115
was looking at these things I suddenly woke up, and it
annoyed me greatly that I had woken up.   I know that that
awakening means that I shall die before the end of these
events comes to pass.   My son, remember how often God in
his goodness has helped you and saved you from death itself,
and how by aiding you greatly in your exile he granted that
you should return to your homeland with good health and wealth.
Now I know that you are destined to win yet greater honours,   123
and I am greatly afraid that the Lord has repaid us both
in this way if we ever did things which pleased him.
Beware of saying this, my son.   For what can we do, who
have nothing save what he gives us?   But whether good or
ill befalls you, give thanks to Him."

exiliens et abire uolens salit undique clamans   M34^r
dum lassus cecidit uix spiramenque recepit.
cui uigor ut rediit ad Ruodlieb humillime dixit
'parce mihi misero, scio quod gratum tibi dico.
5   si me non occideris atque manus mihi solues
monstro tibi censum binorum denique regum,
et patris et nati, qui tecum preliaturi:
nomen habet genitor Immunch, sed filius Hartunch.
a te uincuntur ambo per te perimentur.
10   filia sed regis heres tunc sola superstes
regni totius Heriburg, pulcherrima uirgo,
est tibi lucranda sed non sine sanguine magno
ni quod consiliar facias ego quando resoluar.'
Ruodlieb ait nano 'non occidendus es a me,
15   te cito soluissem tibi si confidere possem.
si me non fallis a me sanus remeabis.
quando potens fueris tuimet nil post mihi dices.'
'absit ut inter nos umquam regnauerit hec fraus,
non tam longeui tunc essemus neque sani.
20   inter uos nemo loquitur nisi corde doloso.
hinc nec ad etatem maturam peruenietis;
pro cuiusque fide sunt eius tempora uite.
non aliter loquimur nisi sicut corde tenemus,
neue cibos uarios edimus morbos generantes.
25   longius incolomes hinc nos durabimus ac uos.
non mihi diffidas, faciam mihi quod bene credas,
si mihi diffidas mea coniunx sit tamen obses.'
hanc uocat ex antro que mox processerat illo,
parua nimis pulchra sed et auro uesteque compta,
30   que ruit ante pedes Ruodlieb fundendo querelas,
'optime cunctorum uinclis mihi solue maritum
meque tene pro se donec persoluerit omne.'

XVIII.1-32   5 me] non oc *m.pr.*   9 uincentur *Schmeller*   13
resorue *m.pr.*

XVIII

(The dwarf) leapt up in his desire to leave, jumped about   1
and cried out loud until he fell down exhausted and could
barely catch his breath.   When his strength returned he said
to Ruodlieb in a most humble manner "have pity on a wretch
like me - I'll tell you what I know will please you.   If you
will not kill me and will untie my hands, I will show you the
treasure of two kings, father and son - the father's name is
Immunch, the son's Hartunch - who are going to fight with you.
Both will be defeated by you and will be killed by you.   But
then the king's daughter, Heriburg, will be the only surviving
heir to the whole kingdom.   She is a most beautiful maiden,
and she is to be your prize, though at the cost of much blood-
shed unless you do as I advise you - when I am set free."

Ruodlieb said to the dwarf "I shall not kill you.   I would   14
set you free straightaway if I could trust you.   If you do
not deceive me, then you shall leave me unharmed;   but when
you are your own master, then you will not say anything to me."

"God forbid that this deceit should ever govern our   18
relations!   For we should not be so long-lived, nor so
healthy, if it did.   Among you men, no-one speaks without
evil in his heart.   Because of this you will not grow to
maturity, you men, for the length of a man's life depends on
how much good faith he has.   We only ever speak that which
we hold fast in our hearts, and we do not eat the different
foods that bring about illness.   And so we last to be hale
and hearty much longer than you do.   Do not distrust me: I
shall give you cause to trust me well.   If you do distrust
me - well then let my wife be a hostage."

He called her out from that cave and she came swiftly.   28
She was small, and yet very beautiful, and was dressed in
gold and fine clothes.   She fell down at Ruodlieb's feet
and poured out her grief to him, crying "best of all men,
release my husband from his chains and take me in his place,
until he has finished all this business!"

EPIGRAMMATA

I

$M1^V$

...............mirabilior famulatus
maxima dum] uirtus dinoscitur esse per actus.
ne merito] follis ullum uel stigma sit oris
exoritur] tantus gelidus dum flauero uentus.

II

detinet] ardorem uetat insudando fluorem
nostro Diet]maro nimis hostibus eius amaro.
nam fauet eque] suis dapibus cum deliciosis,
cottidie] uictu procurat eos et amictu,
5   tollit nil met]uens hostes contra nimis enses.

I.2 maxima dum *Zeydel*   3 ne merito *Zeydel*   fallis *Schmeller*
4 exoritur *Schmeller*   II.1 detinet *Zeydel*   2 nostro
Zeydel   Dietmaro *Schmeller*   nimis hostibus eius amaro]
uirtutibus undique claro *m.pr.*   3 nam fauet eque *scripsi*:
seruit uel *Zeydel*   4 cottidie *scripsi*: heros sic *Zeydel*
5 tollit nil metuens *scripsi*: cum uirtute leuens *Zeydel*

EPIGRAMS

I

................(my) service is most wonderful,
since my exceeding great quality is perceived through
my actions.   Deservedly no mark of shame may mar this
bellows' mouth.   Such a great cold wind comes up
whenever I blow.

II

It keeps off the heat, and stops the sweat pouring off
our Dietmar, bitter indeed to his enemies.   This same
object lavishes the finest fare on his own men, giving
them food and clothing day by day, but fearing nothing it
raises his sword fiercely against his enemies.

III

seruio co]ttidie Dietmaro sat studiose
muscas t]errendo culices uespas abigendo,
a se pro]que meo famulamine nil mage posco
quam post] ut pulchre decet utque reseruer honeste.

IV

equus] ostiolo binis effectibus uno,
nam scit] oppositas uisum depromere causas.

V

n]omina [summa pie Dietmaro congero caute.
exuat ut uestes lassos ut frigeret artus
tu cape me, uirgo, uentum stans assiduando,
maxime quo sit opus studeas miniteris ut ictus
ne noceat musca mordendo culix neque uespa.

VI

has uini plenas tecum deferto lagenas,
propter dulcorem si malis, ferto medonem.
seu sis uenatu seu sis alio comitatu
uim lenire sitis si uis prandere ualebis.
ibis et ad curtem si forte potentis herilem
si pincerna libens tunc est tibi sepe propinans
quando domum remeas forsan repleuerit illas,
caupone nummum cupide quod non dabis unum.

III.1 seruio cottidie *Schmeller*   2 muscas *Seiler*   terrendo
Schmeller   3 a se proque *Seiler*   4 quam post *Seiler*:   quam
hoc *Schmeller*   IV.1 equus *Zeydel*   2 nam scit *scripsi*: binas
Zeydel   V.1 *lacunas replevit Zeydel*

III

Daily I serve Dietmar with zeal, frightening the flies,
driving off gnats and wasps, and for my service I ask no
more of him than that afterwards I be kept nicely, as is
fitting and proper.

IV

It is like a little door with a twofold action,
for it can take the image of things held in front of it.

V

I bear the highest names for Dietmar in holiness and with care.
When he takes off his clothes to cool his weary limbs,
you take me, girl, as you stand applying yourself to fanning
him, and work hard when there is need at threatening to
strike a blow so no f_y or wasp may sting and hurt him.

VI

Take with you these bottles full of wine, or take mead if
you prefer it for its sweetness. Whether you are off
hunting or on any other business, you will be able to slake
your thirst if you want, and to eat. And if by chance you
go to the noble court of a powerful man, and the wine-
steward is happy to keep coming to you often, he might perhaps
fill them when you journey home, so you will not pay a
penny to a greedy barmaid.

VII

hec pari uenatum lia dum uadas uehe tecum.
cum mitis inmitem ceruus restinguet ad amnem
tu mitis extingue succensus litis ab igne,
hoc quod ueneris ut eo citius domineris.
5   et si uectabis quid obest quocumque meabis
prandens in pratis quod potes est tibi gratis.
quin ad mercipolim uenies si nummiuoracem,
nil das caupone quod trudat in ima crumene.

VIII

qui tot efilatas ocreas desideret istas
nunquam uendendos melius, denos dato nummos.

IX

O uassalle bone tibi quam bene congruo crure.
hinc operatori dato quod tibi placet uel illi.

X

militis ad gambas operati nos sumus ambas,
algor ut inmensus non se ledat neque uentus.

XI

Tubalcain inuenit cytharam et organa, Pithagoras
testudinem et harpam, David psalterium et rottam,
Boetius monochordum.
en isti quales repererunt sensibus artes
5   ad consolandos in curis mestificatos.
quiddam celeste nam queuis continet in se.
leniri diras h]is scimus demonis iras.

XI.7   leniri diras his *Seiler*: illis *Schmeller*

VII

Take these identical ones with you when you go hunting.
When the stag quenches his thirst at the fast-flowing river,
you can quench yours, burning from the fire of the chase,
so that you can get there more quickly and subdue him.
And if you go travelling, there is nothing to stop you
wherever you go from eating and drinking in the countryside,
as you please.   But if you come to the moneyguzzling town
of the traders, you will give nothing for the barmaid to
stuff to the bottom of his moneybag.

VIII

Whoever would like such finely-made shin-guards as these,
pay ten pennies, which were never better spent.

IX

O faithful vassal, I fit close to your leg as well as any
may.   Pay my maker a price that suits you and him.

X

We were tailored for a knight's two legs, so that harsh
cold and wind might not harm him.

XI

Tubalcain invented the lyre and organ, Pythagoras the lute
and harp, David the psaltery and the vielle, Boethius the
monochord.   Behold, these men discovered such arts for the
senses as may soothe the sad in their woes.   Each art has
something heavenly within it; by these we know how to soften
the foul tempers of demons.

<u>COMMENTARY</u>

<u>Chief Abbreviations</u>:

DuCange = L. Favre (ed.), *DuCange: Glossarium Mediae Et Infimae Latinitatis*, Paris 1938
Latham = R.E. Latham, *Revised Medieval Latin Word-List*, British Academy 1965
LS = C.T. Lewis, C. Short, *A Latin Dictionary*, Oxford 1879
Niermeyer = J.F. Niermeyer, C. van de Kieft, *Mediae Latinitatis Lexicon Minus*, Leiden 1976
OLD = A. Souter and others (eds.), *Oxford Latin Dictionary*, Oxford 1968, etc.
TLL = *Thesaurus Latinae Linguae*, Leipzig 1900-

Where possible, reference is made to OLD and to TLL; but since the purpose of OLD is stated explicitly in its preface to be to 'treat classical latin from its beginnings to the end of the second century AD', and the author of *Ruodlieb*, like most medieval writers, owes a great deal to patristic authors and the writers of later antiquity, LS remains a valuable if not indispensable tool for this work and medieval studies generally.

I.1   <u>a man</u>: it has been of great concern to the various commentators
on *Ruodlieb* that the hero of the poem is not named until Fragment V is reached.   According to Langosch, this is bacause the
poet initially decided to compose a moralistic tale depicting
an ideal knight, and only later altered his strategy to conform
with the then-fashionable style of Romance which required that
characters be named.   Chrétien de Troyes, in *Le Chevalier de
la Charrete*, does not name that hero for over 3,000 verses,
but he does name other characters, and Lancelot's anonymity
is crucial to the story.   For the stress on the hero's
innate nobility, cf. Venantius Fortunatus, *De Launebode* II
8.39-40, *sed quamuis altum teneat de stirpe cacumen/ moribus
ipse suos amplificauit auos*.
Zeydel points out that various words are used to designate the
hero, such as *miles, exul, princeps, missus, internuncius,
tyro, uenator, compar,* and later on *comes*.   On his circumstances, cf. Barber, *The Knight And Chivalry*, p.32: 'the
poor knight was a common feature throughout the Middle Ages,
ranging from the younger son making his fortune...to the old
knight fallen on harsh times.'

2   According to Seiler, phrases in this line (and others, cf. 25,
77, 99, 135) could have been translated from the poet's own
vernacular German, but it seems more probable that the
unusual nature of the phrasing here and elsewhere has been
shaped by the vernacular tradition with which he was familiar
rather than being a direct rendering of the German.

3   <u>is said to have had</u>:   cf. Ovid *F.* 6.434, *seu pius Aeneas
eripuisse datur.*

9   <u>put his life at risk</u>:   this sentiment is common in medieval
epic;   cf. v.20, and also *Roland* LXXIX, vv.1010-1012, *pur
sun seignor deit hom susfrir destreiz/ e endurer e granz chalz
e grant freiz/ si.n deit hom perdre e del quir e del pel* (for
his lord a man must put up with hardship, and endure great
heat and cold - yes, a man must lose life and limb.)

11   <u>faithless fortune</u>:   the phrase *fortuna malefida* is also found
in Boethius, *Cons. Phil.* I Metre 1.17

12   Zeydel regards the change of tense in this verse and elsewhere
as·being for the sake of the metre, but as Dronke shows, the
poet uses the different tenses far more subtly than has often
been supposed;   here the present may imply 'they are always
making promises...'

16   <u>his mother's charge</u>:   the hero of the story is head of his
household, being the oldest male.   There is no mention
of the nature of his father's death anywhere in the poem;
his mother is merely presented as a widow.

17   <u>for a foreign land</u>:   service overseas is a regular feature
of the careers of knights in the Middle Ages;   cf. Marie de
France's *Guigemar* and *Milun*, both of whom see service in
foreign lands.   While this no doubt reflects actual practice,
this device also affords the poet the opportunity of intro-
ducing magical and mysterious events.   Barber notes (*The*

Knight And Chivalry, p.15) that 'it is essential to the
style of the romances that the knight should wander forth in
search of adventures.'

19   a pack: *entheca* is used to mean 'store' by Augustine, and
in later latin denoted a 'reliquiary' or even 'coffin.'   Here
it clearly denotes a kind of trunk, or baggage.

20   to endure hardship: cf. note on v.9 above.   The phrase
recalls Ovid *M*.9.289, *tolerare labores*.

23   to store provisions: *annone* is written above *ad fodrum*
and is clearly a superior reading, though no correction
mark appears in the MS.

26   at his side: Seiler's conjecture *accinctus* makes the best
sense, though the MS seems to have ....*ictus*.   The
corruption is explicable.

27   a griffin's claw: reference to griffins in writers of
antiquity is rare: cf. Sidonius Apollinaris *C*.22.66, 67
and Claudian, *IV.Cons.Hon*. 30.   In the Middle Ages they
are commonly found in heraldic devices, represented as an
eagle with four legs, wings, and a beak (cf. Fox-Davies,
A Complete Guide To Heraldry, p.167).

30   Zeydel regards this passage as being 'of value in showing how
knights were accoutered in 1050', but this leaves little to
the poet's own creative powers of imagination.   Although
Ruodlieb does not occupy a particularly exalted position in
the society described by the poet, there may yet be a touch
of idealism in the description here.
with pure gold: *obrizo* is late latin, found in the Vulgate.

34   washed with soap: OLD lists *semegma* as 'ointment, cleansing
preparation'; DuCange attests the form *smegma*.

39   a bottle: *uas* is used in its classical sense here (OLD 1a,
'container for liquids').   In medieval latin the word has a
wide variety of applications, as Niermeyer makes clear: 1)
'arms','weapons'; 2) 'sarcophagus'; 3) 'church-bell'; 4)
'baptismal font'; 5) 'vessel', 'ship'; 6) 'sheaf'; 7)
'barn'!
resin: cf. Isidore of Seville, *Orig*.17.8.7, *mastix arboris
lentisci gutta est*.

43   its master: on the interchangeability of *ille* and *iste* in
this work, see Introduction, 'Linguistic Features'.

52   after him: see note below on VIII.125 on the use of *post*
here and in v.54.

53   Braun (p.96) adduces a similar scene to this from Venantius
Fortunatus VI.5, especially vv.37ff.: *tum gemitu fit maesta
domus, strepit aula tumultu/ reginae fletu plorat et omnis
honor/ in populi facie lacrimarum flumina sordent.....*
The portrayal of the mother is much more subtle here, however;
she is careful not to let her grief be seen by the peasantry.
The psychological handling of the characters is very skilful.

58   grief in her heart: the phrase *corde dolorem* is also found
in Sidonius, *C*.XI.64.

60   There is a paragraph mark in the margin next to this verse.

62	the fact that: *quod* must have this sense here, as the following clauses show.
63	feuds: *faidas* is underlined faintly in red in the MS.
65	The syntax in this verse is perplexing: what appears to start out as an accusative-infinitive construction with *se* ends up as a dependent clause with *clientet*; *ipse* or *sibi* would have been preferable. If *clientet* is to be taken with *sicubi, se* is superfluous. Even this poet cannot have taken it as a nominative.
70	nor to desire his death: the sentiment is biblical, and frequent in the Psalms; cf. Ps.27.3.
71	This line is very blurred in the MS, and is copied out at the top of the page in Docen's hand.
75	the stranger: *exul*, as Langosch points out, is used in this work as an exact equivalent of MHG *recke*, 'exile' (as I translate it later), 'stranger', and also 'a man with a small company' (cf. I.80) and 'a fighting man' (cf. I.82).
79	as is often the case: a very delicate and unobtrusive example of *interiectio ex persona poetae*.
80	if he is an envoy: note the skilful handling of the huntsman's thoughts from a psychological viewpoint; the sense of mystery . is heightened by his rhetorical questions.
82	poor in power: *posse* is used here as an indeclinable noun, balancing the phrase *uirtutis opime*.
89	foreign to me as it is to you: the king's generosity to strangers marks him from the outset as standing in the ideal Christian tradition: cf. Venantius Fortunatus VI. 3.17, *si nouus adueniat, recipis sic mente benigna*, for an earlier literary expression of this Christian duty.
92	since: Schmeller's reading *quo* is a misreading of the abbreviation in the MS. Seiler says that *quo* is the regular abbreviation for *quoniam*, and Cappelli lists it from the 8th century onwards. Zeydel thinks that the phrase *quoniam si* is equivalent to German *insofern*.
93	a good omen: the use of the genitive *felicis ominis* is unusual. Cf. I.106, below.
95	One or more lines have been lost before this v. at the top of M4^r.
	the man: *quit* must be understood in the second part of the verse, i.e. *dic, quid hic dare [quit]?* The disjointed word-order may not be clumsiness, but an attempt by the poet to portray realistic conversation.
99	put to the test: cf. *probo* OLD 5.
100	when wheeled about: *gyro* is post-Augustan and very rare (so LS); cf. Vegetius, *Vet*.3.5, *animal difficile se gyrabat*.
103	without measure: there is a possible biblical reminiscence from Luke 6.38, *eadem mensura*.
104	exalts: cf. the Vulgate, Jac. 2.13, *superexaltat autem misericordia iudicium*, for the use of *superexalto*.
106	especial delicacy: the genitive is dependent on *quicquid*.
107	Again, the use of the genitive is unusual; cf. above, v.93.

108	a pact of faith: the MS here has a rare diphthong, *foedus,* but *fedus* is the spelling found elsewhere.
110	The bond entered into here is one of *cumpagniunage,* perhaps best known in medieval literature from the comradeship of Roland and Oliver in the *Chanson de Roland.* This involves oaths of loyalty and sharing in mutual troubles, as well as a kind of mutual vassaldom, as v.121 below makes clear.
112	or better: cf. the German construction *es besser kann.*
113	trusted him and said to him: note the non-reflexive medieval use of *sibi,* here juxtaposed with *illum.*
114	you mean well: *uelle* is used as an abstract noun, like *posse* in v.82 above.
118	you even guessed: *coniciebas* has the MHG gloss *rat* in the right-hand margin.
119	Again, there are some verses missing from the top of M4^v. In the right-hand margin, written vertically, are the words *attinet monasterio Tegernnsee.*
122	explained: for *dispono* in this sense cf. Niermeyer 11.
128	us: i.e. *nobis.* The king often uses the plural of majesty.
130	chasing after: on *post* used in this way, cf. VIII.125 and note.
131	as though to a friend: this whole scene is idyllic compared with the situation that Ruodlieb has left behind; the king's actions illustrate the truth of what the huntsman has said.
135	blessed: for *beatus* in this Christian sense, cf. Vulgate Ps.1.1, Mt.5, and MHG *saelec.*
139	retinue: *clientela* is found as early as Caesar and Sallust in this sense with reference to foreign peoples (OLD).
140	he held: *qui* must be the exile, Ruodlieb; his hound has already been mentioned, in vv.44ff.

II

1	This herb: *buglossa* is mentioned in a handbook on fishing from a later period, but also from Tegernee, as a lure for fish. Pliny says of it only *cui praecipuum quod in uinum deiecta animi uoluptates auget, et uocatur euphrosynum* (*HN* 25.40; cf. Isidore XVII.9.49).
4	into the water: *aquis* is presumably dative; one would expect *in aquam.*
5	can no longer stay: again, the syntax is terribly disjointed: what begins as accusative-infinite ends with a *quod*-clause, with the conditional clause spliced between them. In the margin is the gloss *feruentem,* presumably to explain *aquam.*
7	threw there: in classical latin *dilapido* strictly took the accusative; cf. OLD 1 'to pelt with stones'.
8	Note the lack of conjunctions between this verse and those following.
17	to roast: *assare* occurs as early as Apuleius, *M.*2.10.
20	asked the king: the poet makes clear which speech belongs to which character by noting either *rex* or *uen.* in the margin. Zeydel staggeringly makes these part of his hexameters.
	seines: *sagenis* differ from *retibus* in that they are dragged through the water from a boat: cf. Vulgate, Mt.13.47.

22   at no expense: the nearest usage to this of *gratum* is in
DuCange: *"gratum facere" est debitum soluere, satisfacere
officio, uel id quod alicui gratum est.*

26   After this verse a line is drawn across the page in the MS,
and the sign β appears in the left-hand margin.

34   that was born blind: the reference must be to animals which
only gain their sight after birth; dogs of course come into
this category. The blindness induced by the herb might be
temporary, as *obcaeco* was weakened in late latin. Cf. Itala
Mt.24.29, *sol occaecabitur,* which the Vulgate renders *sol
obscurabitur,* and also Vulgate Sirach 25.24.

37   wolves: *hirpus* is late latin, not in OLD, but is found in
Servius *ad Verg.A.*11.785(LS).

39   in the shade: *sub tegmine fagi* is from Vergil, *E.*1.1.

51   Note how the author himself sides with one kingdom in his
narration from this point onwards.

52   borderers: *marhmanni* is found in Niermeyer as 'a marcher,
habitant of a border region'. Given the unsettled state of
11th century Europe, the situation described here is little
short of idyllic. A harsher reality is shown by HEMOLD.
Lib.I.56, *marcomannos oportet duram habere patientiam* (ref.
in Niermeyer). The *Marcomanni* were a Teutonic tribe.

57   kith and kin: i.e. *compatres.* The translation here is of
necessity expanded. The word is listed in Niermeyer as 1)
'godfather'; 2) steadfast friends. Latham gives the sense
'fathers of the church'. Like German *gevatter* the word had
a wide semantic range. Cf. also XII.3, *commater.*

58   lasted: *duruit* is strictly from *duresco,* and has been confused with *duro,* as Zeydel points out.

59   bonds of peace: the sentiment is biblical; cf. Eph.4.3,
uinculo pacis.

60   the hater of our peace: the reference is to the devil, and
to the parable of the wheat and the tares in Mt.13.24ff.
The present tense shows that this is the poet's own general-
isation. *zizania* is n.pl. in the Vulgate; cf. Mt.13.25.

63   he prevailed: I prefer to take *quo succedente* to refer back
to *exosor pacis* with Seiler and Langosch, as against Zeydel's
quo (semine) succedente, 'this seed grew up'.
a great war: *uuerra* (O.Fr. *guerre,* MHG *werra*) is a medieval
word, attested first in 858 AD by Niermeyer.

64   market-place: *mercatus* is 4th decl. in classical latin; the
2nd decl. form found here is late (TLL lists Jerome *In Ier.*
6.18.6, Prudentius *Apoth.* 710 V^2P^2, with abl. in *-o* and *-is*
and acc. *-os*).

65   because: *pace* Zeydel, *quia* is explanatory of v.64, not a
'mere filler'.

III

5   by the legs: this punishment was normally reserved for Jews
(so Zeydel).

12   like a lamb: The imagery is proverbial and biblical: cf.
Is.53.7, *quasi agnus ... se obmutescet* and the *Agnus Dei,*
and also Prov. 19.12, *sicut fremitus leonis ita et regis ira.*

21	**he may see**: *cernat* has its object in *suam gentem* and also governs *in periculum*; the writing is very skilled.
24	**on their way rejoicing**: the sentiment is biblical. Cf. Act. 8.39 for the sense; the usual biblical phrase is *gaudio magno*.
28	**took back**: the sense is perhaps similar to OLD *reseruo* 4, 'keep alive, intact'.
40	Of the many supposed similarities between *Ruodlieb* and *Waltharius* proposed by Strecker, only two are anything more than coincidental. One is a parallel to this scene, in vv.215ff.: *ecce palatini decurrunt arce ministri/ illius aspectu hilares equitemque tenebant/ donec uir sella descenderet inclitus alta/ si bene res uergant tum demum forte requirunt/ ille aliquid modicum narrans intrauerat aulam/ lassus enim fuerit regisque cubile petebat.* The similarity lies not in the words but in the whole visual image being conveyed. The other parallel passage is with III.59ff., below.
42	**left it at that, adding nothing**: the latin conveys the haste of the messenger and the disjointed phrases he utters as he brushes past the crowd on his way to the king.
43	**handed his sword**: Zeydel claims that he gives up his sword because he is an ambassador; but since he is the king's own servant (and presumably unlikely to be hostile) this action seems more likely to be a part of court etiquette.
46	There are some corrections in the MS here. Zeydel says, in discussion of this verse,'*dic* is over *inque*, which is underlined, i.e. deleted.' However, *faidas* at I.63 is underlined but no correction is appended, and at I.23 *annone* is written over *ad fodrum* but with no underlining. The scribe is not consistent in his practice, and I have decided to treat all superscripts as corrections, underlined or not.
59	Cf. *Waltharius* 140, *quod uolo plus factis te quam cognoscere dictis*, and note on vv.40ff. above.
63	**a good reward**: proverbial. Cf. *Nibelungenlied* 242.4, *des mac man sôlhiu rîchen frouwen gerne sagen*, 'such gifts make men eager to tell news to noble ladies'.
66	**from the balcony**: so Niermeyer, *cancellus* 3, but *per* is odd; perhaps the sense 'over the balustrade' is what the poet is trying to convey.
68	**not only in words**: cf. above, v.59 and note, for a similar phrase.
IV	
5	**say, horses finely shod**: the syntax is again confused. *est ut* has the force 'like unto' (Zeydel equates it with MHG *ist daz*). In v.7, *ad quod* presumably refers to the whole question of what to send. Note that *auxilium* and *consilium* are required in this feudal setting.
6	**finest mottled squirrel-skins**: *crisis* is a variant of *grisis*. Cf. Bernard of Clairvaux Ep.2.11, *uaria griseaque pellicea*. *uaricosis* is an odd word to use; *uariegatis* might be expected. Cf. also O.Fr. *vair*, and Beroul, *Tristan* 1200,

where the leper taunts Iseut with the prospect of living
without *o vair, o gris et o baudor*; and *Nibelungenlied* 59.4
dô gap man sînen degenen ze kleidem grâ unde bunt, 'of
vari-coloured squirrel'. The *pellicium* was short, and could
have red edging (cf.X.124); the *crusina* was longer (cf.XIV.
91) and could also be trimmed (X.126) and lined (XIV.97).

7   After *quid* there is an erasure in the MS.

8   replied: the mood of the vassals seems to be positive, but
in fact they defer judgement to the *philosophus* of v.11, who
then defers back to the king himself, who is thus given the
right to make the decision personally (v.17).

12   This line has the marginal gloss *ad ub loc*. Zeydel thinks
this stands for 'any place'; it might rather stand for
aduerb. locum, i.e. 'note the adverbial use of *a recto quoque*.

15   with the king's wishes: there is a similarity between the
phrase *in regis uelle* and MHG *an sînen willen stan*.

20   to them: *sibi* again is used unreflexively. On *post*, see
VIII.125 and note.

22   terms: *legamina* is a late latin variant of the usual *ligamina*:
so TLL 2, PS-CYPR., and Cassiodorus *Var*.7.47.3, *Inst*.1.32

26   homage: feudal terminology is frequent in this section. Note
that *seruio* is here used as Niermeyer 1, 'perform service as
a vassal.'

32   conclude this: cf. v.119 below. *induciari* is a medieval
word, not in OLD or LS.

35   if you desire: the vocabulary and style of this speech are
courtly, very formal and heavily stylised.

38   frontier: *clausura* is attested only in *Ruodlieb* in this
sense: it normally means 'fence' or 'barrier'.

45   chamber: *caminata* is medieval, found from Alcuin onwards.

48   finest wine: the *trinkgeld* is a frequent feature of this
poem (cf. XIV.14). Cf. *Nibelungenlied* 126.4, *dô hiez man
den gesten scénken den Gúnthéres win*, 'word was given to
pour out Gunther's wine in greeting'.

49   permission: *licentia* here is used in the sense 'leave of
absence' or 'leave to do something'. The envoys' rising
is a mark of respect; cf. *Nibelungenlied* 1780, where
Hagen refuses to do so in Kreimhild's presence.

52   as if to a father: as Braun notes, *rex maior* is the ideal
Christian king, and as such stands in a line that goes back
as far as David and the Old Testament heroes via the
Christian poets of late antiquity. Cf. Venantius Fortunatus
V.1.86, *ut pater et rex sit nullum grauet erigat omnes* and
92-95, *unde alii peccant ignoscendo iste triumphat/ doctus
enim quoniam prima est in principe uirtus/ esse pium quia
semper habet qui parcere nouit/ corrigit ipse prius quod
poscit ut alter emendet*.

56   of your own volition: *ultronee* is late latin: cf. Vulgate,
Ex.25.2.

59   ready: *promptus* with genitive is late and rare (LS).

61   as was decided: *laudatum* in this sense is attested in
Niermeyer 11 *laudo*, and the example from 1090 given in

Rosell. no.218, *per terminos quos ambo laudabunt.* *tu*
refers to the king, who speaks through his envoys. Cf. *de
te* at V.182 below.

65   they replied for their part: the same phrase is at v.8, above.

68   viceroy: *uicedomnus* usually refers to the clerical function-
ary appointed by an abbot; perhaps the man in question here
is a kind of clerk. Cf. also Cassiodorus *Var*.5.14, where
it is used to designate the king's representative in the
Ostrogothic kingdom.

69   fiefs: Niermeyer limits this word *benefacere* to the granting
of fiefs. Perhaps the envoys were given seigneurial rights
over lands in *rex minor's* kingdom, to strengthen the links
between the two realms further.

70   agent: in Horace *AP* 170, *prouisor* = 'caretaker'; here it is
like Niermeyer 8, 'manorial agent'.

85   whose eye is ever watchful: the image derives from Isidore of
Seville, XII.215, *cum dormierint, uigilant oculi;* cf. also
Theobaldus, *Physiologus* I.10, *et quotiens dormit, sua nunquam
lumina claudit.*

92   feudal service: *seruimen* is a medieval word, and is the
equivalent of O.Fr. *vassalage.*

93   removed his crown: again, this is a courtly gesture, a mark
of respect. Cf. Einhard, *Vita K.M.* 23, where Charlemagne
is said to have worn his crown especially *in festiuitatibus.*

94   sat down: note the scansion. Strictly it should be
residens.

95   his people: *suates* appears to be a neologism.

103   wealthy margraves: cf. v.130, below. There is a gap after
locupletibus in the MS, and the mark ⴴ, = *rectificandum,*
something the poet appears to have omitted to do here.

116   it was your pleasure: for *laudo* see note on v.61, above.
It resembles MHG *geloben,* 'decide' or 'vow'.

117   adjourn: so Niermeyer 6. For the alternative meaning of
inducio, 'to decide', cf. v.32, above.

120   early in the morning: *in* would not be necessary in classical
writing, where plain ablative is used to denote time 'when'.

128   were sent for: see note on VIII.125 for this use of *post.*

130   mighty protector: *summique patroni* is gen. sing., as Laistner
pointed out. *patronus* is noted in a wide range of feudal
usages by Niermeyer, and also by OLD 2c 'guardian', 'defender'.

136   ready service: *famulamen* is a medieval latin word, noted
by Niermeyer from 1003 in *D.Heinrichs II* no.44.

141   Zeydel points out that the moral here is proverbial. Cf. also
in the bible I Thess.5.15, I Pet.3.9, and Rom.12.17, *nulli
malum pro malo reddentes; prouidentes bona non tantum coram
Deo sed etiam coram omnibus hominibus.* Note also that
faciens is used instead of the gerund, 'by his actions'.

142   make known: *rescio* is attested only in Gellius 2.19.4 by LS.

143   incomparable: *inequiparabile* is listed by TLL only in Gildas
c.67 chr.3 p.64, *talis species inaequiparabilisque pulchritudo.*

145   pardon: *uenia* here is the equivalent of MHG *genâde* (Zeydel).

154   in Christ's stead: the theological aspect of kingly rule is paramount here. Cf. also Benedict, *Regula* 2.1, *abbas, qui praeesse dignus est monasterio...Christi...agere uices in monasterio creditur.*

156   shield of your good faith: cf. Vulgate Eph.6.16, *scutum fidei.*

158   appointed places: cf. v.61 above for this use of *laudo.*

159   for our part: *de* is either used to designate origin, as OLD 11, Petronius 44.10 *tamquam unus de nobis*, or else a word like *regionibus* must be supplied, to go with *nostris.*

161   furs: *chrusennis* is underlined in red: did the poet intend to provide a gloss? The same phenomenon is found at I.61.

162   Gertrude: this is the oldest reference in literature to St. Gertrude as the saint of peace. Cf. Grimm, *Deutsche Mythologie,* for the later phenomenon of *Gertrudenminne.*

163   he kissed us: these kisses, like those in v.167 and elsewhere in the poem, are part of the court ceremonial. Cf. the same gesture in the *Nibelungenlied* 297.3-4.

166   gave us leave: *condonans* seems to be used absolutely here. *prouisorem* is the object of *simul et dans.* It is not found in this sense in classical latin, but cf. OLD 1c 'to permit' and Plautus *Bacc.*1143. TLL gives the equivalent *remittere.*

170   proper and upright conduct: *disciplinate* conveys one of the poet's ideal concepts for good behaviour.

171   purity of heart: the phrase is Pauline from 2 Cor.1.12, *in simplicitate cordis et sinceritate Dei.*

173   rejoiced at this report: *ouo* takes genitive here, like MHG *sich vröuwen:* in classical latin it takes ablative or a noun-clause (so TLL). Cf. also V.563.

175   looking up to heaven: the concept is biblical, though the Vulgate has *asspiciens* at Mt.14.19, etc.

182   arrangement: cf. above on vv.32 and 119 for *inducio.*

184   Dronke, *(Poetic Individuality* p.43) regards this passage as illustrating a 'lack of diplomacy on Ruodlieb's part', first by rebuffing the lesser king haughtily (v.223) and then trying to cover this error up in a cynical little joke (v. 226). He then takes vv.228-9 to illustrate 'a flash of cruelty' on the king's part. As an envoy, however, Ruodlieb would have been in no position either to accept the stakes immediately, or to be dogmatic in his refusal: it was a point of honour not to take gifts from a defeated foe (cf. note on V.158), and immediate acceptance might have given the impression that Ruodlieb would bow to pressure. Repeated refusals might equally have given the king grounds for breaking off negotiations. The envoy steers a course between the two extremes, and is rewarded to boot. Seen in this light the remarks in vv. 228-230 are not 'cruel' but rather a little joke he shares with his trusted vassal.

187   repeatedly: this brings out the force of *crebro ludo.* The game of chess arrived in Europe in the late 10th or early 11th century, through contact with the Moslems. First mentioned

in the will of a nobleman of Barcelona from 1010, it rapidly
became popular with the aristocracy.   The present passage
is valuable in assessing its introducion into northern
Europe.   See further H.J.R. Murray, *A History Of Chess*,
London 1913; and H.M. Gamer, 'The Earliest Evidence Of Chess
In Western Literature: The Einsiedeln Verses', *Speculum*
XXIX.   A similar scene to this one occurs in the Old French
epic *Gormont Et Isembard*.   Chess is also noted as a pastime
of Charles' men in the *Roland,* v.112, *e as eschecs li plus
saive et li veill.*

192   for me: = *post me*.   Cf. note on VIII.125.   'Carefully' =
       satis.   I take *que dixi* to be a part of the speech, and
       not as parenthetical.

200   poor me: *miserum me* is a phrase found in the comic poets:
       cf. Plautus *Mos*.739 and Terence *Hec*.205, and also Ovid *M*.1.651.

202   if fortune is pleased: the verse is vaguely similar to
       Vergil *A*.12.183.

211   laid a wager: for this use of *depono*, cf. OLD 7b, and Vergil
       E.3.29-31, *ego hanc uitulam.....depono*.

212   a pea: DuCange on this particular reading says that it is a
       'locutio Germanica *niht eine bône*, res minimi pretii.'

226   I refused: = *lorifregi*, which is glossed in the margin
       zugilprechoto, 'I resisted'.

227   presents: for *commoda* in this sense, cf. OLD 4, LS III.2.b.

229   so well-heeled: probably a proverbial saying, lit. 'your
       boots are stitched so well.'

232   as was their due: = *ad honorem*, like MHG *nâch êren*.

233   to return as cavalry: it appears that their rank is changed
       on their homecoming.   Niermeyer renders *equester* as 'squire'
       but gives the adj. *equestris* the meaning 'knightly'.

239   very fine in stature: lit. 'having equal feet'.

242   combat: *duello* and *bello* are not synonymous here as they are
       is classical latin (cf. OLD, LS), unless the poet is being
       crass for the sake of his rhyme; Niermeyer's refs. imply
       that *duello* was used to designate 'judicial combat'.

246   like their masters: = *sibi*.   The lax use of this word brings
       some confusion here.

247   dukes: *satrape* and *duces* are synonymous, as Laistner conject-
       ured.

252   clerks: *scioli* is not found before Jerome, *Ep*.48.18, 58.5,
       125.16, and is used by him pejoratively to mean 'smatterer'.
       In medieval times the word gained a non-pejorative use, as here.

V
1   court: Ford's conjecture *cancellis lata* is based on III.66
       and V.163, but since the court here described is more of
       a camp, and not a permanent fixture, I prefer *militibus*.
       This scene has been claimed to derive from an eye-witness
       report of the meeting of Henry II with Robert of France in
       1023 (so Langosch).   Braun and Dronke both point out
       details in the story which cast doubt on the idea that any
       direct reporting is present here, but the historical anteced-
       ent may have shaped the poet's thought.   See introduction,

6   a path: *podismum* is glossed *gang*. OLD translates the word as 'an area of ground' (from inscriptions only); LS and DuCange give the sense 'a pacing out'. Niermeyer gives only this reference with the meaning 'walkway'.

7   a pavilion: so called bacuse its flaps were spread out like the wings of a butterfly.

11   daily services: = *sinaxis,* which is glossed *cursus uel hora.*

13   more hurriedly: despite his devotion, the king is concerned to get on with the business of the day!

18   embraced him: cf. above, note on IV.163.

20   it should please you: = the polite but firm *ne uelis.*

23   note the odd tenses here - futures would make the sense flow more smoothly.
brought to a close: *adbreuio* is found in the Vulgate, Is.10.22, and Rom.9.28.

28   a single word: = *penitus,* an odd adverb to use.

30   according to their rank: so Niermeyer *ordo* 15, 'rank', 'degree', 'grade': full court etiquette is being observed.

31   his special affection: = *amor ipsus.* This form of *ipse* is found in the comic poets: cf. Plautus *Am.*252*, Mos.*634; Terence *Eu.*546*, Hec.*344.

32   all the clergy: note the powerful role played by the church in this event, reflecting the importance of the Cluniac monasteries, of one of which the poet was a member.

36   by my order: *demando* in classical latin means 'hand over to' or 'to charge (a person)' (OLD); Niermeyer lists the copious variant meanings it acquired in the Middle Ages.

39   may be of one mind: = the barbarous *sint...concordantes.*

47   beneath whose shield: the sentiment is biblical; cf. Gen. 15.1, Ps.5.12, Prov.30.5, and also note on IV.156 above.

49   for us: = *hinc.*

51   even if we refused: = *omnibus inuitis.*

58   this business of ours: *istuc* strengthens *id,* as in the comic poets. The MS *istic* would have to be adverbial, 'there', which jars against *huc,* and gives inferior rhyme. A simple scribal error accounts for the correction.

67   how I treated them: the subjunctive *tractarem* denotes the quality of the behaviour.

70   steadfast friends: see note on II.57, above.

72   an oath: *iuramentum* is post-classical (LS).
by either party: *neutrim* is otherwise unattested.

75   friends: the singular *amicus* is used for the plural, and maintains the rhyme. In view of what follows, *quisque* must refer to the kings.

76   laid out: the subject *rex minor* must be understood with *disponit.* Schmeller printed *disponunt,* but the singulars continue as far as v.100. The sense is obscure at this point; it only becomes clear which king this is later on.

81   thirty: = *bis decapenta.* Cf. introduction, 'Linguistic Features', on the poet's use of Greek words. The order in

which the animals are presented recalls that in Isidore, XII.
1 and 2, where the *pecora* come first, then the *bestiae*.

88   melody: *neumas* is underlined in red; cf. on IV.161.

95   taking their lovely hands: *consertis* is better than *insertis*
(see refs. in LS).

96   stamped very carefully: the impression given is humorous, one
of very heavy-footed bears trying to be graceful. *calco* is
normally used in a bad sense, 'tread down'.
growling very softly: DuCange adds to the one ref. in LS
'in carmine Philom. pro *trissat hirundo* alii legunt *trinsat*'
and also Anselm. *De Re Gramm.* 'anseres trinsiunt'. Zeydel
draws attention to the Bavarian word *trensen*, a kind of gentle
lowing. Dronke translates it 'make gentle murmurs'. Perhaps
the phrase is paradoxical, like *calcant pedetemptim*.

99   lynx: what follows is very close to Pliny, *HN*.37.3.13, 52:
De lyncurio proxime dici cogit auctorum pertinacia, quippe,
etiamsi non electrum id esse contendunt lyncurium, tamen gemmam
esse uolunt, fieri autem adfirmant ex urina quidem lyncis, sed
et genere terrae, protinus eo animali urinam operiente, quoniam
inuideant homini, ibique lapidescere. Esse autem, qualem in
sucinis, colorem igneum, scalpique nec folia tantum aut stra-
menta a se rapere, sed aeris etiam et ferri lamnas, quod
Diocli cuidam Theophrastus quoque credit. Ego falsum id totum
arbitror nec uisam in aeuo nostro gemmam ullam ea appellat-
ione. Cf. also Ovid, *M*.15.413-415, *lyncas dedit India*
Baccho/ e quibus ut memorant quidquid uesica remisit/
uertitur in lapides et congelat aere tacto.

102   jacinth: *ligurius* is found in the Vulgate, Ex.28.19, 39.12.

105   barrel: *butina* is like German *bütte*, English *butt*.

107   a drill: Latham attests *terebello* only from 1310, 1373.

131   cropped: *murcus* is very rare: Niermeyer gives only this
reference, and TLL lists 'GLOSS V.371,19 = *curtus*; Loewe,
Gloss.nom.141 = *truncatus, i.q. curtus* (fort. *vox castrensis*)
Amm. 15,12,3.'

132   baboon: *catta marina* = German *Meerkatz*.

139   ....: *alatis* can be seen clearly in the MS, though whatever went before it has been erased. I have preferred to
leave the MS reading intact; it is possible that there has
been some confusion with the adjective found in Vergil *A*.4.
259, Ovid *F*.3.416, 5.666, where it refers to Mercury's winged
feet. Seiler prints *retalatis* but gives only '?' as an
explanation of it! I wonder if the poet himself was at a
loss to know exactly what to write at this point; from v.185
the sense ought to be 'decorated with gold'. This may be
another example of an unfinished correction in the MS.

152   let your majesty: the subjunctive *reuisat* shows that the
speech continues to the end of the verse, not ending after
id fiat, as Ford punctuates.

156   remember: = *esset*.

158   accept nothing: note that gifts are to be refused from the
vanquished foe, as frequently occurs in the *Nibelungenlied*:

cf.316.2-3 *den sînen vîenden wart daz kunt getan/ ir goldes gerte niemen, daz si dâ buten ê*, 'it was announced to their enemies that no-one wanted the gold they offered', and also 1457, 1458, where Etzel's envoy Werbel is similarly ordered not to accept gifts from those to whom he is sent out of consideration for his lord's reputation. Cf. also above, note on IV.184.

161   shared in a drink: *miscendo* used either as LS IB2 'prepare a drink' or IIB1 'share in'. See also note on IV.48.

163   lattices: see note above on I.52.

169   There is a long gap in the MS between *connexus* and *lince*.

173   jackdaw: *monedula* has the MHG gloss *taha* in the margin.

174   let all these gifts: the visual style of the narrative is noteworthy, and would have given scope for dramatic gestures if the poem was intended to be recited.

179   lesser officials: *ministerialis* later came to denote a knight who entered a lord's service but remained officially unfree in status. The father of Wolfram von Eschenbach, the author of *Parzival*, was one such.

181   so superior: for *superexalto,* cf. Vulgate, Jac.2.13.

183   to each of the twelve: *det* is presumably subjunctive after *quin*, like *donet*. 'Bishops and abbots' is inferred from v.3, above. A line is drawn below this verse in the MS; perhaps another verse amplifying *duodenorum* was to have been added.

191   the brothers: as is clear also in v.210, the author lays some emphasis on the monks, perhaps betraying his own status.

194   counsellors: Niermeyer lists the forms *symmystes, symmysta, summista*. The word can also mean 'associate' or 'companion'.

196   blasting their advice: I follow Ford's exegesis of this peculiar phrase, in his article in *Classica Et Medievalia* 25 (1964) p.202. Grimm interpreted it as meaning 'the sound of acorns blowing in the breeze' or perhaps 'earrings like acorns'; Laistner proposed that *ueluti glandes* was in fact a homonym-like variant for *clandestino*, 'das keinen reim gibt' (*Anzeiger* p.96). Seiler thought it meant something like 'whizzing bullets'; it certainly does not mean 'sea-shells' (as Zeydel wishes it to). Laistner's proposal is not more than a shot in the dark; Zeydel's is based on Langosch's rendering 'rauschen wie Muscheln', from Loewenthal's observation in *Studien zur lateinischen Dichtung des Mittelalters*, pp.132-3, that *glans* is in some sources glossed *balanus* (= Gk. βάλανος) which can mean either 'acorn' of 'a type of shell-fish'. Seiler and Ford take *glandes* to be the object of *flant*. For *glans* used in this sense, cf. TLL II B 1a, and TLL IIIA; cf. also Vergil, *A*.7.686, and Sidonius *C*.23.347, etc.

197   weighty reward: cf. *Nibelungenlied* 242.4, cited on III.63.

212   these men are zealous servants: Dronke takes this to imply that the lesser king is not a Christian. Cf. note on XIII.42, about the topography of the story.

216   whether: *an* is used like *siue*, as in Ovid *RA* 797, etc.

221   to travel: Latham attests *patrio* from 'c.1121'.

222   their own territory: lit. 'under their own jurisdiction'.

223   Ruodlieb: Laistner (*Anzeiger* p.72) did not think that the name was in the original hand: 'hier ist das Wort *R.* von moderner Hand, wahrscheinlich Docens', and elswhere said it was 'unecht'; but recent examination of the MS suggests that his doubts were unfounded. The correction appears to be a part of the author's own revision-process.

228   clerk: on *sciolus* see note on IV.252. The phrase *susceptaque dice* is puzzling: Zeydel renders it 'taking the scroll', Ford 'Ruodlieb took the letter', but none of the dictionaries lists any feminine noun *dicis* or *dix*, and it is unlikely that the poet has intended the imperative of *dico*, which he uses correctly elsewhere.

229   the message: *breuis* is like German *Brief*.

240   the widow and the orphans: this biblical injunction (*religio munda et immaculata apud Deum et patrem haec est, uisitare pupillos et uiduas in tribulatione eorum*, Jac.1.27; cf. Deut. 14.29,16.11, 14, 26.12) is illustrated again by the host at VII.1ff., by Ruodlieb's mother at XIII.68ff. and XVII.86ff., and even (reluctantly) by the mean old man at VI.31ff. It figures as a mark of virtue in many of the Saints' lives.

259   before: see refs. in LS *prae* IA; *pre* here has the same force as *aduersus* does in the Vulgate, as at Ps.22.5, for example.

265   for his mother alone: the ambiguity is present in the latin as well as the English.

268   who were there: = *quin quod fuit*.

271   upright conduct: *moris* resembles MHG *zuht* (Zeydel).

287   when they had been read: Zeydel wonders 'can the king read?' but since in v.228 Ruodlieb had the *sciolus* read the letters for him, the king might have done the same; the latin is not specific. Reading the letters might have been a question of status as much as of ability.
           have pity for: *compatior* is late latin (LS). In Tertullian *Adv. Prax*.29 it means 'suffer with someone'; the sense 'have pity on' does not seem to occur before Augustine, *Ep*.40.29.6, *Conf*.3.2.

291   advise: *reconsilior* is attested only by DuCange (= *consulere*).

293   your brethren: *contribulis* is late latin: cf. Sidonius, *Ep*.8.13, where it means 'fellow-believers'.

299   to treat you well: *te...tribuisse* is dependent on *reminisci*.

305   Easter: in LS and Niermeyer, *pascha* is used only to refer to the Passover, to Easter and the paschal lamb; a wider usage is attested by Latham, but even here it does not mean 'a feast' in general.

314   goldsmiths: *aurificantes* is used because of the metre: the noun is *aurifex, aurifices* (pl.). Bezants were the only gold coin known for a long period in the Middle Ages. The verse is glossed *s. replet*, 'thus he fills them'.

317   with them: = *inde*.

322   <u>well-tried in the fire</u>: cf. *Roland* 132, *tant i avrat de besanz esmerez*, 'refined bezants'.

323   <u>after the city of Byzantium</u>: the repetition of this detail is curious; perhaps, like the episodes of fishing with buglossa, they are evidence that the poet had not finally decided which 'attempts' to excise, and which to retain. Such repetition is however not unknown in medieval poetry.

325   <u>majesty...royal power</u>: Hauck and Zeydel interpret *maiestas* as Christ, and the emperor as *regis potestatis*; Strecker and Seiler reverse this interpretation. The important thing to note is that the poet clearly has a specific type of coin in mind, one that was known to him.

333   <u>eight of them</u>: unusually in this MS, *octaue, solide, recauate* and *capitate* all end in subscript -ę.

334   <u>shaped like snakes</u>: the imagery here is very interesting; again, the author may be building on something he has seen in his description. *capitatus* is very rare (LS); Laistner suggests the meaning 'like the head of a nail' for it.

338   <u>a round yellow mark</u>: Laistner (*Anzeiger* p.96) renders *epaticam* as *aurugineam*, tracing its derivation through epar to Gk. ἧπαρ, 'liver': 'zwar könnte es einfach heissen: eine gelbe mark, wie *eine whîte merk*'.

340   <u>a splendid brooch</u>: Laistner (*Anzeiger,* p.100) and Zeydel (p. 20) regard these pieces as derivative if not copies of the jewellery found in the Gisela treasure, produced c.1026 in Mainz. All these pieces are themselves copies of Byzantine work. Zeydel includes photographs of some of the pieces in his edition; the whole collection is described in Falke, *Der Mainzer Goldschmuck der Kaiserin Gisela*. It seems unlikely, however, that the descriptions here are closely imitative; as Dronke points out (p.47), 'these are masterpieces of imagination in their own right'. Such pieces as are found in the Gisela treasure might have provided the poet with the inspiration, but the items he depicts here are fashioned on an altogether different scale in size, ingenuity, and sumptuousness.

355   <u>bracelet</u>: Niermeyer lists *bauga, boga, boca, bauca,* as 1) 'bracelet'; 2) 'iron collar'; 3) 'leggings'. The syntax of this verse is obscure, to say the least.

356   <u>a smaller one</u>: understand *fibulam* with *modicam*.

357   <u>a lady might</u>: v.358 shows that this brooch is intended for a lady.

362   <u>fine stones</u>: *lapides generosi* can also refer to pearls (Laistner, *Anzeiger* p.101). The next two verses refer to the story of the marriage between the pearl-shell and the heavenly dew, whose offspring was supposed to be the pearl. The whole derives from Isidore of Seville, XII.6.49, XVI.10.1.

365   <u>variegated</u>: some kind of *émail cloisonné* seems to be suggested by *sperule uariate*. Note the tense-change in vv.366-370, showing that these provide the author's own comment.

369   <u>a rough stone</u>: *scabrosus* is late and rare: the only ref. in LS is to Prudentius, *Psych*.106.

370   <u>artificial amber</u>: medieval enamels could be very fine in
        quality; it is noteworthy that Tegernsee was a principal
        centre for their production.

378   <u>lovely twisted shapes</u>: a m.pl. noun is required to account
        for *uariati*, hence *nexus*.
        <u>in amazing ways</u>: cf. Plautus *Mer*.225, Terence *Hec*.179, Vergil
        A.1.354, for other examples of the phrase *miris modis*, which I
        regard as a far more probable reading than *nodis*.

400   <u>comrade</u>: *compar* is classical (OLD 3) and medieval in this sense.

403   <u>to give him a wife</u>: Zeydel thinks that it may have been the
        author's original intention to shape the story in this way,
        or in the manner hinted at in v.413. It is quite acceptable
        to take it as a natural suggestion from the courtiers' point
        of view, though; they are anxious not to see their realm
        weakened by Ruodlieb's departure. Exactly the same attitude
        is evinced by queen Ospirin in the *Waltharius*, vv.125ff.

422   <u>dearest of my men</u>: *cunctigenorum* is a late medieval word;
        Latham lists it from the 11th century.

426   <u>when wealth becomes known</u>: cf. Proverbs 22.1, *melius est*
        nomen bonum quam diuitiae multae, and the example of Solomon
        in III.Reg.3.11.

438   <u>a word of wisdom</u>: Latham gives a wide semantic range for
        uerbum, including 'gospel' (*uerbum uitae*) and 'right of speech';
        cf. also its biblical use as 'a message' in Jer.28.9, 2 Reg.
        (= 2 Sam.) 7.25, 1 Par.16.15, Ps.69.11, etc.

440   <u>ten pounds</u>: Latham gives no ref. earlier than 1274 for *pondo,*
        but cf. Plautus, *As*.2.2.33, *quot pondo ted esse censes nudum?*

444   <u>a poor man has enough</u>: cf. *inter alia* Seneca, *Ep*.1.5,2.6,4.11.

445   <u>I thirst for the taste of wisdom</u>: cf. the example in the bible
        of Solomon, in 2 Par. (2 Chr.) 1.10.

451   <u>a redheaded man</u>: Zeydel wonders if redheads were suspect
        because of the similarity of their hair's colour to that of
        a fox, and adduces the proverb 'Rotbart nie gut ward'.

457   <u>no matter how muddy</u>: the advice given here and in vv.461ff.
        is paralleled in the *Gesta Romanorum*; it is homely,
        common-sense wisdom which fits well with the peasant-based
        feudal community on which the society depicted in *Ruodlieb*
        is founded.

469   <u>foaling</u>: there is a rare instance of the diphthong in *foeta*.

472   <u>do not let any kinsman</u>: cf. Proverbs 25.17, *subtrahe pedem*
        tuum de domo proximi tui, nequando satiatus oderit te.

474   <u>so often</u>: cf. the proverb cited by the earlier author from
        Tegernsee, Froumond: *quod rarum carum, et quod assidue, uile.*

476   <u>never make your maid</u>: cf. Proverbs 30.21-23, *mouetur terra...*
        per ancillam cum fuerit heres dominae suae.

477   <u>your mistress</u>: *consocius/consocia* are late latin (LS);
        consocialis is late medieval (12th century, in Latham).

481   <u>lies with you</u>: *repauso = reposo*, which Latham lists from
        1000/1100. *repausans* is very discreet; presumably they
        had sex too.

485   in order to have children: the need for an heir, to preserve
the stability of a realm, was a paramount necessity in feudal
society. Cf. Marie de France, *Equitan*, and Fragment XVI.1ff.

486   whom you can know of: *cognoscibilem* is late latin (LS).
Braun holds that here it must mean not 'knowable' (so TLL) but
'known'. The precept is illustrated in Fragment XVII.
The *mulier non cognoscibilis* is equivalent to the *mulier
aliena* or *extranea* common in Proverbs: cf.2.16, 6.25,7.5.

487   your mother: Ruodlieb's concern for his mother is not so
absolute as is sometimes supposed: later (XII.7ff.) he is
unaware whether or not she has remarried. Clearly his exile
has cut him off entirely from even news of home.

491   there is no greater fault: cf. Ecclus.33.20, *mulieri...non
des potestatem super te*; also 9.2, 25.30, and *Nibelungenlied*
638.1, *dô begonde vlêgen, der meister wande sîn*, and 673.
Gunther's humiliation at the hands of Brunhild is an excellent
illustration of this precept.

496   wishes to taunt you: *impropero* is mainly late in usage (LS).

498   let no sudden anger: the advice is biblical. Cf. Eph.4.26,
*irascimini, et nolite peccare; sol non occidat super iracun-
diam uestram*, and Ecclus.11.7, *priusquam interroges, ne
uituperes quemquam*.

502   never go to law: cf. Ecclus.8.1, *non litiges cum homine
potente, ne forte incidas in manus illius*.

504   do not lend: again, the advice derives ultimately from
Ecclesiasticus, 8.15: *noli faenerari homini fortiori te
quos si faeneraueris quasi perditum habe*. Braun also
points out (p.14) that a saying in the 'Dialogue of Solomon
and Marcolfus' comes close to this: *contra hominem potentem
et aquam currentem contendere noli*.

511   never let your journey: Zeydel points out that this advice
is found in sermons, and in Old Norse literature, but prefers
to think that like vv.519ff. it originated in a *novela*.

514   bells are rung: *pulso* had the meaning 'knock at a door' in
classical latin; it acquired this sense in late antiquity.
Cf. Benedict, *Regula* 48, *signum pulsat*.

516   share: according to Laistner (*Anzeiger* p.98), *participari*
is used in the same sense as *communicare* in Heb.2.14.

522   if you have crops: this is a warning against greed. Dig
the ditches on your own land, not in the road (thus making
your field bigger), and people will stay off your field.
The advice seems intended for someone who took a personal
interest in the supervision of the working of the land.

524   note the lack of rhyme in this verse.

529   in every way: understand *modis* with *cunctis*.

543   chamberlain: *paranimphus* = 'kämmerer' according to Diefenbach.
The word occurs in late latin writers such as Augustine and
Venantius Fortunatus in the sense 'bridesman' (cf. LS).

545   the servant: *camerarius* = the *paranimphus* of v.543.
Strictly, the word refers to a servant or vassal who had
access to the royal chamber; cf. Beroul, *Tristan* 296-7. 316.

546   which contained: *in quibus...intus* is like German *in denen*
...drin. Zeydel likens this gift to the 'Schenkellaib'
which was given to a servant in Bavaria and Swabia when he left
the household.

563   rejoice in each other's company for so short a time: the
genitive *alterutrius* must be taken with *ouarent, breue tempus*
being the regular accusative of temporal duration. This
usage seems unusual, and may perhaps be influenced by MHG
construction. Cf. above, on IV.173

570   poor fellow: the syntax appears confused at this point also.
a surely cannot govern *sibi* even in this poet, though earlier
translators have rendered the verse as though it did, and
as though the readings of the MS were *fidus...amicus*. If on
the other hand *a* governs *fido...amico, sibi* is then otiose,
unless we emend to the gerund form *disiungendum*. I adopt
the far simpler solution of regarding *a sibi* as an exclam-
ation, like MHG *ah mir* or O.Fr. *aimi*, 'woe is me!'.

580   I shall pray for him: *oramen* is attested only by Niermeyer,
'inde ab Aldhelmo'.

581   and shall always love: this phrase is syntactically
unconnected to the preceding phrases; this practice is far
from uncommon in this author.

594   hood: Niermeyer gives for *cappa* 1) 'cap'; 2) 'hood'; 3)
'hooded cloak'; Zeydel renders it 'cloak', but it has to
be small enough for the redhead to hide it later, tucked under
his arm.

599   armpit: *ascella = axella* or *assella*.
615   duckboard: here, assuming *pons* to be the correct reading
(the MS is in very poor condition at this point), the word
is the equivalent of MHG *stec*.

VI
7   he knew this would turn out: the fate of the redhead is thus
left in no doubt. Such *interiectiones ex persona poetae* are
a frequent feature of medieval poetry. The *Roland* is full
of them, and cf. also *Nibelungenlied* 1393.4.

20   taking in guests: again, the biblical injunction to show
hospitality is illustrated: cf. Ex.20.10, Deut.10.19, and
note above on V.240.

21   little old widow-woman: the MS is blurred beyond *ueluti
ue....*, and Zeydel's conjecture *uxor illius* would insert
the only spondaic 5th foot in the poem, besides not really
fitting the rhyme. Furthermore there ought to be some
reference to widowhood, for the redhead to pick it up in
the following line. Short *-a* for long is not uncommon in
latin of this period.

24   a better one to marry: *nupsisset ad* is rather like MHG
hîraten zuo (Zeydel), though this use of the preposition is
not uncommon in vulgar latin: cf. Strecker p.64, *ad uxorem
accipere*.

30   married a poor man: it would have been unusual for any man
to marry above his station in feudal society, hence Ruodlieb's
question. Cf. also below, XIV.61 and XVI.57.

32   **because it loves the salt**: as Dronke points out, 'salt' is used repeatedly in this fabliau-like story not only to denote the physical substance, which is lacking in the old man's cuisine, but also, symbolically, the quality of life that makes it worth living, like English 'spice' in the phrase 'the spice of life' (latin *sal* is used in this way also). It is precisely this quality that is lacking in the old man's life (cf. vv.35-36, 39-40) but which is supplied by the young man.

44   **hardly a mouthful**: *bucella* is found in *Cod. Theod.*14.17.5, and is also the proper term used for bread given to the poor. Cf. also Gen.18.5, Ruth 2.14.

48   **cupboard**: this is surely the sense of *toreuma* here, though only in this place does it bear this sense; elsewhere it means 'couch' (DuCange) or 'curtain' (Niermeyer).

50   **early or evening meal**: as in V.16, *prandium* and *cena* are the two main meals of the day.

72   **cheap ingredients**: *causa* is like O.Fr. *chose, cose*, found as early as the 'Strasbourg Oaths' of 842.

85   **some cakes**: cf. the *Tegernsee Kochbuch*, which speaks of *geschmalzen brôt* and *begozzen brôt*.

86   **and long straight ones**: lit. 'like a penis'. *mencla* is a variant form of *mentula* (TLL; cf. also Ford, 'Notes de Lecture', *Latomus* XXIV (1965), 168, 169, 170).

87   **shall not increase**: having listed the variety of bread he can make, the young man must now assure the old miser that he will not make too many loaves. Ford's *non deminuo* takes *numerum* to mean 'amount', i.e. 'you'll get just as much bread this way', but does not fit the context so well; Zeydel's conjecture lacks the negative found in his translation, and in Ford's words 'makes the text mean the opposite of what he wants it to'.

106   **they kept it to themselves**: = *corde tenus*. At this stage they had not formalised their relationship, though Zeydel interprets their churchgoing together as a sign that they were man and wife. Undoubtedly it would set tongues wagging, but it may have preceded a formal marriage. Cf. *Nibelungenlied* 528 for an example of a couple sleeping together before they had had a church wedding.

107   **they who...together**: the odd moods and tenses suggest that this is a proverb, hence my punctuation. Cf. also the situation with the nephew and his young lady, X.62ff.

110   **father**: Zeydel regards this as 'typical of a patriarchal relationship', but this seems excessively slavish and literalistic. The poet is more likely using the 'names' to stress the harmonious nature of their household: the young man is fully accepted by the servants.

112   **a couple**: *contectales* is found only here in this sense. In the singular, the word is used to mean 'spouse'.

118   **is there an old man here**: as is clear from VII.34, the redhead already knows this woman - she is his niece.

1   cut the bread up: according to custom, the host's duty was
    to cut up his guest's food.   Tacitus says of a much earlier
    generation's habits *separatae singulis sedes et sua cuique
    mensa, Germania* 22; here, there is more than one to a table
    (cf. below, X.65, XVI.28).

5   our own festival: as Hauck points out in 'Rituelle Speise-
    gemeinschaft in 10. und 11. Jahrhundert' (*Studium Generale*
    III, 1950), what is described here is a ritual of lay commun-
    ion deriving from pagan German roots as much as from the
    Christian eucharist.   For a similar practice, cf. Bede, *HE*
    III.6.

12 walnut goblet carved from the hardest wood: *tuber* here must
    refer to the knots in the wood; so Pliny, *HN* 16.16.27,etc.
    Such goblets carved from various types of wood, with intricate
    and ornate detail, were not uncommon, and were known in
    German as *maser*; this, however, appears to be their earliest
    attestation.   Alternatively, *summi tuberis* might be taken
    as a genitive of description, 'of a very round shape' (lit.
    'of the utmost swelling'), which fits well with the illustra-
    tion of a walnut goblet included by Zeydel in his edition;
    this resembles an old-fashioned champagne glass, rounded and
    very shallow.

23 how he could: *qui* is the adverb here.
29 come with me: understand *ire* with *uelles mecum*.
30 you'll get what you're looking for: such *praemonitio* or
    'signposting' is a regular feature of medieval poetry; cf.
    VI.7.   The ominous tone of these words here finds a parallel
    in Ganelon's reply to Charles' men in *Roland* 336, *'seigneurs'
    dist Guenes, 'vos en orrez noveles'*, 'you'll hear of it soon
    enough'.

38 someone open the door: the MS seems to have *-es* or *-as* here.
    Cf. Ovid, *M*.10.457, *fores aperit*.

45 rode shamelessly: the broken narrative, with its sense of
    rapid movement conveyed by the abrupt phrasing, shows the
    poet's artistry with the language he elsewhere seems to find
    so difficult and awkward.   The violent temper depicted here
    is supposedly typical of a redhead.

58 of a different kind: *alius* is the rare genitive form (cf.
    Cicero *ND* 2.48.123; Varro *LL* 9.40.62, etc.(refs. in LS).

65 there is a young man: the situation set up by the redhead
    is typical, with a 'viel gelus' and a lovely young woman to
    be rescued by a 'gallant' knight.   It must have been common
    enough for the poet to make humorous use of it in such a stock
    manner.

67 fair-skinned: lit. 'of fine wheat-flour'.   LS gives only one
    reference to *similagineus*, Ecclus.39.31.   Pale skin was
    though to be a sign of good breeding.   I refrain from the
    possible pun 'well-bred'.

75 melodious horn: cf.I.32 for the horn-blowing motif.
81 in a well-bred way: *disciplinate* is one of the poet's chosen
    terms for courtly behaviour: cf. IV.170.

84	the redhead: the marks *R, N, R, H,* in the MS refer to the speakers, *rufus, neptis, herus.*
85	sleep with me: *succumbas* = 'submit' and also (lit.) 'lie beneath'; hence *succuba,* 'concubine' or 'female devil'.
86	do it ten times: the woman's tone here is definitely not courtly! As has already been remarked, this episode has all the marks of a *fabliau.*
88	give me your counsel (to go): *praecipio* is not found in exactly this sense in classical latin (but cf. OLD 6, 'advise, recommend'); Zeydel's 'permit me to leave' and Ford's 'bid me leave!' are a little imprecise.
91	whatever is ours: note the irony of the old man's words.
107	ordered: *iubeo* takes dative very rarely: cf. LS Iδ, and the ref. to Macrobius *S.*1.12.28.
109	sat between them: only TLL attests the very rare usage of *intersedeo,* from a legal gloss in *Cod. Paris Gr.*1357, 'Α ἰντερσεδειν'. TLL also notes that all MSS of Tertullian *Adv. Nat.* 1.12.13 read *intersedit* for *intercedit.*
115	watched through an auger-hole: the role normally reserved for the 'viel gelus', (like the *senex* in Plautus), is exploited to the full, with the cuckolded husband reduced to spying on his own wife. *ad secretum* is marked for correction, though only Schmeller among previous editors seems to have noticed it.
117	wretched: = *infeliciter.* Once again the poet indulges in *praemonitio,* pointing the moral of the redhead's downfall in advance for his readers.
127	my lady: these verses underline the old man's weakness, already seen in vv.88ff. He is not even master over his wife (and cf. the king's warning in V.491, above).

VIII

8	forgive these people: cf. the *nunc dimittis* for perhaps the best-known example of *dimitto* in this sense, and also OLD 7a.
11	when morning came: Braun, p.66, draws attention to the trial-scene in Apuleius *Met.*X.2-12 as a possible parallel to this part of the poem. The similarities are superficial, however.
20	the murderers themselves: TLL lists both *mordris, is* and *mordrida, -ae* as a 'vox germanica legis Salicae', giving the example *quis femina...et occisa fuerit et mordrida fuerit,* LEX *Sal. Merov. cas.* 8.1, 8.2, 8.3. Here, though, it has the sense 'murderer', not 'murdered person': cf. Latham, who gives only the form *murdritor,* c.1115.
28	that young girl: as Braun notes (p.64) the use of *ancilla* points back to V.476, of which precept this story is an illustration.
37	I made no advances to you: on *post* used thus, cf. note on VIII.125.
45	if you want me: the remarkable hyperbole here ('hang me by my own hair') is paralleled by that found in Iseut's speech at the start of Beroul's *Tristan,* vv.33ff.: *mex voudroie que je fuse arse/ aval le vent la poudre esparse/ jor que je vive que amor/ aie o home qu'o mon seignor,* 'I would rather be

burned and have my ashes thrown to the wind than live a day
in love with any other man than my lord'.   This is a regular
feature of Iseut's charcter in Beroul's version (cf.vv.403ff.
for an 'encore' of the above) as it is of the country girl in
this work: her excess in self-denigration matches her lust,
seen in VII.86, and in this at least she is consistent.

53   on the outside: this usage of *deforis* is only found in the
Vulgate and later; cf. Gen.7.16, *inclusit eum Dominus
deforis,* also Mt.23.25, Lk.11.40.

56   fierce crocodiles: Laistner (*Anzeiger* p.105) makes the point
that unless the author intends us to imagine that Ruodlieb's
homeland is far from Germany, *cocodrillis* is an anachronism:
V.585 has already made it clear that he is nearing his home.
Laistner thought that 'dragons' might be meant; it seems on
the whole better to take it as a part of the author's fantasy
world.

58   fires of hell: cf. Mt.5.22, *reus erit gehennae ignis.*

73   wholeness of body: = *salutem.* The jury prescribes no
mutilation as punishment for her crime.

76   mistress now: *amodo* is a mainly ecclesistical-latin usage.

79   cut off my nose: Marie de France gives a similar, though
not identical, fate to the wicked wife in her tale *Bisclavret,*
vv.235, 311ff.

103   kept watch: the MS is very blurred at this point, and only
et....auit is visible. *ueniauit,* proposed by Schmeller and
followed by Seiler, Langosch, and Zeydel, is impossible;
Ford's *u[el adi]uit* is better, but does not give sufficient
continuity with v.104. *uigilauit* seems to fit very well,
especially with its overtones of 'praying till she sweated'.

106   burned down: Latham attests *cremo* in this sense c.1362, c.1380.

109   for a little while: cf. OLD 6 for examples of the phrase
ad breue in classical writers.

112   no authority for herself: *potestas* is attested with the mean-
ing 'dominion, area of authority' in Latham, 9c., 948, etc.
The variant spelling *uendicat* for *uindicat* is frequent in
MSS of this period.

114   played with no-one: like English 'play', *ludo* can have sexual
overtones; cf. Plautus, *Most.*5.2.36, and LS II B.

116   her: note *hanc* and *eam* used identically in the same verse.

125   to send for him: on this unusual use of *post,* cf. TLL IIC,
Fulgentius *Myth.* 3.10, p.77, 13 *post quam Euridicen maritus
ad inferos descendit,* and Jerome, *Ep.*29, 2, 4 (I Reg.22.20)
fugit post David, where in the Vulgate he wrote *ad David.*
Cf. also Vulgate Mt.4.19, *uenite post me, et faciam uos....*

129   noble knight: *miles summe* is the equivalent of *edler Ritter.*
IX

2   he stands against everything: *obuio* is post-classical (LS II).
In Jerome, *Ep.*1, 5 and Vulgate Ps.84.11, it means 'to meet';
here it is used in the sense 'prevent', hinder' (LS IIB).

6   avoid me completely: *deuito* is rare, pre- and post-classical:
cf. Plautus, *Rud.*1.2.79, *saluae sunt si illos fluctus deuita-
uerint,* and also the Vulgate, Eccl.2.3.

X

5   <u>upper room</u>: so Niermeyer I, Latham c.1115, for *solaria*.

6   <u>welcome here now</u>: = *bene ueniatis*. Cf. the etymology of
both the English and German equivalents.

20   <u>a boat</u>: cf. the previous episode of fishing, II.1.

28   <u>the knight frightened them</u>: Schmeller began his chapter XIII
with this verse, but there is clearly no break in the sense.

29   <u>young ladies</u>: Latham lists *dominella* from c.1200 as 'damsel'.

38   <u>had been caught</u>: note the use of *fuerant* for *erant*; the
auxiliary verb is in effect a main verb, with *capti* used
adjectivally.

39   <u>the pike</u>: Many of the fishes named here are also to be found
listed in the *Fischbüchlein* from Tegernsee; they would in
all probability have been well known to the monks, and simply
because lists such as this one form a stock rhetorical device
used by poets in the Middle Ages (cf. *Nibelungenlied* 1122,
1123, for example) it need not be assumed that the poet is
not speaking in his *propria persona* here: v.48 is one of
the rare times when the voice of the narrator intrudes on the
story. Laistner, *Anzeiger* pp.102ff., and Braun, pp.88-89,
both give a full description of the fish names found here.

50   <u>piled high with white bread</u>: I follow Seiler and print *latis.
similia* = lit. 'fine wheaten flour', and hence 'white bread'
(so Niermeyer). *latis* is the adjective used adverbially.

52   <u>after her</u>: Zeydel's *postquam* is an error, further compounded
by his translation, 'then soon many nimble squires hurried
along'; for *post* used in this way, see note on VIII.125.

55   <u>when she went out</u>: the comparison of the girl with the moon
is common in medieval poetry: cf. *Nibelungenlied* 283. 1-3:
*sam der liehte mâne vor den sternen stât/ des scîn sô
lûterlîche ab den vilken gât/ dem stuont si nu gelîche vor
maneger frouwen guot*, 'Kreimhild outshone many good ladies
as the moon does the stars when its light shines clear from
the sky...'. Cf. also below, XV.3.

59   <u>asked for water</u>: apart from its obvious hygienic function,
washing is also part of the etiquette of the society portrayed
in this poem.

61   <u>sat down</u>: *consido* is 'frequent in all periods and species of
composition' (LS); cf. Vergil, *A.4.573, considite transtris*.

65   <u>a single loaf</u>: the sharing of a meal denotes an especial
closeness of relationship, a personal sharing of hospitality.
Cf. below, XIII.18, and the following passage from John of
Salisbury, *Met.4.42*, describing the warm welcome afforded him
by Nicholas Breakspear: *et cum Romanus pontifex esset, me in
propria mensa gaudebat habere conuiuam; et eundem ciphum et
discum sibi et michi uolebat et faciebat, me renitente, esse
communem.*

66   <u>that hound</u>: Zeydel says in a note on this verse, 'trained dogs
were popular among the mimes', but the dog is presumably that
belonging to Ruodlieb, introduced in I.44ff. The dog recalls
Husdent, Tristan's faithful hound in Beroul, which like this
one was remarkably gifted in a variety of ways.

71	titbits: so LS, which gives *gustum* as a collateral form of the more usual *gustus, -us* in Apicius 4.5. TLL also attests its usage by Fulgentius, Jerome, and in *Schol.Iuv.5.24*.
87	an evil spirit: as is clear from LS, Latham and Niermeyer, *daemon* was used in a neutral sense only by the pagan writers of antiquity; in ecclesiastical and medieval writers, it definitely refers to an *evil* spirit (as in the Gospels, too).
89	to the man: one would expect *cui* for *cuius*; the pronoun is attracted into the genitive to govern *ea*.
97	showed its delight: only the deponent form *gratificor* is found in classical writers (cf. OLD); TLL lists the active form 'inde ab *Itala*'. LS refers to Cassiodorus *Var.7.6*, and to Eph.1.6, in the Vulgate.
97	now to this man, then: note the visual aspect of the dog's running from group to group, paralleled by the latin's repeated *nunc...nunc...nunc*.
98	take you by the hair: lit. 'take your hair to himself' (assuming *sibi* is reflexive here); the writing is very powerful and dynamic in this passage.
102	the dog leapt: like the episode with the dancing bears in Frag. V, this event may not be to modern taste, but obviously appealed to the poet - and, one presumes, to his audience.
106	after many courses: cf. the almost identical verse, XIII.24.
110	hazel-bark: a *hapax legomenon*, noted only by Niermeyer.
111	...every place: note the tautology in the phrase *undique passim*.
114	bands: Lucca, in northern Italy, is still a centre for textiles. These bands are presumably items of luxury, and they add both verisimilitude and a heightened sense of grandeur to the narrative.
116	slippers: *pedulis* is attested c.1200, 1324 by Latham. *calceolus* is 'shoe', slipper' in OLD, but here must refer to something like 'puttees' or 'spats'. It is not recorded in any of the dictionaries with this meaning. *sericatus* is found in Suetonius, *Cal.52*, and Sidonius *Ep.2.13*; *sericosus* is another *hapax legomenon*, a variant on *sericatus*.
124	trimmed with fine fur: again, *gulatus* is a *hapax legomenon*, rendered 'adorned with marten throat-fur' by Niermeyer. Latham gives *gula*, 'fur from the throat of an animal', from 1176.
127	the ring which the young mistress: this cannot be a reference to the ring won later in a dice-game (XI.69ff.), unless this is another occasion when the poet has sacrificed consistency in his narrative for the effect of the moment. The word *herilis* does not suggest a reference to the *scurra* with whom the nephew was earlier involved. Is a third young lady, unspecified, to be understood - or has the poet himself been confused by his earlier mention of *ligamina* in v.53?
130	cloak: *mantel* is a German form, not latin: both *mantellum, -i* and *mantile, -is* are attested by Latham. As Dronke notes. the shedding of the old clothes and putting on of new ones is symbolic of the new life the nephew now lives.

1   then they ate: trained and talking birds were a popular
      diversion in medieval society: cf. Marie de France, *Laüstic*,
      where the bird forms the centrepoint of the story.   The
      fashion for such birds came to the West from Byzantium.

2   their little houses: *doma, -atis* is late latin, found in
      ecclesiastical writers.

5   became used to this: *consuefacio* is mainly ante-class.(OLD).

6   little door: *ostiolum* is post-Augustan; cf. also the Vulgate,
      Dan.14.20.

8   with soft words: = *leniendo*.

9   were eager: = *certatim*.

14   little house: the form *domicella* = *dominella*, 'damsel', in
      both Latham and Niermeyer; but cf. Latham *domicellum, -i*,
      c.1150, 'little house', 'shed'.

24   as best they could: *quam* is used here as it is in such phrases
      as *quam celerrime*, but with a verb: cf. Plautus, *Men*.6, Ovid
      Tr.3.4.75, *Pont*.4.8.37.   It does not mean 'before', as Zeydel
      claims, despite his assertion that it is so used in ecclesiast-
      ical latin.

26   harpers: the *harpatores* are the same as the *mimi* of V.87.

27   the tune: = *rithmum*, which normally refers to the words,
      rather than the melody; perhaps the harpers played and sang.

31   my brave husband: = *meus heros*, which resembles the way in
      which Kreimhild speaks about Siegfried in the *Nibelungenlied*.
      It is not merely a metrical substitute for *herus*, as Zeydel
      maintains; the lady's character is delineated with great care.
      Here, she clearly looks back with longing to the times when
      her husband was alive, and is still devoted to him.   It is
      noteworthy too that she is not beyond making very subtle over-
      tures to Ruodlieb himself, both in this episode (note the
      little touch about the harp: no-one has played it since her
      husband died, but he may play on it), and in their eating
      together.   Note also the stress on love in v.32.

32   grow weak with love: *langueo* is a common term used to descr-
      ibe love-sickness in medieval lyric: cf. *Carmina Burana* 1.2,
      with the refrain *O langueo, causam languoris uideo*, etc.

34   play melodies on it: the deponent form *modulor* is usual,
      only Priscian, *Gramm*.II.396,12 gives the active form as well
      (TLL).   Ruodlieb, like Tristan, is a master-harpist.

38   playing some improvisations: the sense-order is *nescius
      omnino saltandi uel agendi neumas manibus hec ambo citus
      perdisceret*.   *saltandi* and *agendi* are genitive of the
      gerund, dependent on *nescius*.   *manibus neumas uel agendi*
      must refer to the arm-movements in the dance or to clapping,
      as only one person seems to be intended by *nescius*, i.e. a
      prospective dancer, and the other harpers are shamed into
      silence, not encouraged to join in, by Ruodlieb's playing.
      On the other hand, Niermeyer gives only 'melody' or 'note'
      as renderings of *neuma*.   *perdisceret* is a qualitative
      subjunctive, 'anyone who had no knowledge...might learn'.
      It makes no sense to refer these lines to Ruodlieb.

44   dare to play: see note on v.34 for *modulo*.
48   variations in harmony: *sistema* and *diastema* are technical
     terms, found in Pseudo-Hucbald, *Musica Enchiriadis,* from the
     10th century (so Niermeyer).
49   with wonderful grace: *decenter*, like *disciplinate*, is a word
     used by the poet to stress the courtly quality of the action.
51   like a falcon: despite claims made to the contrary, this
     does not seem to be a description of a swallow-falcon folk-
     dance, but rather a poetic representation of the way that the
     two dancers moved. Zeydel is right in saying that 'this is
     the first courtly dance in literature'. Falcon-imagery is
     also to be found in the famous lyric of Kürenberc, where a
     lady pictures her lover as a falcon whom she has trained, but
     who has forsaken her.
53   she seemed to float: cf. X.57 above for the same image.
54   neither...anyone: there is one negative too many in the latin.
     The order for understanding is: *neutrum saltasse, uariasse*
     neumas manibus quo nemo (=ullus?) posset corrigere si
     uoluisset.
61   gave them leave: *faculto* is another *hapax legomenon*.

XII
3   become a godmother: Ruodlieb's confusion is due to the
     ambiguous sense of *commater*, as the refs. in Niermeyer make
     clear; it can mean either the godmother in relation to the
     father or the godfather, or the mother, in relation to the
     godfather. Nowadays we stress the relationship with the
     child. The lady's words do not make it clear whether she
     or Ruodlieb's mother has had a child.
7   could have married: as Zeydel points out, second marriages
     were permitted but not encouraged for women.
16   the messenger's bread: cf. *Nibelungenlied* 553.1, 1216.3, for
     other references to this customary gift for the purveyor of
     good news, the *botenbrôt.*
26   changing their sexes: cf. Laistner, 'Die Lücken im Ruodlieb',
     p.14, on this feature; perhaps in their zeal to express their
     devotion to one another, they confused the case endings by
     accident, though the solecism is found in the early MHG love-
     lyric *Ich bin dîn, du bist mîn*, which also originates from
     Tegernsee, and in Gottfried von Strasbourg's *Tristan*, 11.1356
     ff., *sus was er sî und sî was er/ er was îr und sî was sîn.*
30   would have slept together: Zeydel claims that there is 'no
     sign of courtliness here', but cf. *Nibelungenlied* 528, and
     Hatto's comment that 'according to medieval notions, once the
     consent....had been given, (the couple) were free to consumm-
     ate their marriage'. It is worth pointing out, too, that many
     instances of 'courtly' love are explicitly adulterous.
67   of cherries: from this point on, the text contained in M26^V
     is written vertically without breaks between the verses
     in the right-hand margin.
75   Ruodlieb: this is the first time since V.223 that the hero
     of the poem has been mentioned by name.

1 He did not scrape his beard: there is no attestation for Ford's conjecture *barbiciam*, though *barbitium, -i* is used in Apuleius.

2 no-one so cunning: note that in this verse the rhyme occurs at the end of the third foot, and is not coincidental with the caesura.

5 got out of the bath: apart from its practical function, bathing had a ceremonial and courtly role: cf. Einhard, *Vita Kar. Mag.* 22, Marie de France, *Equitan* 269-270.

10 the count: *comes* is not used elsewhere of Ruodlieb, but it must refer to him here. A new paragraph begins with this line, which makes it unlikely that 'companion' is meant.

12 submissively: *subiectiue* is used in an otherwise unattested adverbial form. Ruodlieb shows respect to his mother out of filial and feudal duty, and in accordance with the king's precept. Later in medieval latin, the word was used as a term of logic, to mean 'subjectively'.

18 companion and partner: cf. X.61ff., above. They share a single plate and cup as a sign of intimacy.

21 jackdaw: *monedula* has the MHG gloss *taha*.

23 walk to and fro: *perspaciens* is otherwise unattested.

24 many courses: cf. the almost identical verse, X.106. With each course a different wine is served; cf. Einhard, *Vita Kar. Mag.* 24, *super cenam raro plus quam ter biberet*.

27 Only at this point in the work do the manuscripts from Munich and St. Florian preserve the same fragments of text. The Munich copy is in a very poor state at this point. Its readings are as follows: 31...*e plus tribuletur/...t illo cum caruisse/...totam regionem/...letatum sat abunde/* 35 *dum secretumque sibi fit/...ilecta sibi matre/...hecam quo sibi ferret/...traxit opes preciosas/in chrusinis in pelliciis c../* 41 *post poscit peras quas s.../43 quos dum produxit matri i../* 45 *hos mihi rex dederat m.../* 47 *quam bene sint sapidi uid.../* 49 *educens cultrum quo pan.../* 51 *pollen ut abrasit iubar ar.../* 53 *comminuens lima cito.../* 55 *tam strictim iunctos...*

35 opportunity to speak in private: *secretum* is not so much 'an unnoticed opportunity' (Zeydel) as 'a secret conversation' (LS 2b, OLD 3: cf. Pliny, *Ep.*1.5.11).

39 in the form of skins: for *in* + abl. used like this, cf. OLD 44b, Vergil *A*.1.640, Apuleius *Met*.3.11.
other kinds: the genitive form *alius* is rare: cf. Cicero *ND* 2,48,125, Ammianus 30.5.10. The long *-i* is clearly marked in the St. Florian MS.

40 The St. Florian MS has *que* with subscript *-e* in this line.

42 in the Africans' land: Braun points out (p.10) that here, and in v.67 and XVI.5, the poet's use of this term 'has nothing whatsoever to do with eleventh-century Moslem Africa' (my trans.). Zeydel claims that 'Saracens were sometimes called *Africani*', but Dronke points out that the passage from Liutprand on which Zeydel bases his case refers rather to Saracens

brought to southern Italy from Africa by the Byzantines, and
concludes that, as Ruodlieb does not seem to undertake any
sea-voyages,'the poet had in mind a principality in southern
Italy which was still surrounded by Saracens from Africa'.
This suits the references to border-dwellers and to inter-
marriage (II.52ff.), and to the chess match. It might be
objected that the lesser king is never stated not to be a
Christian, but he does seem to need to have the role of monks
explained to him in V.210-214. One might also adduce the
confusion about Islamic theology so apparent in the *Roland*
as an illustration of the ignorance of Islam at the time,
though the author of *Ruodlieb* avoids the strident excesses
of the vernacular work, and in any case his interest lies less
in the theological aspect of the situation than in the
courtly and godly behaviour of Rex Maior (Braun, pp.23ff.).

44   I have earned these: in classical latin, *deseruio* means 'be
devoted to' or 'serve' (OLD); only in late medieval latin
does it take on the notion of merit. Cf. also TLL II.B.1,
where the sense *praesto esse* is also noted.

47   well-flavoured: there is a pun on *sapidi*, which means both
'tasty' and 'wise'.
    African loaves: see note above on v.42.

48   look at them alone: the tone of Ruodlieb's words seems to
indicate that something out-of-the-ordinary is expected.

63   blessed: *beatum* carries connotations of wealth as well as of
divine favour.

65   his lord's own king: the latin is ambiguous. 'King' might
refer to the African king, beloved of God (cf.v.73), or to
Christ, 'the King of glory'. 'Lord' would then refer to God.
On the other hand, the latter might be taken in a feudal sense
and 'king' would then refer to God. The general sense is
clear, however: Ruodlieb attributes his good fortune to God
and to Christ.

68   pitiable wretch: note the biblical phraseology, which one
would expect in a prayer; cf. I Cor.15.19, Ps.41.17, etc.

71   I see once again: Zeydel wonders if the poet originally intended to bring Ruodlieb back to the great king's court. As
an alternative, this sentiment may be taken as a rhetorical
flourish, an expression of heartfelt gratitude.

XIV

2   some of our own dear relations: *quidam...nostri* ought to be
accusative after *credo uenire*. It may have been attracted
into the nominative by v.3 - or it may just be carelessness.

4   your daughter: so Zeydel. *ille* and *iste* are interchangeable
in the latin of this period (cf. Strecker, p.63).

5   comrade: *communis* is rendered 'united under one lord' by
Zeydel, 1246. Zeydel's 'retainers' is possible, but the
translation 'comrades' seems better. 'on both sides' refers
to her own kinsmen and those of her deceased husband: cf.
also XVI.15, below.

11   to their chambers: *secreta* = MHG *kemenate* (Zeydel).

14	to show their service to him: *illo* must refer to the bride-groom. This seems to be some kind of lay communion binding her servants to his service before the marriage; cf. the lay communion described in VII.1ff., and the wine poured as a greeting at IV.48.
29	burned in the fire: a punishment reserved for adulteresses.
35	damnable prostitute: from here to v.49 the text is written vertically in the right-hand margin.
38	betrothed: *desponso* is post-Augustan and biblical (LS).
40	dowries: gifts given by the bride and groom are common in all periods and in all cultures: cf. Tacitus, *Germ*.18.
43	fretfully: *morose* might mean 'hesitatingly' as an alternative (so Latham), or 'in a captious manner' (OLD), but not Zeydel's 'decorously', despite his equating it with MHG *hövesch*. The girl's modest reaction is paralleled by the behaviour of Rüdiger's daughter in *Nibelungenlied* 1684.
44	stood up: a mark of respect for the ladies, as at IV.49.
47	relations: the form *contribulus* is listed in Latham c.685, c.1125; see also note on V.293.
49	the conjecture must contain a reference to the young man smiling (cf.v.51 *parum quoque ridet*); the idea of her 'serving him as lord' is suggested by her reference to him as her slave.
50	my supplying this line, totally erased in the MS, means that the numeration in my edition is one digit ahead of previous editions from this point on in this Fragment of the text.
53	should I not want: the girl's initiative recalls Beroul's sparkling characterisation of Iseut, among other medieval literary creations. The bridegroom's previous entanglement with the harlot gives her a moral advantage, which she uses to brilliant effect, as Dronke notes. For the use of *an* as introduction to a question suggesting the answer 'no', cf. OLD 1, and Vergil, *E*.5.53.
56	serve me with all his might: the reversal of the usual roles of man and wife is highlighted again; *seruio* has feudal connotations (cf.IV.26) which the poets of the Middle Ages took delight in, applying it to the situations of love. A detailed exploration of how feudal relationships could be jeopardised by romance is provided by Marie de France, in her Lai *Equitan*. The sexual innuendo here must be intentional, as it often is in the feudal imagery of courtly love. Cf. also the king's teaching in V.491ff.
58	roar of laughter: *risus magnus...atque cachinnus* is a hendiadys.
61	status and wealth: lit. 'power of riches'.
62	they took counsel and decided: *discutio* is used in the sense 'investigate', listed in Latham from the 8th c. In classical latin it means 'tear asunder'.. 'decided' is *censent*.
64	scraped it along the stonework: *pyramide* is very obscure. LS renders it 'pyramid', Latham as 'canopy' from c.700, '? coffin lid' c.1180, 'roof or gable' 1519. Ford takes it to mean part of the sword, 'at its point', but Zeydel before him has the most plausible explanation, whereby it refers to the

column of a stairway or *Handgemal*, which could symbolise a
freeman's hereditary estate, and also served as a judge's
bench.   The sword is then whetted on the 'foundation of
domestic jurisprudence' (Zeydel) to symbolise the oath and the
solemnisation of the civil marriage.

67   encircles: Niermeyer gives only this ref. for *circumcapio*;
Latham also attests *circumcaptus* from *circumseptio*, 12th c.

76   for Adam: cf. Genesis 2.21-23.

78   when you go off wenching: the form *meretricor* is found only
in late antiquity, as TLL's refs. show, ITALA Am.7.17, August.
In Psalm. 136.9.   LS also lists the *Gloss. Philox.*, which uses
it in the sense 'to play the harlot'.

81   there are plenty: for this use of *tot* cf. OLD 2a.   *quo* might
be an error for *quot*.

87   those terms: = *ea lege*.

96   gave them: the repeated *dat...dat* are omitted in the translation; their principal force in the latin is to stress the
opulence and great number of the gifts.

98   lined with scarlet: Zeydel renders the phrase 'dyed scarlet',
which seems an odd thing to do to ermine.   *coccum* is 'red
cloth', as in Sil.17.396, Suet. *Nero* 30.   LS renders *super-
duco* as 'draw over', but the sense seems to be 'lined' here.
migalinam, 'ermine', is otherwise unattested.   A possible
derivation for it is suggested by DuCange's *migale = pica*.
Might the sense not be 'piebald', and hence 'spotted', as
ermine is?

100   why should I worry: cf. *Nibelungenlied* 1680.1, *Swaz sich sol
geflegen, wer mac daz unterstên*, which Hatto renders 'who
can thwart the workings of destiny?'   Zeydel regards this line
as 'a jest such as Wolfram von Eschenbach might indulge in',
and adduces V.491ff. as a comparison.   However, there seems to
be no comedy of role-reversal at the end of the fragment; the
girl has made her point, gifts have been exchanged, and all
seems perfectly happy.   It is better to take this verse as
Dronke does, to be indicative of the poet's assurance that they
will get on very well together - since they have a good under-
standing of the basis of their relationship within the
marriage, as v.87 makes clear.   The poet's intervention is
a neat way of tying up this sub-plot so that he can get on with
the story of Ruodlieb proper.

XV

3   the flower of her youth: note *iuuente* for *iuuentutis*.   *Flos*
could be used alone in this sense (cf. Terence, *Eun*.2.3), or
with *aetatis* (many refs. in LS).
as lovely as the moon: cf. XI.55, above.   This whole section
has a remarkable similarity to the 15th century poet Villon's
Ballade de la Belle Heaulmiere.

7   foully snivelling: *muculentus* is post-classical;   cf. Prudentius, στεφ.13.282.

13   firm round breasts are now: on *ceu trochi* Laistner (*Anzeiger*
p.95) says 'nicht "wie Kreisel", sondern = *schîbelot*, wie ein

Kinn, ein Schwertknauf, gescheibt'. DuCange says of *trochus*
'notus fuit trochus vel pro *turbine qui flagello percutitur*
vel pro *rota quam currendo pueri regunt*, ut habet vetus
Scholiastes Horatii'.

21 dragged through a hedge backwards: this proverbial English
phrase seems an adequate rendering of the latin, which would
seem to be its earliest attestation in literature. Seiler
mistook *anuatim* for *annuatim*, 'yearly'; Langosch rightly links
it with *anus*, 'buttocks'. The word is otherwise unattested,
and might well be a neologism.

59 set me free: cf. St. Paul, in Romans 7.24, *quis me liberabit
de corpore mortis huius?*, and also Cicero, *Rep.6.14.14.* Zeydel
compares the verse to Propertius II.13.50, *O mors cur mihi sera
uenis*, and says of it 'the identity is striking'; Dronke also
regards it as evidence that the *Ruodlieb*-poet's reading of
Roman poetry may have been 'exceptional'. Against this it must
be admitted that most of the verse is conjecture, and that the
similarity may not be so striking after all. According to R.J.
Tarrant in *Texts And Transmission,* p.324, art.'Propertius',
'Propertius seems to have been virtually unknown from the
end of antiquity to the middle of the twelfth century'.

XVI

2 what will happen: the concern for an heir is paramount in
many medieval stories; cf. the various versions of *Tristan*,
and Marie de France, *Equitan* 194ff.

5 with the Africans: see note on XIII.42, above.

16 are not defective: a similar image occurs in William of
Malmesbury, *Historia Regum Anglorum* Prol.: *absque literarum
patrocinio claudicat cursus temporum in medio.*

26 Ruodlieb arranged their seats: the guests are arranged
strictly according to rank and status.

27 designated: *certifico* is only found in medieval authors;
LS does not list it.

28 one table: cf. notes on X.65 and VII.1, above.

29 one higher chair: as is the modern custom, there is a 'high
table'; note that Ruodlieb again pays deference to his mother
and does not presume to equate his own status with hers.

33 a crown: cf. Apocalypse 2.10 and Jacob.1.12 for *coronam uitae*
and also I Cor.9.25.

35 when they had eaten: the tense of *manducauit* is odd; the
stress is clearly on 'finished eating'.

36 the doors were closed: privacy is crucial for such negotiations, as at IV.124 above, and Marie de France, *Equitan* 191,
les us des chambres furent clos.

43 what great grief...suffering: lit. 'with what great grief my
mother and with what labour/ endured many things'.

57 noble breeding: cf. I.2 for similar phraseology.

61 Christ: the MS reading is x̄p̄c̄, deriving from the Greek. Here
it must be an abbreviation for the nominative *Christus*, and
it introduces a very rare instance of elision if the earlier
conjectures are retained. As elision does not form part of

the poet's regular practice, I have put *quis ditauit*.   Despite
the occurrence of *mantel* above at X.130, I see no justification
for printing *Christ*, as several other editors do.

65 <u>make her a match for you</u>: lit. 'is made a match for you'.

XVII

1 <u>she herself</u>: this personal service denotes intimacy and a
special honour.   Braun (p.12) points out that this episode
serves to illustrate the precept laid down at V.484ff.

6 <u>there is nothing I have meddled in less</u>: cf. Latham *intro-
mitto*, from 1227 and 14c., and TLL IAlb, CAES. AREL. *serm.*
193.1, *per haec ille malorum artifex se intromisit.*

7 <u>womaniser</u>: *scurra* means 'man about town' and later 'buffoon'
in the writers of antiquity;   it later came to have the
sense attested by DuCange in the *Gloss. Lat. Sangerm.*,
'scurra, lechierres...'

9 <u>I bow to them</u>: the nephew (for he it is) is gracious to the
ladies, but keeps his distance.   He has clearly changed his
ways from the time when he had the affair with the harlot.

11 <u>I send him</u>: = *de me*, lit. 'from me'.

13 <u>delights in birds</u>: Laistner, *Anzeiger* p.95, notes that some
two centuries before *Ruodlieb*, the poet Otfrid had written
thesses liedes wunna, frides wunnon.   H. Walther, in *Z.f.d.
Altertum* 65 (1928) pp.258ff., draws attention to a *carmen
gratulatorium* which includes such couplets as *sit tantum uobis
a Christo dante salutis/ sol quantum radii retinet uel aura
uolucris*, and *quot siluis frondes insunt, quot in equore
pisces, aere quot uolucres, tot uobis opto salutes*.   He
traces the device back as far as Ovid.

29 <u>garters</u>: lit. 'bindings of her legs'.   In classical latin
crus refers to the lower leg;   Zeudel's 'knee-garters' is
a little too specific in intent as well as being slightly
inaccurate.   *cydarim* is MHG *schapel*, chaplet;   cf. IV.93.

30 <u>the clerk</u>: as Dronke's edition of the delightful 'Love-verses
from Regensburg' in *Medieval Latin And The Rise Of The
European Love-lyric* demonstrates, ladies who learned latin
ran every risk of falling in love with their teacher, who
would of course have been a *clericus*.

33 <u>she doubted</u>: there are two possible conjectures: *ignarus*
gives the sense 'she doubted that he was unaware', and the
lady's shame is thus doubled because she fears that the messenger is aware of the gift which Ruodlieb has sent her.
nec uerus, Laistner's proposal, is rendered 'does not doubt
that he is truthful who was feigning' by Zeydel, thus reveal-
ing the inner contradiction in the latin, and is paraphrased
by Ford 'doubted that he...was aware of what was in the box'.
If the suggestion did not jar with Ruodlieb's straightforward
character, one might even propose *nec clerus*, 'she did not
doubt that the clerk was the messenger in disguise' (= *is qui
simulabat*), which would require that the entire situation with
the clerk was engineered by Ruodlieb himself.   At all events,
the lady is extremely flustered.

40   he swore by him: the disjointed grammar aptly conveys the messenger's nonplussed state of mind, and illustrates the poet's skilful use of language very vividly.

49   to undo any deceit: note the irony in the scene. The messenger has already unwittingly uncovered the lady's own deceit, and his words enrage her still further, which explains her lack of courtly manners in the way she dismisses him.

50   note that there is no leonine rhyme in this and the following lines. vv.51 and 52 rhyme at the caesura, and have assonance at the end.

72   forgotten something and not given: 'something' must be inferred unless *non* is taken with *oblitum*, 'pretending I had just remembered to give...' The tenses used make the latter unlikely, despite the poet's strange use of tenses on various occasions.

83   I need to ask: Zeydel detects a change in the style of the poem from this point on: a lack of verbs of speaking, the introduction of end-rhyme, and a variety in the scansion of *Ruodlieb* in vv.87 and 91. The script in the MS is even throughout, however.

84   said Ruodlieb: this is taken from the margin, *Ruo.*, which Langosch and Zeydel staggeringly make part of the hexameter!

86   Christ's poor: the injunction from biblical teaching is again laboured. See note above on V.240.

89   in her dreams: cf. the dreams of Kreimhild, *Nibelungenlied* 921, and of Charles in the *Chanson de Roland*.

94   a linden-tree: the linden-tree was a commonplace in German poetry before the period of the Minnesinger. Zeydel sees a link between the vigil of King Mark in *Tristan* at the lovers' tryst, and this verse and XII.67; but apart from the fact that a tree and a lookout are included in both scenes, there is little to link the two works. Braun (p.71) traces the tree's prototype back as far as Herodotus I.107f., and adduces parallels from other sources, such as Suetonius, *Galba* 1, which are not at all convincing. The dreams clearly point forward to the conflict with Inmunch and Hartunch, predicted in XVIII.

97   as though ready for war: cf. V.61 for similar phrases.

98   a snow-white dove: the picture is a compound of biblical imagery: cf. Matt.3.16, *et uidit Spiritum Dei descendentem sicut columbam*. *coronam* shows that Ruodlieb will eventually be a king in his own right.

101   loving kisses: *sauia* is ante- and post-classical, and frequent in Plautus.

102   saw all these things: cf. Mary in Luke 2.19, *Maria autem conseruabat omnia haec, conferens in corde suo*.

104   portend: *pretitulo* is medieval, listed from 1006 by Latham.

108   she told him: note that the poet makes use of his characters to tell us about the dream, even though their divine source is not in doubt.

113   Once again, there is no leonine rhyme here.

124   of saying: this must be inferred. Ruodlieb's mother fears the sin of pride.

XVIII

1   (The dwarf) leapt up: the character of the dwarf in this
     fragment is of especial interest. *Nibelungenlied* 497ff. also
     has reference to a dwarf who guards the treasure of two kings.
     The famed longevity and upright moral character of the dwarf,
     backed up by Laistner, *Anzeiger* p.106, contrast sharply with
     the cunning and devious nature of dwarves in other medieval
     works, such as Beroul's *Tristan*, esp. vv.638-640. This may
     explain Ruodlieb's suspicion of the dwarf, and his fear that
     he may be planning to betray him, in vv.15-17. The dwarf is
     even used by the poet as a vehicle for his own moralising
     comments on infidelity among men, in vv.20ff.

2   catch his breath: *spiramen* is rare in classical latin, and
     is used by Christian writers to refer to the Holy Ghost.

3   most humble: note that in this verse, 'h' does not make
     position, as it often does in medieval poetry; cf. *Walt*.172.

4   I'll tell you: the present tenses here ought really to be
     futures, and are peculiar in their context.

5   This line is defective, having no caesura, and no leonine
     rhyme. The rhyme in fact becomes very sporadic in this
     fragment.

6   of two kings: note that *denique* is otiose.

8   Inmunch...Hartunch: the German names are noteworthy. Lang-
     osch believed that they were more common in the latter parts
     of the poem because the poet wished to make his work conform
     to the then-fashionable romances, in which characters were
     more carefully drawn (though this is true of the earlier part
     of the work as well) and were named.

9   will be defeated: the MS clearly has a present tense here;
     perhaps the force of it is 'are already defeated'.

18   God forbid: cf. with these vv. the words from the *Collatio
     Alexandri cum Dindimo* cited by Braun, p.75: *cum locuti
     fuerimus - non dicimus nisi ueritatem - et statim tacemus.
     uos autem dicitis multa, quae debeant fieri, et non facitis*
     and *subitam mortem non patimur, quia per sordida facta ipsum
     aerem non corrumpimus.*

20   evil in his heart: the thought is biblical. Cf. Jer.17.9,
     prauum est cor omnium et inscrutabile. doloso is rare in
     classical latin, but common in the Vulgate. 'you men' is
     expanded from *uos* in order to stress the comparison.

24   we do not eat: cf. another statement from the *Collatio
     Alexandri cum Dindimo: de talibus cibis implemus mensas
     nostras, qui nos non nocent, et proinde sumus sine aliqua
     egritudine.*

25   hale and hearty: *incolomes* is a regular medieval spelling.
     Cf. Siguinus, *Ars Lectoria* pp.7, 10, *et 'in' pro 'sine, ut
     'incolomis', 'sine columna', ...'u' in 'o'...columna/
     incolomis.*

29   she was small: *sed et* is padding, to make up the metre.

31   my husband: *mihi* illustrates the classical use of the ethic
     dative, from which the looser uses derive, especially of *sibi*.

32	finished all this business: this phrase prompts the question, how did the story end? There is clearly a more fabulous quality to the narrative in this latter part, and the MS breaks off unfinished, with room for several more verses at the foot of the page. It is possible that the poet intended to have Ruodlieb fulfil the dwarf's prophecy, marry the princess Heriburg, and perhaps even return to the Great King's land (cf. V.385, 403, 539; XII.44, 71ff.), but the imagination can easily run riot in tying these loose ends. Braun compares the sudden end of the work to the abrupt dénouement found in Wolfram von Eschenbach's *Parzival*.

Epigrams

The Epigrams are found on sides 1^V and 34^V of the Munich MS, but as Zeydel points out in his article 'Die elf Epigramme...' they have nothing to do with *Ruodlieb*, though they are written in the same hand. Seiler (p.208) regarded them as the work of the same poet, and Schmeller put V-XI as his fragment XVIII and I-IV as his fragment XIX. Similar epigrams are found in the work of the medieval poet Froumond, amongst other writers, and the tradition as a whole may be traced back to Martial, who found many imitators in the Middle Ages.

I	This epigram is about a pair of bellows.
II	The subject of this is unidentified; perhaps a gauntlet is intended (this at least answers the riddle, 'what feeds our men and fights our enemies?').
2	Dietmar: Hauck thought this *Dietmar* or *Thietmar* was a count of Formbach and a vassal of Henry III.
3	Zeydel's conjecture does not scan.
4	food and clothing: cf. *Ruodlieb* I.97, V.276.
5	raises: Zeydel's *leuens* should be *leuans*.
III	This epigram is about a fly-swat.
IV	Subject unidentified: a mirror?
V	Like III, this seems to be about a fly-swat. Beside it in the left margin are written the words *ridens enodans*.
3	applying yourself: *assiduo* is not found before the Vulgate (LS). 'threatening to strike a blow' = *miniteris ut ictus*.
VI	This and VII are about bottles or flasks: cf. *Ruodlieb* I.38.
7	for your journey home: = *quando domum remeas*.
VII.1	The tmesis here in *pari...lia* is extraordinary, and without parallel in the rest of this poet's work.
2	thirst: = *sitim*, written as *mitis* here and in v.3 to avoid hiatus (so Seiler, p.159).
3	fire of the chase: = *litis ab igne*. Zeydel renders *litis* 'Gefechts'; the word is normally found in legal contexts.
7	moneybag: *crumena* is common in Plautus.
VIII.2	which were never better spent: *uendo* usually refers to things for sale, but the case-ending here links it with *duos nummos*. Alternatively, the change to masc. might be done because of the

rhyme, in which case *uendendos* would refer to the shin-guards: 'none better were ever up for sale'.

IX   This and X are etiquettes for hose or trousers.

XI.1 <u>Tubalcain</u>: In Gen.4.21-22, Jubal, not Tubalcain, is called *pater canentium cithara et organo*. Tubalcain is a smith. The poet's interest in music is seen also in *Ruodlieb* V.81-83, XI.27ff.

2   <u>vielle</u>: *rotta* is an early type of viol: cf. MHG *hrôta,* O.Fr. *rote.*

7   <u>David</u>: the story of David is told in I Reg.16.23, *igitur quandocumque spiritus Domini malus arripiebat Saul, David tollebat citharam et percutiebat manu sua, et refocillabatur Saul, et leuius habebat; recedebat enim ab eo spiritus malus.*